Why UNIX? Why the Instant Guide?

The UNIX operating system is one of the most versatile and flexible operating systems available. Its power derives from the ease with which any UNIX user can customize their environment and tailor it to their own needs. There are many different flavors of UNIX, but all the variants are descendents of one parent system and, therefore, do not radically differ from one another. With UNIX you can access the Internet, connect networks, communicate via a Graphical User Interface similar to Windows and get to grips with the vast amount of free software and utilities that are scattered across the globe.

As with all of the Instant guides, this book is for you if you want a thorough, yet fast-paced, guide to UNIX. The first part of this book begins by teaching the commands that are necessary for working and maneuvering within the UNIX environment and introduces some common utilities. The second part of the book branches off into the many different aspects of the UNIX user's world. The whole book should act as a biblical reference guide, your gateway to a whole new world.

What is Wrox Press?

Wrox Press is a computer book publisher which promotes a brand new concept - clear, jargon-free programming and database titles that fulfill your real demands. We publish for everyone, from the novice through to the experienced programmer. To ensure that our books meet your needs, we continuously carry out research on all of our titles. Through our dialog with you we can craft the books that you really need.

We welcome suggestions and take all of them to heart - your input is paramount in creating the next great Wrox title. Use the reply card inside this book or mail us at:

feedback@wrox.demon.co.uk
or
Compuserve 100063, 2152

D1479621

Wrox Press Ltd.   **Tel:** (312) 465 3559
2710 W. Touhy   **Fax:** (312) 465 4063
Chicago
IL 60645
USA

Instant UNIX

Andrew Evans
Neil Matthew
Richard Stones

Wrox Press Ltd.®

Instant UNIX

Published by Wrox Press Ltd. Unit 16, 20 James Road, Birmingham, B11 2BA, UK
Printed in the USA
Library of Congress Catalog number 95-60740
ISBN 1-874416-65-6

Credits

Authors
Andrew Evans
Neil Matthew
Richard Stones

Technical Editors
Chris Ullman
Julian Dobson

Series Editor
Adrian M. Sill

Technical Reviewers
Steven Berkovich
Steven Dawes
Ian Wilks
James Lambeth
David Gray

Indexers
Ian Wilks
Simon Gilks

Managing Editor
John Franklin

Operations Manager
Gina Mance

Production Manager
Deb Somers

Book Layout
Eddie Fisher
Greg Powell
Neil Gallagher
Graham Butler

Proof Readers
Pam Brand
Jenny Nuttall

Cover Design
Third Wave

For more information on Third Wave, contact Ross Alderson on 44-121 236 6616
Cover photo supplied by The Image Bank

Trademark Acknowledgements

Wrox has endeavored to provide trademark information about all the companies and products mentioned in this book by the appropriate use of capitals. However, Wrox cannot guarantee the accuracy of this information.

UNIX	UNIX is a registered trademark in the United States and other countries, licensed through X/Open Company Ltd.
Netscape	Netscape Communications
SCO UNIX	Santa Cruz Operation
SCO Open Desktop	Santa Cruz Operation
AIX	IBM
Ethernet	Xerox Corporation
Kermit	Henson Associates
VT-100	Digital Equipment Corporation
MS-DOS	Microsoft
MS-Windows	Microsoft
Windows NT	Microsoft
OS/2	IBM
NDIS	Microsoft/3Com
NFS	SUN Microsystems
Solaris	SUN Microsystems
PC/TCP	FTP Software
Trumpet Winsock	Trumpet Software Pty Ltd.
Chameleon NFS	NetManage
WinQVT/Net	QPC Software
JSB Multiview	JSB Computer Systems Ltd.
XVision	Visionware
Wabi	SUN Microsystems
MKS Toolkit	Mortice Kern Systems
Unixware	Novell
BSD	Regents of the University of California at Berkeley
System V	AT&T
Postscript	Adobe
Ghostscript	Aladdin Enterprises

About the Authors

Andrew Evans is a software engineer, technical instructor and entrepreneur, living in the Washington, DC area. His computing career so far has led him from UNIX systems engineering and X Windows application programming to Microsoft Windows and Macintosh programming. In addition to his extensive programming experience in C and C++, Andrew has designed and taught courses on subjects ranging from object-oriented software engineering to electronic music. He is also co-founder and president of Compass Point Software Inc., a software engineering consulting firm specializing in high-performance GUI application development.

Neil Matthew has been using and ministering to UNIX systems since 1979. A mathematics graduate from Nottingham, he now specializes in software engineering and software quality assurance.

Rick Stones is a graduate of Nottingham University and started using UNIX over ten years ago. He specializes in communications and real-time applications written in both C and C++.

Author Acknowledgements

Neil would like to thank his wife Christine and his children, Alexandra and Adrian, for enduring disrupted weekends while this book was being written.

Rick would like to thank his wife Ann and his children, Jennifer and Andrew, for their patience during the writing of this book.

Neil and Rick would also like to give heartfelt thanks to Richard Neill for giving up sleeping time on the train to make numerous helpful comments and suggestions on the early drafts. They would also like to thank the Internet for being there, US Robotics for inventing Sportster modems and Linus Torvalds, the Free Software Foundation and a cast of thousands for bringing UNIX functionality, in Linux, to the people.

We would also like to thank Julian and Chris at Wrox for their help in putting this book together.

Andrew Evans would like to thank his wife, Lori, for putting up with all this. Special thanks go to Network Computing Devices Inc. (NCD) for supplying the X terminal photograph in Chapter 7. Thanks also go to Cliff Stoll for graciously taking time out of his busy schedule to look over Chapter 12. And last but not least, thanks to Wrox for making it all possible.

INSTANT

Summary of Contents

INSTANT

UNIX

Table of Contents

Table of Contents

Table of Contents

Table of Contents

Table of Contents

Table of Contents

INSTANT

Introduction

Welcome to the latest Instant Guide from Wrox Press, Instant UNIX. This book has been designed as a guide to using and administering the UNIX operating system. Introducing everything you need to know about UNIX, this book will enable you to understand the UNIX system and how it integrates with the rest of the computing world. As UNIX is no spring chicken, this book will give you an insight into the background behind UNIX and bring you right up to date with how it is progressing towards the new millenium.

What Can UNIX Do for Me?

Most people will have come across the UNIX operating system, even those without very much computing experience. A great many of you will have been put off by the sometimes user-unfriendly presentation and cryptic responses to commands. The same people might also have been discouraged by the reputation that UNIX has attained as a hackers' operating system, requiring excessive expertise to complete the most simple tasks.

Persevere however, and you will find that UNIX is one of the most versatile operating systems around. Once you've mastered the UNIX commands, you will find it very simple to rebuild and customize the system to your own personal preferences. Like Windows NT and Windows 95, it is a true multi-tasking, multi-user 32-bit operating system, and in the form of X Windows, UNIX has a graphical user interface to rival MS Windows.

Who Should Use This Book?

Instant UNIX contains the information necessary to transform the reader from a person with little or no UNIX knowledge, to one who is a competent UNIX user and system administrator with the ability to understand and design UNIX networks. The type of people this book is likely to benefit are:

- The DOS programmer unfamiliar with UNIX who wishes to quickly understand the system and perform system administration.

- The UNIX user who wishes to progress to system administration.

- The network manager who needs to integrate UNIX systems into the network.

- Everybody who requires a concise and informative guide to all the aspects of the UNIX operating system.

How to Use This Book

The aim of the book is to teach a novice UNIX user how to use and administer the system. UNIX is an 'Open System' and is increasingly replacing legacy systems, running on a range of platforms from large supercomputers to desktop workstations. Instant UNIX is written with network connectivity in mind and will describe typical network architectures and the principles of network administration. Methods of connecting DOS systems to UNIX networks will also be addressed.

What You Should Know

To get the most out of this book, you should have some basic programming knowledge; you don't need to have spent five years of your life learning assembler, but you should understand the basic concepts that are familiar to most programming languages. You should ideally have some experience of a DOS system and Microsoft Windows - we will be making frequent parallels to both of these systems throughout the book. Since we are going to take this tour at a fast pace, we won't be dwelling on superfluous programming and operating system features, such as what a program or window is, although we will explain how these terms relate to UNIX.

If you don't have any UNIX experience don't worry - we start from the very beginning. We even detail how to log in and we don't assume prior knowledge of any UNIX features and quirks.

Conventions Used

To enable you to find your way around this book easily, we have used various different styles to highlight different references. Each style has been selected to enable the reader to succesfully understand the content as efficiently as possible.

Dialog

The UNIX operating system is predominently text-based and highly interactive - two components that conveniently form a smooth dialog style. All commands, programs and immediate output are highlighted with a gray background, so you can find them easily:

```
$ ls; ls -l; date
report.txt
total 5
5 -rw-r-r-   1 neil      users        4553 Dec  8 10:52 report.txt
Fri Dec  9 20:18:38 GMT 1994
```

Fonts and Styles

Throughout Instant UNIX we will consistently be using the following styles and fonts for a variety of textual distinctions:

- When code or a command is mentioned in the middle of a sentence, we write it in **this_style**, so as to emphasize its origin.

- Important words are introduced in **this style**. These are significant words that we are meeting for the first time. Subsequently they will appear as normal text.

- Actual keys that you press will be displayed in *this style*, for example press the *Return* key. Note that *Ctrl-K* depicts the depression of a *Control* key and the *K* key, together.

- Text that appears on your screen such as field names, menu items or headings appear in this style.

3

When we introduce the syntax of code, we will use the following
bracket styles:

[   ]   Optional

<   >   Obligatory

> **When an important piece of information needs to be *really*
> emphasised, we will place it in a box like this.**

UNIX Variance

UNIX isn't very graphically sophisticated and so relies a great deal on the
written word. Unfortunately, this spawns a host of different modes and
environments where conventions differ. When using UNIX, you must bear in
mind that different systems, variants and versions *will* produce different
responses and output.

Tell Us What You Think

One last thing. We've tried to make this book as enjoyable and accurate as
possible. The programming community is what we're here to serve, so if
you have any queries, suggestions or comments about this book, let us
know - we are always delighted to hear from you.

You can help us ensure that our future books are even better by simply
returning the reply card at the back of the book or by contacting us direct
at Wrox. For a quick response, you can also use the following e-mail
addresses:

feedback@wrox.demon.co.uk
Compuserve: 100063,2152

Please return the reply card at the back of the book, and tell us what you
think of the book, the style of presentation and the content. We are always
ready to listen to comments and complaints (although we do prefer
unadulterated adoration...).

Let's Learn UNIX

Thank you for buying Instant UNIX. We hope you enjoy it and learn about this fascinating operating system as smoothly as possible. All our efforts have been aimed at bringing you maximum satisfaction and if you want to learn UNIX, then we are convinced that this book will fulfill your requirements. Anyway, you've bought this book to learn UNIX, and we shall hold you from it no more. Dip in and enjoy!

Chapter

The UNIX Operating System

Welcome to the vast and varied world of the UNIX operating system. Shortly we will be embarking on a whirlwind tour of the major bodies in the UNIX universe. We'll consider briefly its origins and its history, and then we'll look at the position it has attained in the highly competitive operating systems market. After that we will be able to get to grips with some of the different strains of UNIX available. And finally, we'll examine how UNIX compares to other popular operating systems.

This chapter is designed to give you a grasp of why UNIX is still such a successful operating system, and why you should want to use it. The main topics of discussion in this chapter are:

- The origins of UNIX
- The main variants of UNIX (System V, BSD, OSF/1, Mach and Solaris)
- Client/Server architecture
- X Window System
- Comparison of UNIX/X Window System and DOS/Windows system

The Background of UNIX

Unlike DOS or OS/2, UNIX is a multi-user operating system. It has been developed continuously over 20 years and, as a result, a great collection of customizable programs are widely and freely available to all users.

We'll start by taking a look at how UNIX came about and how it managed to develop into one of today's foremost computer operating systems.

The Origins of UNIX

In the late 1960's AT&T Bell Laboratories, General Electric and The Massachusetts Institute of Technology (MIT) embarked on a project to produce a computer operating system that would support multiple users. They wanted all their users to be able to cooperate with one another on-line, sharing files and other resources while still maintaining privacy for personal use. They wanted the proposed operating system to take full advantage of the power of the best computer systems available at the time.

Bell Laboratories eventually pulled out of this development effort when it began to feel that the project (known as Multics) wasn't going to fulfill its initial promise. Several of their top developers who worked on it, including Ken Thompson and Dennis Ritchie, began to produce an operating system for use inside AT&T Bell Laboratories solely to help them with their work. They initially named the operating system, "Unics", a pun on the failed Multics system. The name soon became **UNIX** and it has stuck fast ever since.

AT&T then began offering UNIX to universities and it quickly became a favorite amongst computer science researchers and students. This could largely be attributed to its software-development orientation. Its open architecture and flexibility also enabled UNIX to form the universal basis for research into new concepts of operating system design. Students leaving university often took UNIX with them into the commercial engineering world, where it is still dominant today.

The Relationship between UNIX and C

The first versions of UNIX were written in PDP-11 assembler, but in 1973 the bulk of the operating system was rewritten in the C programming language.

The beauty of the C language is that it only has a very small core of basic functionality. The remainder of the functionality can be accessed via the various system libraries particular to your machine. This means that only the core needs to be ported to a new hardware platform - the rest can simply be included on compilation.

The power in the relationship that has developed between UNIX and C lies in the portability of UNIX programs from platform-to-platform. Software written in C for one UNIX system can frequently be moved with minor or no modification to another UNIX system with an entirely different architecture simply by recompiling it on the target platform. A huge body of free UNIX software has emerged, largely distributed via the Internet. Popular packages distributed this way typically contain minor changes to account for the major system variants (like System V or BSD) but they usually auto-detect the variant and compile correctly without any user intervention. Since some variants of UNIX run on nearly every popular hardware platform available today, this portability allows developers to serve a vast and diverse audience very efficiently.

X/Open

The main problems with operating systems in the past have been badly fragmented environments and confusion with standards. This has led to a wide variety of operating systems, all of which offer individual benefits such as graphical user interfaces (GUIs), application interfaces and distributed processor architectures.

To make sense of the bewildering array of features offered, the X/Open Company Ltd has been formed to bring standards together within the industry, so everybody (users and vendors alike) is working towards the same common objective. For a product to be X/Open branded, it has to pass many strict tests of conformance. X/Open maintain that this brand is 'a promise by the vendor to conform to the specification.'

One aim of the X/Open brand has been to create a single UNIX specification. This common specification has been designated **Spec 1170**. This initiative came of age when Sun Microsystems, IBM, Hewlett Packard, OSF and Novell/USL jointly organized a plan to provide a single common definition of UNIX services. This would provide a stable system for developing future applications as well as preserving the portability of existing applications. The UNIX brand name, incidently, is now owned by the X/Open Company Ltd.

UNIX Variants

As UNIX has evolved over the years and emerged from AT&T Bell Laboratories to face the world, several major variants of UNIX have arisen. While these variants sparked off 'religious' wars in the UNIX community for many years, efforts are now underway to bring them all back together again under one common standard.

The following variants have all played, or are playing, some part in the development of UNIX systems:

BSD

The Berkeley Software Distribution (BSD) UNIX flavor arose out of operating system research at the University of California at Berkeley (UCB). In the UNIX world, the BSD variant of UNIX is considered to be the most technically advanced and research-driven. Many of the key enhancement features to UNIX have come from BSD and have made their way into other variants too.

System V

The first commercial release of UNIX from AT&T, surfacing around 1982, was called the UNIX System III. System V, with several enhancements over System III, was released about a year later. The latest release is System V Release 4, which contains elements of BSD and SunOS as well.

AT&T recently sold its UNIX business (UNIX Systems Laboratories, or USL) to Novell, the PC networking giant. Novell has continued to support and develop the AT&T-style UNIX in a "new" operating system product called Unixware.

OSF/1

The Open Software Foundation (OSF) is an industry consortium formed by some of the larger hardware vendors (like DEC, IBM and HP) to help establish a system of software that enables computers from multiple vendors to work together in an open systems computing environment. OSF strives for maximum portability, scalability and interoperability of the technologies it develops and promotes. OSF hopes to eventually establish OSF/1 as the central UNIX standard for all vendors and a GUI - MOTIF - to go with it.

Solaris

Solaris is the core operating system product of Sun Microsystem's SunSoft unit. Solaris is a UNIX System VR4 variant with a number of key extensions, including a multithreaded kernel with support for symmetric multiprocessing, real-time scheduling for critical tasks, security enhancements and standards compliance (including POSIX, X11R5 and ISO 9660). It is probably the most complete and advanced commercial UNIX operating system available.

Linux

Linux is a free, independent implementation of UNIX that complies with the POSIX specification. Linux is the kernel or core operating system. The original author is Linus Torvalds, who still directs people wishing to customize Linux and hold their own copyright to their code.

In the last two years a cottage industry has sprung up around Linux, which is freely available on the Internet. Linux still has no company, no advertising and no marketing budget. It has spread primarily to individual users and colleges. It does have commercial applications, such as at the Roger Maris Cancer Center in Fargo, ND, which has been running its entire operation on Linux-based workstations since 1993. Linux will be discussed in greater detail in Chapter 13.

Mach

There is a lot of talk (and even more confusion) about Mach in the UNIX world right now, so it rightly deserves some discussion here. Mach is a project at Carnegie-Mellon University aimed at producing a highly-portable, multithreaded operating system. IBM and Microsoft have both adopted the Mach approach for some of their own operating system projects, and these operating systems appear to be the wave of the future.

The UNIX Family Tree

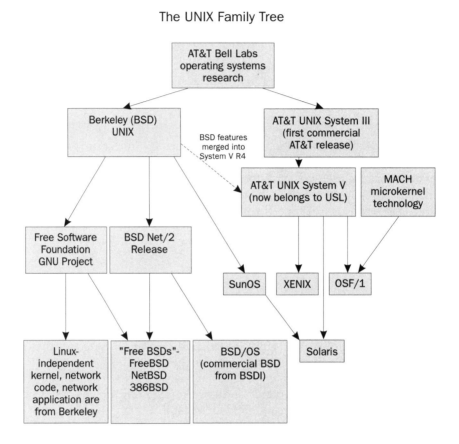

UNIX in the Marketplace

Because of its strange licensing background and the numerous variants, UNIX has had a tough road to acceptance in the commercial marketplace. AT&T were originally barred from selling UNIX due to complications with its antitrust settlement. The University of California at Berkeley among others, helped form a tangled web of licensing confusion that persisted until both AT&T and UCB left the UNIX business in the early 1990's. As many of the licensing and standardization issues were gradually sorted out and more commercial vendors distributed and supported UNIX, it became increasingly more accepted. Now it is the most widely used operating system in the industry, able to run on the most diverse set of platforms.

The Versatility of UNIX

UNIX was designed to support multitasking, and so it wasn't too great a departure to include multiprocessor architectures in the definition. With the advent of symmetric multiprocessor (SMP) machines, UNIX was the natural choice of operating system. SMP companies like Sequent and Tandem chose SMP-capable variants of UNIX for their machines. UNIX variants built on the Mach microkernel architecture are extremely SMP-friendly.

As more and more UNIX vendors hop onto the microkernel bandwagon, mainstream UNIX releases are able to run on everything from 80386-based PCs to massive, parallel supercomputers. No other operating system boasts as wide a dynamic range of supported processor architectures as UNIX does; this has allowed it to make crucial early market inroads into cutting-edge, high-performance hardware technologies.

The Movement to Open Systems

Despite the commonalities that the various flavors of UNIX share, there has been enough "drift" in the features to make it inconvenient to port large, complex software systems from one UNIX variant to another. In the 1980's, efforts were launched to create a set of standards and application program interfaces (APIs) to form a common universal standard that software developers could code towards.

> An application program interface (API) is a collection of lower level functions that are used by programmers to connect an application to a program. There are specific APIs for every application.

The best-known of these is the POSIX effort by IEEE (The Institute of Electrical and Electronic Engineers) which has been adopted by many organizations, including the U. S. Government. Competition in the operating system marketplace has sparked further efforts to standardize UNIX in the form of the Open Software Foundation (OSF) and the Common Open Software Environment (COSE).

Client/Server Architectures

"Client/Server" was the great information-processing catchphrase of the 1980's. As more and more organizations looked to downsize and decentralize their information-processing systems, Client/Server systems became increasingly important in the computer industry.

Clients: Desktop machines running client (front-end) components of distributed application - user-interface, data entry/reporting, etc.

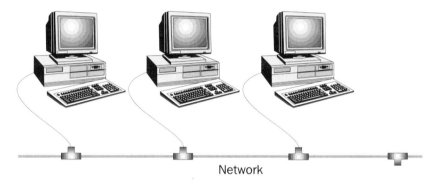

Network

Server: Larger machine running server (back-end) components of distributed application - DBMS server, file server, etc. Commonly has more system resources (disk, memory, CPU speed) than desktop machines.

The Client/Server model harnesses the power and flexibility of putting desktop computers on everyone's desk, without losing the sharing of information and the connectivity offered by the mainframe.

In the Client/Server model, software on the desktop machines acts as the client. A client front end to a server-based database usually handles most or all of the user-interface and application logic on the client machine, only communicating with the database server when records of data need to be stored or retrieved. This lets each machine specialize in its own particular function, improving the efficiency of the resources. Client/Server computing could in fact be considered to be a form of parallel processing - one processor handles application logic and user interaction while another handles only data storage and retrieval, interleaving requests from multiple clients.

Okay, so if the desktop computer is running the client software, then what's running the server? Since much of the work has been offloaded to the client machine, the server machine probably doesn't have to be one of those room-filling behemoths from the mainframe era. In fact, minicomputers or large microcomputers are the most popular choices for server machines. The main considerations are the ability to handle high network transaction rates, the ability to manage large and complex file systems, and to multitask efficiently. Aging linear operating systems like DOS don't measure up here. Some vendors have built custom operating systems for servers, like Novell's Netware products.

An ideal candidate operating system for servers is UNIX due to its ability to handle the above requirements with its wide availability and acceptance on the hardware platforms of choice for server-sized machines. Many Client/Server concepts can be traced back to distributed computing features first tried with UNIX (for instance, NFS). UNIX has become a key player particularly in the database server arena.

Common Roles for UNIX Systems

Over the years, UNIX has found its market niches quite comfortably. The dominance of UNIX within these areas is principally due to the power of the operating system. The following sectors have been particularly dominated by the UNIX bandwagon:

Servers

Client/Server computing originated in the UNIX world, so it's not surprising that UNIX is the dominant choice for server implementations. This has held true even as client applications moved closer and closer towards personal computers running DOS. For instance, UNIX machines are frequently seen running as database servers for distributed Client/Server MIS applications with DOS or Windows-based clients.

High-End Workstations

UNIX is the favorite operating system of the scientific and engineering communities. Because of the work of companies like Silicon Graphics and Sun Microsystems, UNIX has gained a reputation for power and flexibility. A great deal of powerful graphics hardware and software exists in the

UNIX market solely for this reason. Because of the large body of existing UNIX code (and knowledge) in these areas, newer entrants to this market (like Microsoft's Windows NT operating system) will have a hard time breaking UNIX's dominance.

Multi-User Time-Sharing Systems

Mainframe-style time-sharing isn't dead yet - there are still many applications for this type of computing. Many supercomputers still use a time-sharing model for managing accounts, and UNIX is still prevalent in this field. Also, the providers of Internet services to end-users have sparked a resurgence in UNIX time-sharing. A user will rent time-sharing ("shell") accounts on UNIX systems in order to gain access to the Internet.

The X Window System

As operating systems have evolved, the way users interact with them has changed dramatically. This is due at least in part to the changing and increasingly sophisticated ways these operating systems inherently work.

The **graphical user interface (GUI)**, with its windows, icons, mice and pointing devices, has become the de facto standard for how people interact with computers. The windowing technology allows multiple tasks to present their information to the user in an organized and standardized fashion. Windowing GUIs are a must-have feature for modern operating systems, and UNIX now uses a common windowing GUI - the X Window System.

UNIX/X Versus DOS/Windows

UNIX often competes in the same market-place as the DOS operating system. Both can run on the same hardware, yet each have a very different structure and background. While there are similarities between the two (like their ability to use windowing software), their differences are quite profound. The subsequent extensions to MS-DOS, Microsoft's Windows environments, have a little more in common with UNIX, but still differ considerably.

The Limitations of DOS

Problems tend to arise with DOS when attempts are made to squeeze more functionality out of it than was originally intended. DOS must usually be painstakingly patched or augmented to do many things which UNIX does naturally, and even then UNIX usually does a better job. DOS, by virtue of being designed to run on a lone personal computer, wasn't intended to support more than one program running at once, and provides no support for multiple users.

The original machines for which DOS was developed had processors that could only address 1 megabyte of memory. Over time, as application software and uses for the desktop PC evolved, this limit soon became a liability. The stubbornness and inflexibility of the original specification is causing more and more crippling problems for today's users. DOS of course, is predominantly text only, which was the major catalyst in the development of Windows.

What Windows Adds (and Doesn't Add)

Microsoft has developed its MS-Windows (or Windows) product to effectively patch the problems caused by DOS and to provide more features of a modern, graphical operating system.

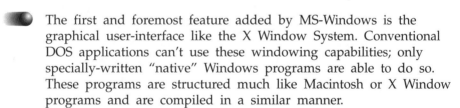

The first and foremost feature added by MS-Windows is the graphical user-interface like the X Window System. Conventional DOS applications can't use these windowing capabilities; only specially-written "native" Windows programs are able to do so. These programs are structured much like Macintosh or X Window programs and are compiled in a similar manner.

The windowing environment is a natural for multitasking, because the screen can be shared by many applications at once. MS-Windows adds multitasking (albeit non pre-emptive) to DOS. Multiple DOS sessions can be run at once and can be intermingled with native Windows programs.

True multitasking systems, like UNIX, are fully pre-emptive. The most contemporary Windows systems such as Windows NT and Windows 95 are also pre-emptive.

● Windows doesn't attempt to address the issue of having more than one user connected to the machine at once. It is still designed to support the single-user, desktop computing model as fashioned by DOS. This isn't so much a limitation, as it is a decision to optimize the operating system for a particular type of use.

● The original Windows doesn't change the basic 16-bit nature of DOS, so all the same old memory problems still persist.

The 32-bit Windows Versions

The UNIX implementations that run on the same platforms as DOS and Windows are all 32-bit, which means that they can treat the memory on a machine (up to 4 gigabytes) as one contiguous address space rather than having to juggle with memory extenders. Microsoft has decided to move away from the DOS 16-bit model into true 32-bit operating systems with its two latest offerings: Windows NT and Windows 95.

These new systems have, amongst others, the following influences on the operating systems market:

● Both NT and Windows 95 utilise 32-bit addressing and pre-emptive multitasking.

● NT is aimed at the high-end workstation and server market, currently dominated by UNIX.

● NT features the same portability functionality that UNIX has - a very important factor in the future of operating systems.

● Both feature advanced GUI environments and extensive networking capabilities.

● Windows 95 features the Plug-and-Play architecture, which allows users to connect new peripheral hardware without having to wrestle with interrupts, jumpers, channels etc.

UNIX to DOS/Windows Connectivity

UNIX is still the dominant server platform and, despite the encroachment of Windows NT on this market niche, will probably remain so for a little while at least. However, DOS and MS-Windows based machines are very important on the client side of the Client/Server model. Because of this, connectivity between DOS and UNIX machines has become very important.

The principal solution to this problem historically has been to bring UNIX-style networking to the desktop PC rather than to make UNIX machines conform to DOS-only networks. Gradually, DOS TCP/IP implementations from third-party vendors have actually become increasingly more sophisticated and even quite serviceable. Microsoft has now acknowledged the importance of TCP/IP by including it with Windows NT and Windows 95. As a result, we can expect to see TCP/IP established as a networking standard across several platforms for many years to come. Furthermore, socket support through the WinSock API makes it easier to port TCP/IP network code between the two platforms.

On the application side, X Window display servers for Windows allow X Window applications to be run on Windows machines across a TCP/IP network. Conversely, tools like SoftWindows and Sun's Windows Application Binary Interface (WABI) allow DOS and Windows applications to be run locally on UNIX workstations.

Summary

In this first chapter we have established that UNIX is an operating system with a long and varied history. We have discussed the concepts behind its success and durability through which it has remained a prolific market leader. We took a sideways glance at how UNIX's competitors have fared in their bids for a stake in the market. We have also brought you right up to date with how the market stands right now.

Enough of all this theory, let's take a closer and practical look at the UNIX system.

Chapter

UNIX File Systems

So, now that you have had a brief flirt with the theory and background behind UNIX, you should be eager to dip in further and get your hands really dirty. There are many different ways of looking at UNIX, but to start with we will focus on the view of the UNIX file system observed by the user and the view encountered by the system administrator.

The system administrator is primarily interested in how files are physically arranged in the system, whereas users are mainly concerned with file manipulation. Looking at some of the more integral and important files, we will discover how they are structured and accessed within the file system.

We will be taking a look at how you can securely and efficiently manage all your valuable data, and how it can be backed up and restored in the event of corruption. The main entries on the menu in this chapter are:

- Getting into the UNIX system
- The UNIX file system from the users' point of view
- File permissions
- The administrators' view of the file system
- Systems administrator tasks
- Backing up the system

Logging In

UNIX is said to be a multi-user, multitasking operating system, which means that many people may use it at the same time. Each of these users may run many programs at the same time, subject to system limitations (such as available memory). Multi-user operations are supported by the allocation of user identities or login names. This is the work of the administrator of the system. Each user is given a unique login name and a personal password system to prevent others from manipulating their personal files without permission.

DOS contrasts with this because it has no concept of a user, although a password system may be implemented to prevent unauthorized use. Typically though, all the users of a DOS-based personal computer have unlimited access to every file and directory. A user's files in UNIX are stored separately from every other user's files and are generally inaccessible to other users.

Microsoft Windows does allow some level of multitasking for an individual user and with some versions it is possible to support more than one user identity. It isn't usual, though, for more than one person to use a Windows PC at the same time. Most PC-based versions of Unix do allow this.

When you want to use a UNIX system, the first thing you must do is sign in. UNIX will first ask you for your user name followed by your pre-determined password. If you type it all in correctly you will be presented with the UNIX prompt. Note that the password isn't echoed to the screen, so people can't look over your shoulder and see what your password is.

```
Welcome to the UNIX System
tilde login: jim
password: password-not-echoed
ACME Computer Ltd. Accounts
Please note this system will be unavailable from 5pm this evening.
You have new mail.
$
```

You have now independently logged into the UNIX system and everything is ready for you to start your work.

> Remember that UNIX is case sensitive and when logging in be sure to enter your user name in lower case. If you enter your user name in capital letters, some systems will automatically assume that you are using an upper case only terminal. Yes, such machines do exist, and these systems will expect you to use back slashes to indicate lowercase letters. The best thing to do in these circumstances is to log out and log back in again!

If you still haven't logged in properly and you are convinced that you've entered your user name and personal password correctly, it is recommended that you see the system administrator. If you aren't sure, then try again.

> We shall examine the UNIX equivalent of `AUTOEXEC.BAT` and the whole login procedure in all its glorious detail later, in Chapter 5.

A User's View of UNIX

The typical user of any computer system will log in with the sole intention of fulfilling a task or series of tasks. Users who are familiar with DOS will notice many striking similarities. One of the major differences between the two is that UNIX appears to the user to be very simplistic.

As we shall see in this chapter, one of the most important features of UNIX is that it treats everything as a file, even input, output and directories.

Another feature of UNIX is that it makes no distinction whatsoever between different types of file. Whether a file is executable, a data file, a link library or binary code - they're all treated in exactly the same way by UNIX.

In DOS, text files terminate their lines with both carriage return and line feed characters, whereas UNIX uses a single line feed character as a line terminator. Also a directory is only a file that contains a list of other files. Even devices such as serial ports are files, although rather a special sort of file.

All UNIX files are arranged in a single tree hierarchy, in a similar vein to how a hard disk is arranged in DOS. In UNIX there aren't any disk drive specifiers like A: or C: for you to worry about. Indeed, the user will often neither know nor care how the files are physically arranged across the one or more disks that actually store the data. Imagine all your DOS drives rolled into one universal disk space - this is how the UNIX file system operates.

The Layout of Files and Directories

The top level of a UNIX file system consists of a single directory, referred to as the root directory or simply 'root' or 'slash'. All manner of files and directories descend down and expand from the root directory. A simple example is shown below:

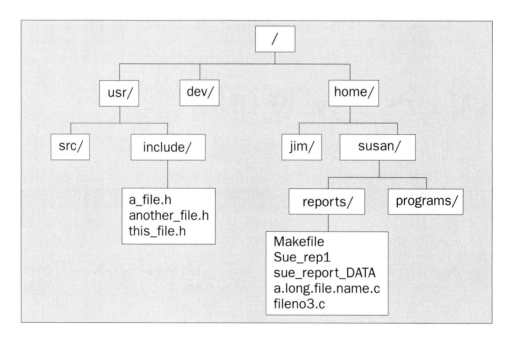

This hierarchy has been universally accepted as the standard file system structure for nearly all computer systems.

Moving Around the Hierarchy

Moving around the tree and examining files is very simple. If you are familiar with DOS, then the only major difference is that the slash between directories is the forward slash, **/**, rather than the DOS backslash, ****.

Suppose we are in the directory called **susan** shown on the previous page. We say we are in the directory **/home/susan**. This is what is known as a pathname. In this case, it is the directory that the user Susan starts in when she logs in - her 'home' directory. To change to the **reports** subdirectory we use the **cd** (change directory) command (the $ is the UNIX prompt.):

```
$ cd reports
```

If we forget or lose track of where we are in the system hierarchy, we can use the **pwd** command to tell us which directory we are in.

```
$ pwd
/home/susan/reports
```

We can view the contents of the current directory with the **ls** command. Here the output will be a list of names:

```
$ ls
Makefile Sue_rep1 sue_report_DATA a.long.file.name.c fileno3.c
```

We can see the contents of a file by using the **cat** command, which simply outputs the contents to the screen (like **type** in DOS). If a file is larger than can be displayed on one screen, it will scroll on regardless. To prevent this happening, there is another command, **more**, which displays the contents of a file one screen at a time.

```
$ cat Makefile
This is the contents of the file Makefile!
```

We move up in the hierarchy using the **cd ..** command, and we move down via the **cd subdirectoryname** command.

```
$ pwd
/home/susan/reports
$ cd ..
$ pwd
/home/susan
```

> The . and .. notation is something that should already be
> familiar to DOS users. These dot notations originally appeared
> in UNIX and have long since been emulated by popular DOS
> systems. The command cd . simply directs the system to the
> current directory whilst cd .. takes the user to the parent
> directory of the current directory.

The parameter to the **cd** command can either be an absolute path from the
root directory, i.e. the path starts with a **/**, or a relative path where the first
character isn't a slash. For example, to change from the directory **/home/
susan/reports** to **/home/jim** both the command **cd /home/jim** and the
command **cd ../../jim** will have the desired effect. Of course, that is
assuming that we have the appropriate permissions.

```
$ cd /home/susan/reports
$ cd ../../jim
$ pwd
/home/jim
```

Most UNIX systems allow a shorthand for a user's home directory,
~username, often referred to as 'tilde', 'twiddle', or 'home'. Assuming that
the directory **/home/susan** is actually Susan's home directory, we can change
to it from anywhere in the directory tree with the command **cd ~susan**.
Susan can also use the even shorter version, **cd ~**, as a tilde on its own
refers to the user's own home directory. Additionally, if you type **cd** without
any arguments, you will also return the user to their home directory.

```
$ pwd
/usr/include
$ cd ~susan
$ pwd
/home/susan
```

The Structure of a Typical Root Directory

The root directory structure is usually divided up into a series of functional
areas, each relating to the purpose of its contents.

A typical set of top level directories and their uses are shown here:

Directory	Contents of directory
/	The root directory has a variety of sub-directories. Some files are used for starting up the system, most notably **UNIX** or **VMUNIX**, which are operating system kernels.
/boot	Files used for the system start-up (normally referred to as 'booting'). Contains device drivers and loadable modules.
/bin	Important system command files.
/sbin	Static binary files, similar to **/bin**.
/tmp	A place for temporary, short-lived files. They are normally shared between all users and may be deleted on reboot.
/lib	System libraries.
/dev	Devices. All UNIX devices appear as files.
/usr	These are files that are required to support multi-user working, but are not owned by users. User programs and compiler files are stored here. A network of computers may share a common **usr** Sometimes a user's home directories are put here, although for security reasons this practice is not recommended.
/etc	Important system configuration and control files, normally only accessible to the system administrator.
/var	Variable files. Files that are machine specific are stored here. These include files such as printer configuration files, mail files, log files, spool files. (Smaller machines sometimes use **/usr** for these.)
/u **/home** **/users**	A user's personal files are usually stored in one of these directories, depending on which system variant you are using.

As you can see, the structure is divided up by purpose. This allows the most critical and stable parts of the system to be neatly separated from the less important and more unreliable files. Similarly in DOS, the root may include directories such as **mouse, temp, DOS, windows, cmd** and **backup**.

Often the UNIX directories **/, /etc, /bin, /lib, /sbin** and **/boot** will physically be on a separate disk from the remaining directories. These are normally the only directories required to boot a UNIX system and rarely ever change. Keeping them physically separate from the other files is a sensible precaution against corruption.

The **/dev** directory mainly contains special files that only access physical devices. Normally only the system administrator needs to use these, except for one special file, **/dev/null**. This is always an empty file. If you want to execute a command but don't want its output, you can write the output to **/dev/null**, which discards it efficiently.

> Some UNIX variants (such as the UNIX System V) also have a **/proc** directory. This is a special pseudo-file system used to allow utility programs to obtain the status of executing programs.

Swap Area

There is also another part of the file system that may be present, a **swap area**, which the operating system uses for managing its virtual memory. This area is used to execute more programs than will fit in the physical memory at one time, and allows an individual program to use more memory than physically exists. If you are familiar with Microsoft Windows, the swap area serves a similar purpose to the Windows swap file. Although the swap area does have a structure, it is normally quite different from the other file systems.

File and Directory Naming

The naming rules that exist for files and directories in UNIX are actually very flexible. Unlike DOS or VMS, case *is* significant, so **freds_file** is a completely different file from **Freds_file**. All commands are files as well, so case is significant in commands too - **ls** is a command but **LS** will not be recognized.

UNIX files can have names, like the 8 character name with 3 character extension that DOS uses, but in UNIX there is no need for these extensions. There is a limit to the length that a filename can be, but on modern UNIX variants this is likely to be around 250 or more characters - more than enough. File names may contain any sequence of characters, including spaces (which should, however, be avoided), along with the following:

```
* . < [ ] { } > \ / ! |  & ; ( ) <tab>
```

as well as any other non-printable characters and control codes.

Asterisk Wild Cards

UNIX uses wild cards to refer to groups of files, rather like DOS. Unlike DOS, however, the shell program is responsible for expanding the wild cards and passing the resulting file names on to the program being run. Suppose we have a directory with a number of files that we want to manipulate, like the following one:

```
$ ls
We.Like--longer.file.names--   file2        file4.txt file1
file3
```

If we wish to delete the files beginning with '**file**', we can use the **rm** command like this:

```
$ rm file*
```

Just as it does in DOS, the asterisk stands for any sequence of characters. If we only wanted to delete the files **file1**, **file2** and **file3**, we would use a question mark to act as a single character wild card. Like this:

```
$ rm file?
```

The difference between DOS and UNIX wild cards is that when this **rm** program is run, it is given a sequence of three arguments, **file1**, **file2** and **file3**. The equivalent DOS command, **DEL**, is given a single argument, **file?** and has to expand the wild cards itself. In DOS, wild cards can only be used with programs that cater for them - because some don't take advantage of this feature. In UNIX, the shell expands the wild cards, so the programs don't have to bother with them, thus making them much simpler.

	UNIX	DOS
User types:	**rm file?**	**del file?**
Program sees:	**rm file1 file2 file3**	**del file?**

This also means that wild card expansion is totally consistent for all UNIX programs. Because the shell automatically expands wild cards as file names, we can use them with any command. For example, the **echo** command:

```
$ echo file?
file1 file2 file3
```

Unlike the DOS asterisk, the UNIX version can be followed by more characters or wild cards, making complex file specifications possible.

Note that the file specification ***.*** matches those files containing a dot in their name and not all files:

```
$ echo *.*
We.Like--longer.file.names-- file4.txt
```

Use ***** on its own to match all files. If there aren't any files matching the pattern, UNIX passes the unchanged pattern to the command, just like DOS. So a command given ***.xyz**, where the current directory hasn't any files of that extension, will be passed an argument ***.xyz**.

Pattern Matching

The shell also supports other file name wild cards, or patterns, notably square brackets, to denote character classes. Thus:

```
[...]
```

matches any one of the enclosed characters. Take the following example:

```
$ echo file[31]
file1 file3
```

This matches all files that begin with **file3** or **file1**.

Ranges

A pair of characters separated by a minus sign denotes a range and enables you to match any character within that range. If ! or ^ follows the first bracket, then only characters not enclosed in the brackets are matched. If you need to match a dash or an actual square bracket, you must include it either as the first or last character in the set. Finally there are a special set of files which we must consider seperately.

Dot Files

Files and directories starting with a . are considered hidden and are not normally displayed. Unlike DOS, being 'hidden' isn't an attribute, it is purely a naming convention. The `ls` command and shell programs ignore all hidden files by default.

> Applying `ls -a` will show you all the hidden files and subdirectories in a given directory. You may be quite surprised to see just how many hidden files you have lurking in your own directory!

File Permissions

As UNIX is a multi-user system, it has various access controls for files and directories. These can be used to restrict access to data or programs that you don't wish other users to use, see, modify or even know exist.

A single UNIX user is considered to be both distinct from other users and able to belong to one or more groups of users. In addition there will always be one 'special' system user, the system administrator, who is commonly referred to as the superuser, or 'root' user. This superuser has access to all files and areas in the system. Most UNIX systems will also have several different administration logins, called pseudo users, for different administrative purposes such as configuring devices, making backups or shutting down the system in an orderly fashion.

Each file and directory:

- Has an owner.
- Is associated with a group.
- Has (at least) twelve flags associated with it.

File Permission Flags

The twelve flags are arranged into four categories. There are three for managing permissions and one for other special purposes, usually only of interest to the system administrator.

The three permission categories that control the access allowed to three different classes of user are:

- The 'owner' - the person who owns the file.
- The 'group' - people in the same group as the file owner.
- The 'others' - all other possible users.

In each of these three categories, there are three permissions, 'read', 'write' and 'execute', which may be set to either true or false.

Viewing and Understanding Normal Permissions

As we have seen, files and directories are displayed with the `ls` command. There are many options to the `ls` command, but the most commonly used is `-l`, which gives a more detailed listing than the list of file names.

> In UNIX, almost all options to a command are introduced with a dash rather than a slash as in DOS or VMS.

When a file or directory is shown with the `ls -l` command, the first part of the output tells us the file type and permissions. The file type indicator is a dash for a normal file, or `d` for a directory. We will return to the other types later. The permission categories are shown opposite:

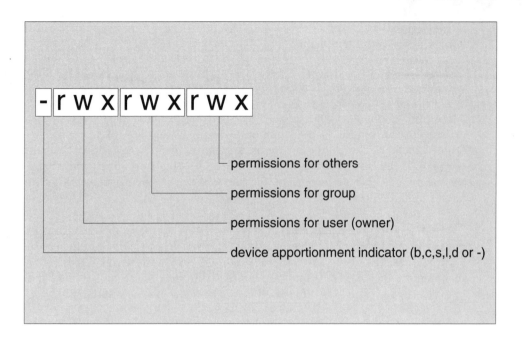

The position of each **r**, **w** or **x** character is fixed. If an **r,w** or **x** is present, then a permission is granted. A dash indicates that no permission is granted. The meanings of the permissions are shown in the table below:

Permission	ID	On a file	On a directory
read	r	Allowed to read	Allowed to read the directory to show information about files in the directory, but only if the filenames are known.
write	w	Allowed to write (and overwrite)	Allowed to create and delete files in the directory.
execute	x	Allowed to execute	Allowed to search the directory, i.e. able to discover what files are present.

If we were to now try and run the command `ls -l` in user Jim's directory, you will see output like this:

```
-rw-r----- 1 jim  softdev   2654 Jul 27  9:33      report_data
-rwxr-x--- 1 jim  softdev  53456 Jul 21 13:36      run_report
```

After the twelve flags that are set for permissions, the next attribute you can see in the output is the number of links, normally a **1** for a file or **2** for a directory. The following items are the name of the owner, the name of the group, the size in bytes, the modification date and time, and bringing up the rear is the all important filename. We will have a closer look at links later in this chapter.

The file **report_data** has one link, is owned by Jim, is in the group **softdev**, contains 2654 bytes and was last written to at 9:33 a.m. on the 27th of July. The user Jim can both read to and write from the file, members of the **softdev** group may read but not write to the file, and no-one else apart from the superuser can access the **report_data** file.

The file **run_report** is an executable file, and Jim has granted it the same permissions as the data file, plus the additional permission for both himself and members of the **softdev** group to execute the file. Note that UNIX doesn't look for **.exe**, **.bat** or **.com** files to execute - only the name of the file can signify whether a file is executable or not.

Loopholes in Permissions

You should take care with permissions on directories. Even if you create a file in your directory with no write permissions for anyone but yourself, the file may still be deleted by other users if you have granted them write permission on that directory. For example a file with these permissions:

```
-rw-r--r-- 1 jim  softdev   2634 Jul 21 10:31    undeletable_file
```

could be deleted if it were within a directory with these permissions:

```
drwxrw-rw- 2 jim  softdev   1024 Jul 21 10:25    deletable_dir
```

If you haven't got permission to a file and you try to access it, then access is denied. For example, if the user Jim belonged to the group **softdev** and there was a file that was owned by root and had the following permissions, then user Jim wouldn't be able to read the file:

```
-rw----rwx  root softdev     1024  Jan 1 9:50  foo1
```

Although the file has read, write and execute flags ON for all users, user Jim won't be able to read it because he belongs to the group **softdev.** Access will be denied, because the group **softdev** doesn't have read privileges.

Special Permissions

Permission	ID	On a file	On a directory
Set uid or gid	s	Runs as though executed by the owner of the file	Meaningless for directories.
Sticky	t	Hold in memory even if not running	Only the owner of a file may delete that file from the directory.

The fourth category is the 'special' group of permissions. They have the unusual names **setuid**, **setgid** and **sticky**. All processes running under UNIX have an effective user and group to control access to files. Normally when a user executes a program, the program is run according to the permissions that apply to that user. If a file has the 'setuid' flag set and is an executable file (other than a shell script), then when it is executed it runs as though it was executed by the owner of the file. This is useful for allowing users to access information in other files, without allowing them to actually read the file. In our earlier example, let us assume that Jim would like to permit all the other users on the system to run a summary report that shows only some of the information in the **report_data** file. He could create a new report named **summary_rep** that produces the correct information and allows all users to execute it. The directory could now have the following three files:

```
-rw-r----- 1  jim  softdev   2654  Jul 27  9:33      report_data
-rwxr-x--- 1  jim  softdev  53456  Jul 22 13:36      run_report
-rwxr-x--x 1  jim  softdev  24732  Jul 28 16:52      summary_rep
```

Unfortunately, if the program **summary_rep** is executed by a user Rob, who isn't a member of the **softdev** group, and the program tries to read data from the file **report_data**, it will fail. This is because Rob hasn't got permission to read the file. This difficulty can be overcome by adding the 'setuid' permission to the file.

Set Uid Permissions

The following listing displays the execute permission for the owner as **s**, to show that the program will run under setuid.

```
-rw-r----- 1  jim  softdev   2654  Jul 27  9:33      report_data
-rwxr-x--- 1  jim  softdev  53456  Jul 22 13:36      run_report
-rwsr-x--x 1  jim  softdev  24732  Jul 29 16:52      summary_rep
```

When Rob runs the file **summary_rep,** it executes as though it had been run by Jim (since it is owned by Jim and is setuid), and it is able to read the file **report_data** successfully.

Set Gid Permissions

The setgid flag is the equivalent flag for setuid, but it is applied to groups and is shown as an **s** in the 'execute by group' position. These flags should be used with caution, since they reduce the security of the system considerably. If the file **summary_rep** allowed any other command to be executed, then Rob could potentially ask **summary_rep** to delete files owned by Jim, since the system allows the program to have the same permissions as Jim himself.

Sticky Permissions

The last special flag is the sticky flag. This is shown as a **t** in the 'execute by others' position of a file listing. It tells the operating system that the executable program with this flag set is to be held in memory if possible, even if it isn't running. This was useful for small, frequently run programs, but is becoming less popular these days as UNIX becomes much faster, cheaper and far more advanced. On some UNIX variants the 'sticky' flag may be used on a directory. It then has the special meaning that only the owner of a file may delete that file from the directory. This is commonly used on temporary directories shared by many different users, such as **/tmp**.

Changing Permissions

Now we have looked at the concept of file permissions, it is time to get down to the business of changing the file permissions if they don't suit you. This is accomplished with the aid of the **chmod** command, via one of two methods.

chmod Command (Simple Method)

The simplest method is to use the following which adds or subtracts permissions:

$ chmod *<who><add or subtract><what> <filename>*

<who> denotes which user's permissions are to be changed, **u** for user (i.e. the owner of the file), **g** for group, or **o** for others. To *<add or subtract>* we simply use **+** or **-**, and *<what>* presents the new permission, **r** for read, **w** for write or **x** for execute. These may be combined. Given the following:

```
-r--r----- 1  jim  softdev   4536  Jul 21 9:33 report
```

we could add the permission for the owner to write to it using:

```
$ chmod u+w report
$ ls -l
-rw-r----- 1  jim  softdev   4536  Jul 21 9:33 report
```

To add permission for the user, group and others to execute the file we could use the following command:

```
$ chmod ogu+x report
$ ls -l
-rwxr-x--x 1  jim  softdev   4536  Jul 21 9:33 report
```

Instead of using **ogu** in the last example, we could have used **a** to state all types of user, so the previous command could have been expressed as

chmod a+x report. It would have had the same effect:

```
$ chmod a+x report
$ ls -l
-rwxr-x--x 1  jim  softdev   4536  Jul 21 9:33 report
```

chmod Command (Absolute Form)

The other method is known as the absolute form. This ignores the current state of the permission flags and sets the flags as an octal string. To repeat the success of the above example we need to set the user's **rwx** flags, the group's **rx** flags and the others' **x** flag. As a bit-pattern this is 111101001 or in octal 751. The command we would require is:

```
$ chmod 751 report
$ ls -l
-rwxr-x--x 1  jim  softdev   4536  Jul 21 9:33 report
```

As you can see, the absolute form can be quicker, but it can also be quite laborious to apply. A common octal series is 755 for programs, which represents the permissions, **-rwxr-xr-x**.

chmod Command and Special Groupings

The special setuid, setgid and sticky bits are set with the **u+s**, **g+s** and **o+t** options respectively, using the **chmod** command. They can also be set using the absolute form where they are the fourth octet of bits, before the permission octets. The command **chmod 5755** sets the setuid and the sticky bits, as well as granting read, write and execute to owner, with read and execute to both group and others.

> There are many more commands for manipulating files and directories besides those for setting the permissions. As a quick start reference guide, you will find a summary of the main ones together with their closest DOS equivalents at the end of this chapter.

38

Hints and Tips

There are several common dilemmas that often baffle less experienced users, among which 'How do I copy a directory tree?' and 'I can't delete this file' are two well known examples. Here we will try to de-mystify the processes involved in solving such problems.

Moving and Copying Directories

In most cases UNIX allows you to move a directory simply by using the **mv** command. This even works when the directory is being moved to a different level in the directory tree, for example:

```
$ mv /home/susan/test/jimcmd /home/jim/newcommand
```

will move the **jimcmd** directory to the **newcommand** directory.

However, if you want to move a directory across file systems, or you want to copy a directory tree, you can't use the **cp** or **mv** commands.

Some versions of UNIX have a special command for copying directory trees, or they have a **cp** command that takes the **-r** or **-R** options. These options can be used to copy directories. In Linux, the **-r** option is used to copy directories and their contents. For example if you decided to copy the **jimcmd** directory to the **newcommand** directory, instead of moving it, you would use:

```
$ cp -r /home/susan/test/jimcmd /home/jim/newcommand
```

Copying Directories with tar

If neither **cp** or **mv** are available, then to copy a directory tree from **/src** to **/dest** directories you can use this rather strange looking incantation:

```
$ cd /src; tar cf - . | (cd /dest; tar xfp -)
```

This changes to the source directory, invokes the **tar** program to backup the current directory and tells it to write any output to the standard output. The bracketed command then starts a shell, changes to the destination directory and uses the **tar** program to restore the data by reading its standard input. We will look fully at these concepts in later chapters.

Deleting Files That Won't Go Away

If you have a file that won't be deleted or if you can't get UNIX to admit that a file exists, it is usually due to one of two things. Firstly, check the obvious! Do you have permission to delete the file? Remember - you need to have write permission on the directory in order to delete a file in that directory.

The second possibility is that you have accidentally created a file with a name that contains a non-printable character. If you can't delete a file that is apparently called **bigfile,** type in the following:

```
$ ls b*e | od -h
```

This will list all the files starting with **b** and ending with **e**, converting the output into hex. This will let you see, amongst the hex output, any non-printable characters in those file names (such as those resulting from *Ctrl+H*). You can then delete files with strange names by using the command **rm** with the **-i** parameter. In our example then, we could write **rm -i b*e**. For each file matching **b*e**, **rm** will ask if you want the file removing.

There is one last tip for using **rm**. A parameter starting with a dash is taken by the **rm** command to be an option, not a filename. If you try and remove a file called **-f**, **rm** thinks that the **-f** is an option, not a file name. To avoid this, ask **rm** to delete two files, making the second one the file **-f**, even if the first file doesn't exist. For example:

```
$ rm not.a.file -f
```

The **rm** command will then interpret the second parameter as a filename - even though it starts with a dash. Alternatively, the parameter **--** is often interpreted as meaning the end of options, so this should work too:

```
$ rm -- -f
```

> Beware - once you remove a file, you can't get it back. There
> is no undelete function in UNIX, although some versions help
> you by supplying a 'waste bin' which can be restored.
> However, in Chapter 6, we will be taking a look at an
> alternative version of the **rm** command that will enable you
> to recover deleted files.

The Administrator's View of UNIX

As you might expect, the administrator's view for files is rather more
complex than the one presented to users. Usually a UNIX system will have
its actual disk space split into more than one partition, perhaps over several
physical disks. All this complexity is hidden from the user and managed by
the administrator.

Devices

Before we can look at the file system from the point of view of the
administrator, we need to know a little more about devices, the special files
that normally appear in the **/dev** directory. An important concept of UNIX
is that all hardware is accessed via the file system. There are two types of
device files: 'character special' and 'block special'. Both types are created
with the **mknod** command.

Block devices are normally used to access hardware that supports random
access, so disks are usually block devices, and serial and parallel ports are
character devices. There is a restriction that a block device must be read
and written in a multiple of its own 'natural' block size. This is commonly
1 kilobyte, but it may be larger or smaller. Since disks can be accessed in a
serial fashion as well as randomly, it is usual for a disk to have both a
block and a character device.

Most systems will have two filenames for some physical devices - a normal
name and a name preceded by '**r**', for **raw** device. Thus both **/dev/mt1** and
/dev/rmt1 may both refer to a magnetic tape drive, but the second device,
the raw device, accesses the hardware without using the operating system's
internal buffers.

The type of a special file is indicated in the 'directory' flag position of a long listing: **b** for a block device or **c** for a character device. A typical listing of part of the **/dev** directory might look like this:

```
crw--w--w- 1     root  root  21  1 21 Jul /dev/console
crw------- 1     root  root  21  2 19 Jul /dev/serial
brw------- 1     root  root   2  1 21 Jul /dev/dsk/0s0
brw-r--r-- 1     root  root   2  2 21 Jul /dev/dsk/0s1
brw-r--r-- 1     root  root   2  5 21 Jul /dev/dsk/1s0
brw-r--r-- 1     root  root   2  6 21 Jul /dev/dsk/1s1
crw------- 1     root  root   7  1 21 Jul /dev/dsk/r0s0
crw-r--r-- 1     root  root   7  2 21 Jul /dev/dsk/r0s1
crw-r--r-- 1     root  root   7  5 21 Jul /dev/dsk/r1s0
crw-r--r-- 1     root  root   7  6 21 Jul /dev/dsk/r1s1
brw-r--r-- 1     root  root   2 14 21 Jul /dev/floppy
crw-r--r-- 1     root  root   7 14 21 Jul /dev/rfloppy
```

The above shows two character devices, **/dev/console** and **/dev/serial**, four hard disk devices (typically two physical disks, each with two partitions) and a floppy disk device. Both the hard and floppy disk drive entries have block and character devices.

Remember, the block device transfers data in groups of characters. The character device is a raw device and allows more direct access to the underlying data, transferring data character by character. A character device can both produce and/or consume streams of characters. The main character devices are keyboards and printers.

The two columns of numbers between the group owner (**root**) and the date are the major and minor device numbers. The operating system uses these to access the physical device. The first number, the major device number, is the type of device and interface. Devices that use the same device number also use the same device driver. The second, minor device number, identifies the particular device being accessed. Terminals, for example, have minor numbers to identify them.

Other File Types

Before we move on, there are still a couple of file types that we haven't encountered yet. We will take a look at sockets and links right now.

Sockets

Sockets are used for inter-process communication and are denoted by an **s**. These are created with the **mknod** command, like the other devices. The socket is a data-pipe with a name. (We'll look at pipes between two commands in Chapter 3.) A command or program can write data into the pipe, and an unrelated program can read the data out again, on a first in first out (FIFO) basis. The difference from standard files is that a second program can start reading before a first program has finished writing - the named pipe acts as a buffer. The operating system will automatically suspend the data generator if it tries to write to a full pipe and only restart it when space is available. Equally, it will suspend the data reader when no data is available and restart it when data becomes available. This allows two unrelated programs to pass data without them having to worry about synchronization.

Links

A link file type is created with the **ln** command and is represented by an **l**. This allows two different names to refer to the same set of data. As we will see later, names in the file system reference a structure called an **inode**, which then points at a set of data blocks. Where two or more names refer to the same file, the different link names refer to the same inode.

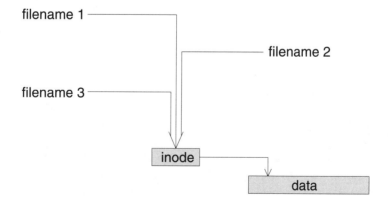

The link count in the **ls -l** command is shown after the permissions flags. Each inode maintains a count of the number of names pointing at it and, if the count becomes zero (i.e. there are no names referencing it), both the inode and the data it references are no longer in use and are marked as free.

Hard and Soft Links

There are two types of link, both created with the **ln** command - hard links and soft links. Hard links are only allowed between two files in the same file system, whilst soft links (also known as symbolic links) are more flexible and allow links across different file systems. An example of a hard link would be:

```
$ ln myfile linkfile
```

This would create a new file **linkfile** which is linked to the file **myfile**, except now there are two filenames pointing to the same file. You can't use hard links across file systems and you can't make a hard link to a directory. The hard link does have the advantage that the link and the original file are identical and the extra link takes up no disk space.

The format for a soft link is **ln -s**. An example of a soft link would be:

```
$ ln -s myfile linkfile2
```

This actually creates a new file **linkfile2** which is also a pointer to **myfile**. Soft links can be used across file systems and if you use the **ls -l** command you will be able to see which file the link is pointing to.

As there is only one copy of a file, a change made to a file through one of its links can be seen through all of its links. The **rm** command does not remove a linked file, it removes the links to the file. The file is deleted when the last link is removed.

It is also possible to link directories; for example, the directory **/usr/lib/news/spool** may be a link to the directory **/var/news/spool**. This can be confusing, because **cd ..** may not return you to the directory you expect, although some UNIX shells will recognize the special case and change to the expected directory. This unexpected behavior is shown in the following example:

```
$ pwd
/usr/lib/news
$ cd spool
$ pwd
/var/news/spool
$ cd ..
$ pwd
/var/news
```

Preparing a Disk

Assuming that you have decided how much disk space you need, or more likely how much you can afford, you must do some preparatory work before you can utilize the physical disk that is connected to your machine.

There are three stages: preparing the physical disk, dividing the disk into one or more partitions and then creating UNIX file systems in those partitions.

Format

The very first step is the low level format and bad track check. Since these can take a very long time it is perhaps fortunate that IDE and SCSI disks are normally preformatted and already have a bad track list. This saves the busy administrator a great deal of time consuming work.

Partition

The next step is to partition the disk. For each separate file system you must have a separate partition, but you don't need to create a file system in each partition. There will always be a swap partition and at least one other file system partition - a master partition for the root directory itself - from which UNIX will boot. Normally there is at least one other partition for user files. The commands for partitioning a disk depend upon your hardware and particular version of UNIX, though most UNIX implementations use the **FORMAT** command to do this task (e.g. HP, SUN and IBM do). Consult your system manuals for more details.

45

Deciding on the size of a partition is an important step, since they are not easily changed on most UNIX variants, and a partition may not extend over more than a single disk. The temptation for many users is simply to make the disk have a single root file system containing /, and put all the files, both system and user files, into the same single file system. Since the partition sizes can't be changed, this would seem an obvious choice. However, even for small systems with limited disk space this would be an inadvisable choice, since it mixes system and user files in the same file system. The experienced system administrator would usually separate the fairly stable root and **/usr** files from the more frequently changing user files, and, if possible, keep the rapidly changing **/tmp** file system away from all the other files. This minimizes the risk of corruption occurring to the system files.

For larger installations you should have at least three file systems, one for booting from, one for the **/usr** files and one for the actual user files. If you have the disk space, you should consider going still further and having a root partition for booting from, a partition for **/usr**, a partition for **/tmp** and one or more additional partitions for the actual user files. Depending on the physical disks on your system, these partitions may reside on a single physical disk, or be resident across several physical devices.

The master partition and **/usr** partition shouldn't change in size significantly once the system is installed, however some of the software packages do modify **/usr** and some also modify root, kernel patches and OS upgrades. Therefore, it is very important to make your root and **/usr** large enough for the future installs and upgrades.

File System Structure

After partitioning the disk (or disks), the basic file structure must be written to the disk. This is done with the **mkfs** (make file system) command. This is actually a front-end for various file system builders - consult your system manual and the UNIX help system for more details. The procedure for the master partition is often slightly different, since the files required for booting must be created. This will be detailed in your system manual.

There are many different forms of the UNIX file system, such as the System V file system, the BSD file system and the ACER file system. Some UNIX variants are even able to directly access DOS file systems. Since all details of the file system implementation are hidden in the kernel, user programs normally only need be aware of the underlying file system when restrictions are imposed. For example, if the underlying file system is DOS, then the definition of filenames is much more restricted than is normal in UNIX.

The internal structure of a UNIX file system depends on the type of UNIX you are running, but most variants have the same basic details. The items in a file system are:

- A super block
- A list of inodes
- A list of data blocks

There is always at least 1 super block, and normally several copies of it for safety. The super block normally contains:

- The size of the file system
- The number of free blocks
- A list of the free blocks
- An index to the next free block
- The size of the inode list
- The number of free inodes
- A list of the free inodes
- An index to the next free inode
- A 'dirty' flag, indicating if the file system needs checking

Inodes are the index into the file system. Each inode normally contains:

- The owner of the file
- The group owner of the file
- The file type
- The permission flags
- The access and modification times
- The size of the file
- The initial data blocks
- The disk address

The data blocks are simply where the data is stored. This is either the actual data in a file, or the data comprising a directory entry.

As we mentioned before, the filename . stands for the current directory, and .. refers to the parent directory of the current directory. Unlike DOS, the . and .. UNIX directory entries are actual entries in the directory file table. The algorithm used for finding data from a filename is quite complex, and the arrangement of the file system is rather more complex than presented here. However the basic sequence of events for finding a file is as follows:

1 Read the root inode (this is in a fixed location) which will point to a data block containing the directory file for /, and contains filenames and inode numbers for the first level of files and directories.

2 Search for the entry for the next level file or directory you want and retrieve its inode number, which is stored in the directory.

3 From the super block entry use the inode number to find the physical inode entry which contains information about the file, including its size and the block number of its first disk block.

4 From the super block use the data block number to locate the actual disk block containing the data from the file or directory.

This sequence is repeated as the tree is traversed until the required files' inode and data blocks are located.

If the path is a relative path, then the search starts from the current directory rather than the root directory. Sophisticated algorithms and caching strategies ensure that this search is efficient.

Mounting File Systems

Once a disk partition has a file system, it needs to be 'mounted' to make it appear as part of the standard tree structure.

Suppose a very small UNIX installation on a single disk has exceeded the disk space available. The existing tree structure might be something like:

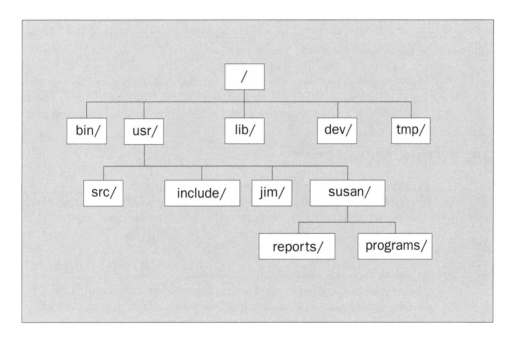

To expand the disk space available, a second disk is purchased and a file system created upon it. We now need to attach this second disk into the tree structure. We do this with the **mount** command. A sensible choice is to move the user files from **/usr/jim** and **/usr/susan** onto the new disk, since it is normally the user files that will grow, and we would like them separated from the system files anyway. We first create an empty directory to attach to; in this case we will use **/home**.

We then mount the new disk onto the **/home** directory with the command:

```
$ mount /dev/dsk/1s0 /home
```

The name of the actual device **/dev/dsk/1s0** will depend on your version of UNIX. Now we have all the free space on the new disk available in the directory **/home**, and we can copy the user directories from **/usr** into their new location under **/home**.

> If **/home** wasn't an empty directory, then mounting a file system on it will have the effect of hiding all the files.

To ensure that the new file system is automatically mounted for future reboots of the system, you may need to edit a configuration file. Where such a file resides depends upon your variant of UNIX, but quite a common location is the file **/etc/fstab**. Note the 'mount point', the place where we attached the new file system to the old directory tree. It could have been at a lower level. If we had wanted to, we could have created a new sub-directory under **/usr/jim** and added the new file system there.

Read Only Mounting

The most important parameter to the **mount** command is **-r**. This mounts the file system as 'read only'. This can be useful when you want to check the contents of a file system without risking changing any important data, or when the file system doesn't allow writing, such as a file system on CD-ROM.

> File systems are dismounted using the **umount** command. UNIX will prevent you dismounting a file system if any process has a file on the file system that is currently open.

For further information on the **mount** and **umount** commands see Chapter 9.

Maintaining Integrity - fsck

The structure of the file system is checked and corrected by a program called **fsck**, in conjunction with the 'dirty' flag in the super block. During normal use of the file system, this flag is set and can only be cleared (or unset) on a clean system shutdown. When the system tries to mount a file system, it always checks the 'dirty' flag. If this is set, then it can tell that the system did not shutdown cleanly and the integrity of the file system should be checked.

The **fsck** command performs a similar function to the DOS **scandisk** command. It is normally invoked automatically on boot, but may be run at any time if required. Apart from on the root file system, which can't be dismounted, **fsck** should only be run on a dismounted file system, otherwise user programs could be trying to write to the file system while **fsck** is trying to repair it. Some variants of UNIX have a special flag (usually **-r**) to **fsck** to signal that it is to be run on a root file system. If you do need to run **fsck** on the root file system, ensure UNIX is running in single user mode and that there is little or no system activity before continuing.

The **fsck** program makes several passes to correct problems and will often ask seemingly complex questions before proceeding. Fortunately this isn't a problem. If you want **fsck** to check a file system, but not change anything, use **fsck -n**, meaning answer NO to all questions. To repair a file system run **fsck -y**, meaning answer YES to all questions. Very few experts know more about a file system than the authors of the **fsck** program. They did a good job, so trust in **fsck**'s ability to do a good job for you. If you run **fsck -y** on a file system and **fsck** reports it has made changes, then you should run **fsck -y** again. Often **fsck** will require two or even more invocations before a badly corrupted file system is properly repaired. If it was the root partition that **fsck** was cleaning, then the system should be rebooted once **fsck** has finished.

Most UNIX variants have an additional program **fsdb**, for file system debugging. This enables you to directly manipulate the structure of a file system. This should only be used in the most serious cases and only after careful consultation of the manual. The only 'undo' feature is the previous backup!

Backing Up the System

If you have important information on your system, you need a strategy for ensuring it gets backed up safely. Usually you must make some trade-offs between cost and the time available. Just think of the amount of disk space or memory you could afford if you are able to do without that tape drive!

Remember that backups are not just for those very occasional system failures, they come in very handy for those times when users delete a file and then want it back. In fact, this is a much more common reason for needing to restore data from a backup than the corruption of a file system or a physical failure of a disk drive.

You should occasionally test your backups, to ensure, that the backup media is readable and that you can restore files from it. It's best to test the restore function in your backup strategy before your system gets corrupted!

Strategies

- A typical UNIX installation will have significantly more used disk space than can be stored on its backup medium in a single pass. However, you will probably only need to back up a subset of the entire system at any one time.

- The most obvious reduction isn't to back up all the permanent system files. Remember that even if all your user files are in **/home**, there will still be configuration files, password files and so on, in the rest of the file system. Once you are used to running the system, your configuration will rarely be much different from when you originally installed it.

- A sensible compromise might be to install the system, keeping notes about how it was set up and then in future only back up those files that have changed.

- If, like most UNIX systems, it is impractical to back up every single file on each backup, you must decide what to back up, when and how often. It is up to you to find a sensible compromise between taking too much time for backups and not backing up the system frequently enough.

- Always backing up every file ensures that everything gets backed up. However, unless you have a disproportionately small disk and a large backup device, the time and cost of your backup media will make this option fairly expensive.

- Incremental backup ensures only modified files are replicated. This reduces the number to be saved, but increases the complexity of the backup. A simple strategy would be to back up the whole system on the first of the month and then have a daily incremental backup, copying only those files that have changed since the full backup.

Single Timestamp File

For small systems, it may be possible to install the system and then create a special 'timestamp' file. Each time you do a backup, you need only backup the files that have changed since that timestamp file was created. The problem is that, over time, the number of new or changed files will continue to increase. Suppose you install a new compiler or a new database? The size of your backup will suddenly increase considerably. You could then perform a new complete backup, create a new timestamp file and backup future changes. This is probably satisfactory for small systems, but isn't a tenable long term solution for larger installations.

Interleaved Full and Incremental Backups

Most UNIX installations use a system of full and partial backups. From time to time a complete backup will be performed, and incremental backups are used to keep more up-to-date copies of working files. As we will see, UNIX has a host of tools and utilities for performing backups, so even a complex backup strategy can be quite easy to implement.

There are two common methods of mixing full and partial backups - the differential method and the incrementing level (or towers of Hanoi) backup procedure. To explain the difference between these two, take the following example. Suppose we decide on a full backup every Monday and some form of incremental backup on other weekdays. Most backups are performed late at night when no users are on the system.

The Differential Method

The differential method does a full backup on Monday. Then, for Tuesday's backup, only files changed since Monday's backup will be stored. Wednesday's backup also consists of all files changed since Monday and so on through the week. This is assuming that a 'timestamp' file is being created every Monday. Suppose on Thursday morning our hard disk fails and all the data on it is lost. We need to restore Monday's tape and on top of it restore Wednesday's backup. The system is now back to the state it was in first thing Thursday morning.

The difficulty with this system is that each of Tuesday's through to Friday's backup is larger than the previous evening, because not only does it include that days alterations, but all changed files since Monday evening. By Friday we could have accumulated a very large backup. The advantage is that only one incremental tape was needed to restore all the files, and changes are often backed up onto more than one tape, which is useful if an incremental tape were to fail.

The Tower of Hanoi Method

The tower of Hanoi method does a full backup on Monday, on Tuesday it backs up all the files changed since Monday, on Wednesday it backs up all the files changed since Tuesday, etc. The disadvantage is that when our hypothetical system failure occurs on Thursday, we must now restore not only Monday's full backup, but also Tuesday's and Wednesday's backups, and a failure on any of these tapes will prevent us fully restoring our system. The advantage is that the size of each incremental backup tends to be relatively small.

Depending on the size of your system, the number of files changing daily, the size of the backup media and the complexity involved, each system administrator needs to choose the most suitable strategy for their system. The good thing is the amount of choice available, so that various backup strategies can easily be implemented.

One thing to bear in mind is that backup media is often less reliable than the media you are backing up from. If you do a long sequence of 'tower of Hanoi' backups, then to restore a complete file system you not only need the base backup, but every subsequent incremental backup as well. The more sets of backup media you have to use to recover your file systems, the more chance there is that one of these backups could be corrupted.

Backup Commands

There are three main backup commands - **tar**, **cpio** and **dump/restore**. Each have their place and we will look at each one in turn.

Two other commands fall into this section, the **dd** and **mt** commands. The **dd** command stands for disk to disk copy and is self-explanatory. It can be used to copy between file systems and backup media, but isn't a good form of backup because there is no way of restoring individual files. It is occasionally useful because it runs very quickly. A backup tape may be checked by using the **dd** command which reads and then discards the data:

```
$ dd if=/dev/rmt0 of=/dev/null bs=10k
```

The **mt** command is for positioning on a tape. This could be used if you have several file systems backed up as separate files on a single tape. If you need this command, you should consult your manual for the parameters applicable to your backup device.

The tar Command

This command is universally available, has a simple syntax and is easy to understand. Some variants are unable to backup device files or named pipes, however these do not often require backing up, since they are normally only created when the operating system is installed. The most common choice for small backups is **tar**, because it is so easy to use.

An example command would be:

```
$ tar cvbf 1024 /dev/rmt0 .
```

This means **c**reate a backup with a **v**erbose list of files, **b**lock the output and write to a **f**ile in blocks of **1024**. **/dev/rmt0** is the device to write to. The final **.** is the directory you want to backup. All the files in this directory and its subdirectories will be backed up. Blocking the output to 1024 means that **tar** will collect all the data to be saved until it has 1024 blocks to write. It is normally much quicker to write a few large blocks rather than lots of small blocks. In fact some tape drives require you to write in multiples of 10k.

To restore from the backup, you would change to the directory to be restored and use the command:

```
$ tar xvpbf 1024 /dev/rmt0
```

As you can see, the syntax is very similar to that for backup. The differences are that **c** is replaced by **x** for extract, and **p** is added. This **p**reserves file ownership and permissions when the files are restored. You must be in the directory that the backup was initially taken from if the files are to be restored correctly in the same place. This is because **tar** will write the restored data straight into the current directory.

> If you add the syntax | grep *filename* to the end of the **tar** command, you can specify the individual file you wish to restore.

The command for listing the contents of a **tar** backup is:

```
$ tar tvbf 1024 /dev/rmt0
```

This produces a **t**able of contents, without actually restoring the tape. You should be aware that this isn't a means of testing the integrity of the backup - **tar** is able to read a header record, skip the actual data and read the next header record. This makes the table of contents command run much quicker, but would make it oblivious to any corrupt data.

The **tar** command is often used to create a backup of a simple hierarchy by specifying the source directory as '.', which has the effect of creating a **tar** file containing all files in the current directory and all sub-directories. Some versions of **tar** have an option **-z,** which automatically compresses the archive being created. This combination is often used for packing directory hierarchies for transfer over a network, since a single compressed file is both easier and much more efficient to handle than a large directory tree.

Most versions of the **tar** command have an option that allows you to specify a file containing a list of files to back up. This is very useful if you want to use **tar** to create a backup of a specific list of files you have created. If your version of **tar** doesn't support this option, you may be unable to use **tar** to back up a large pre-determined list of files, since the length of the command line required may exceed your system limits.

> In Chapter 9 we will look at how to extract specific files using the tar command, from an ftp site.

The cpio Command

The **cpio** command is also widely available. All variants can back up device files as well as normal files. The command is more flexible than **tar**, but has a much more complex syntax. When transferring data between different machines, **cpio** has a special 'character header' mode for increased portability between different variants of UNIX. Its ability to take a list of files from standard input can be useful when writing complex shell scripts for backups.

The **cpio** command expects a list of backup files to be presented on its standard input, and it will write the backed up data to its standard output. The input file list is often generated with the **find** command, but could easily be from a file. A typical backup command would be:

```
$ find . -print | cpio -oBcv > /dev/rmt0
```

This finds all files in the current directory tree, outputs them in blocks, in character and in verbose mode to the device **/dev/rmt0**.

> The > character indicates that the data flows from the output of the command to the device.

The equivalent restore command would be:

```
$ cpio -iBcv < /dev/rmt0
```

The output flag is simply replaced with the input flag, and data is read rather than written to the tape.

> The < character indicates that the data flows from the device to the input of the command.

The command for listing the contents of a backup is:

```
$ cpio -iBcvt < /dev/rmt0
```

57

This produces a table of contents, without actually restoring the tape. Like **tar** you shouldn't assume this is a way of testing the integrity of the backup.

The dump and restore Commands

The **dump** and **restore** commands are not as universally available as the **tar** and **cpio** commands. They were written for backing up and restoring whole BSD file systems and are often the chosen backup command on larger systems. The **dump** command maintains records of which file systems have been backed up and when this was done. Full and incremental backups are catered for. An example command would be:

```
$ dump 0dsbf 54000 600 1024 /dev/rmt0
```

This means do a level **0** backup, tape density **54000** bits per inch, size **600** feet, blocking factor **1024** and backup file **/dev/rmt0**.

An example restore command would be:

```
$ restore xvdsbf 54000 600 1024 /dev/rmt0
```

The only differences here are that we are extracting it in verbose mode. This would restore an entire file system. To restore a smaller number of files, **restore** has an **i** flag which gives an interactive mode. This allows you to read in the tape header, and then examine the names and dates of files and directories on the backup, tagging those you wish to restore, before actually extracting any files.

The backup level to the **dump** command is most important. A level 0 dump dumps all files, whereas levels 1 to 9 dump all files that have been modified since the last dump at that (lower) level. This is often ideal for backing up large file systems, because it allows both differential and incremental backups to be made. They only backup and restore a single file system however, so you may need a non-rewinding tape device and a sequence of backup commands to backup your entire installation. If you have the **dump** and **restore** commands available, they should be your first choice for backups. Some UNIX variants without **dump** have an equivalent 'backup' command.

Commands for Manipulating Files and Directories

UNIX	DOS	Command Effect
basename *<filename>*		Converts a full pathname to a local name. The command **basename /tmp/jim** gives the output **jim.**
cat *<filename>*	type	The command **cat report** will display the contents of the file **report** on the screen. The name is short for 'concatenate' - multiple files may be given.
cd *<path>*	cd	Changes directory to *<path>*.
chmod *<mode> <filename>*	attr	Changes mode (permissions).
diff *<file1> <file2>*	filecmp	Compares the contents of two files. The UNIX version gives a lot more information than the brief DOS version.
cp *<srcfile> <destfile>*	copy	Copies one file to another.
df	dir	Disk free. Shows the free disk space.
du *<directory>*	dir	Disk used. Shows the disk space used.
ed *<filename>*	edlin	A simple (but very powerful) line editor.
emacs *<filename>*		A powerful file editor from the GNU project, available on many UNIX systems.
find *<path> <expression>*		Locates files matching a pattern in a directory tree.

Continued

UNIX	DOS	Command Effect
grep *<pattern> <filenames>*	**find**	Searches file(s) for a pattern. **grep fred *txt** searches all files with names ending in **txt** for the string **fred** and prints each line containing **fred**.
head *<filename>*		Shows the first few lines of a file.
ln *<oldfile> <newname>*		Link. Makes another name refer to an existing file.
ls *<options> <pattern>*	**dir**	Lists the contents of a directory. Different versions of UNIX have slight differences. The most useful options are **l** (gives a long listing), **t** (chronologically sorts with the newest files first) and **r** (sorts alphabetically).
mkdir *<directory>*	**mkdir**	Makes a directory.
more *<filename>*	**more**	Displays by pages. Unlike the DOS command **more**, the UNIX **more** accepts a filename as a parameter.
mv *<oldname> <newname>*	**rename** **move**	Moves (or renames) a file. UNIX also permits directories to be renamed.
od *<options> <filename>*		Octal dump.
pr *<options> <filename>*		Prints listing. Displays a formatted listing of the file on the screen, suitable for printing.
pwd	**cd**	Prints the working directory. Displays the path to your current directory.

Continued

60

UNIX	DOS	Command Effect
rm *<filename>*	**delete**	Removes a file. The command **deltree rm -r mydir** recursively removes the directory **mydir**, including all files and directories in it (and of course any files within those directories, etc.).
rmdir *<directory>*	**rmdir**	Removes a directory.
sort *<filename>*	**sort**	Sorts the lines in a file and displays the output on the screen.
tail *<filename>*		Shows the last few lines of a file.
touch *<filename>*	**touch** (only found in DR-DOS)	Updates the time of modification of a file, without changing its contents. Unlike DOS, this creates the file if it did not exist.
uniq *<filename>*		Outputs the file to the screen, removing any repeated lines.
vi *<filename>*	**edit**	Visual edit. The standard full screen UNIX editor. Powerful, but very difficult to learn.
wc *<filename>*		Counts the words, characters and lines in a file. Some effort to learn, but the rewards are considerable.
file *<filename>*		Uses a data file and an heuristic algorithm to determine the type of file. The result isn't guaranteed to be correct, but usually is.

Summary

In this chapter we have taken a look at both sides of the UNIX file system fence: the user's view and the more integral administrator's view.

As a user, you have learnt about directory hierarchy, file permissions and many useful file system commands. You will now be able to traverse the UNIX system and complete many file management tasks, including directory and file manipulation.

As a UNIX administrator, you have learnt about different file types, preparing a disk, the structure of a file system, mounting and backing up your data. You should now have a grasp of how to set up and backup, and understand how the UNIX file system works and evolves.

You should now be ready to move on from file permissions and plow into the vast array of useful commands that UNIX offers the user.

Chapter

General UNIX Commands and Utilities

In this chapter we will learn more about using UNIX to get work done - how to run and control programs and manipulate their output. UNIX has a large number of tools, each of which perform specific tasks, which may be used collectively to perform useful work. It is very much a part of the UNIX culture that programs be reusable and many jobs may be accomplished by reusing and adapting existing tools, rather than writing new programs. This chapter begins at the most basic level of UNIX commands and briefly details the most useful commands and utilities available to the user. We will cover:

- Definitions of UNIX terminology
- Basic UNIX commands
- Information commands
- Input and output within UNIX
- Processes and job control
- Regular expressions
- Different editors available with UNIX

UNIX Terminology

There are a number of terms related to running programs that you must understand before we progress any further. These are:

Shell

When you login, UNIX automatically starts a shell session, which means that you begin a dialog with a program called a **shell**. This is an ordinary program running on the computer alongside other shells for other users. The main function of the shell program is to accept commands from you and perform them. You type the name of a command and the shell runs it for you. It bears a similar resemblance to the **COMMAND.COM** program in DOS, but is ultimately much more powerful.

Command

A command is an instruction to the UNIX operating system that tells it to perform some action, i.e. whatever the user types in to the shell. The shell may perform the action itself if the command is built into the shell. This is similar to a DOS internal command.

Program

A program is an executable file. The shell will run the program whose name is given as the first word of a command. It finds the program to run by looking in those directories specified in the environment variable, **PATH**. This operates in a similar fashion to DOS external commands and **.EXE** files.

> Beware - if you give a program the same name as a command, the program won't execute. For example, you may have problems if you named a program **test**, since there is actually a **test** command. To get round this, you need to specify the whole path with a program name.

Process

When a program is running it consists of code that is executing and data that the program is working with. Together with some stack space and any open files, these form a process. Each time a program is run, there will be a distinct process. When a program is running for one or more users, there will be two or more processes, each executing a copy of the same program. This is similar to the way in which many MS-Windows applications are able to run at the same time.

Arguments and Parameters

Commands often need arguments or parameters to specify their actions and these normally take the form of files to act upon. These are the words in a command that follow on after the command name. Each UNIX command can be given parameters, or program arguments, to work on. All parameters are case sensitive. The **echo** command, like the DOS equivalent of the same name, simply prints its arguments to the screen.

```
$ echo Hello World
Hello World
```

Here, the **echo** command is given two arguments. The first is the word **Hello** and the second is the word **World**. The **echo** command prints each of its arguments separated by a single space. The shell ignores spaces before the command and between arguments so that, even if we spread out the arguments, **echo** produces the same result:

```
$   echo       Hello         World
Hello World
```

To include spaces in an argument they must be placed inside quotation marks. Single quotes or double quotes may be used, but they must be matched consistently. The shell treats all the characters between the quotes as a single argument. So the following example has two arguments:

```
$ echo "  Hello     World"   ' again'
  Hello     World again
```

The subtle differences between the two types of quoting are that single quotes are used to create an argument precisely as written, and double quotes allow the expansion of shell environment variables and escape sequences.

```
$ echo "Hello $HOME World"
Hello /usr/neil World
$ echo 'Hello $HOME World'
Hello $HOME World
```

The **HOME** environment variable defines the user's home directory (environment variables are covered in detail in the next chapter).

Options

Options are indicators that can be affixed to a command in order to control or modify what the command does. Options are normally indicated by a single letter which is preceded with a dash ('-'). This is similar to DOS notation which uses '/' instead of a dash.

The following example, using the **ls** command, shows how options can affect the operation of a command:

```
$ ls
report.txt
$ ls -l
total 5
5 -rw-r--r--   1 neil      users        4553 Dec  8 10:52 report.txt
```

Combinations

Some programs allow options to be grouped together so that:

```
$ program -a -b -c
```

is the same as:

```
$ program -abc
```

We can also run one command after another by separating them with semi-colons. The shell looks for the semi-colons and runs each command in turn. For example:

```
$ ls; ls -l; date
report.txt
total 5
5 -rw-r--r--   1 neil      users       4553 Dec  8 10:52 report.txt
Fri Dec  9 20:18:38 GMT 1994
```

Information Commands

Given the wide range of commands available under UNIX, it is just as well that help is at hand. Possibly the most useful and informative feature, for both novice and expert users, is the **man** command.

man

The **man** command, prints the UNIX manual page for the command given as its argument. There is even a manual page for the **man** command itself:

```
$ man man
man(1)                                                        man(1)
NAME
     man - format and display the on-line manual pages
SYNOPSIS
     man [-adfhktw] [section] command ...
DESCRIPTION
     man formats and displays the on-line manual  pages.  This
     version...
```

Most manual 'pages' consist of a lot more information than will actually fit on one page, in these cases you will have to scroll through the information using the space bar. Nearly all pages follow the same format: different sections describe the command use and the options available.

The section that a manual page comes from appears in its title line in parentheses. **man(1)** indicates that the **man** command was found in section 1. The sections are:

1 User commands

2 System calls

3 Library calls

4 Devices

5 File formats

6 Games

7 Miscellaneous information

8 System administration

Multiple Entries

There may be two entries in the manual for the same name; for example, the program `crontab` has an entry in section 1 and the file format used by `crontab` has an entry in section 5. By default, `man` will print the first entry it finds, so to see the section 5 entry, the section argument must be given.

```
$ man 5 crontab
CRONTAB(5)                                              CRONTAB(5)
NAME
 crontab - tables for driving cron
...
Man includes the following options
      -a      Display all the manual pages that match the given
              name, not just the first.
      -k      Display the title line for all manual pages that
              include the name as a keyword.
```

apropos and whatis

On some systems the command 'apropos' is an alternative name, or alias, for `man -k`. The `man -k` command is very useful if you are looking for all references to a command throughout all help files. It can only be used once the `whatis` database has been created (the `whatis` database being a set of files containing short descriptions of system commands for keywords). The command necessary to create this database varies according to which variant of UNIX you are using. For details on how to create the `whatis` database on your particular implementation of UNIX, type `man whatis`. For further options, see `man man`.

date

On UNIX, like DOS, the **date** command is used to both report and set the date. However, only the superuser may set the date on UNIX computers. Unlike DOS, the **date** command also reports and sets the time. The UNIX **time** command has a different purpose - it times programs, as we shall see later.

```
$ date
Fri Dec  9 20:20:03 BST 1995
```

Here you can see that the **date** command tells you both the time and the date. The format of the result can be altered in many ways.

To set the date and time, as superuser, use an argument of the form **MMDDhhmmYY.ss,** where **MM** is the month, **DD** is the day of the month, **hhmm** is the time (using a 24 hour clock), **YY** is the year and **.ss** are the seconds.

```
# date 05082020
# date
Thu May  8 20:20:01 GMT 1994
```

The year and seconds are optional.

who

The **who** command provides information about users of the UNIX system. It lists all the users logged on, when they logged on and where they have logged on from. The format of the output varies but this is a typical response:

```
$ who
neil     tty1      Dec  9 20:03
neil     ttyp1     Dec  9 20:03 (:0.0)
chris    ttyp2     Dec  9 21:16 (alex)
unclbob  ttyp1     Dec  9 21:20 (192.168.1.111)
```

This shows the user Neil logged on once from the system console, **/dev/tty1**, and once in a command window running under the X Window

71

System (:0.0 denotes an X Windows display). The user Chris has logged on across the network from a computer called Alex, whilst Uncle Bob has also logged on to a terminal called 192.168.1.111.

whoami

There is a special option to **who**, used mainly by programs, to find out who the user is. This is the **-m** option, or '**who am I**' command:

```
$ who am i
tilde!neil        ttyp2      Dec  9 20:03 (:0.0)
```

Often a separate program, **whoami**, fulfils the same function.

finger

The **finger** program gives information about a particular user. This information is gleaned from the system and also from special files in the user's home directory. For example:

```
$ finger neil
Login: neil                          Name: Neil Matthew
Directory: /usr/neil                 Shell: /bin/bash On since Fri Dec
9 20:03 (GMT) on tty1,  idle 13:01
On since Fri Dec  9 20:03 (GMT) on ttyp1, idle 1:45, from :0.0
On since Fri Dec  9 20:03 (GMT) on ttyp2, from :0.0
New mail received Sat Dec 10 09:02 1994 (GMT)
Unread since Sat Dec 10 08:46 1994 (GMT)
Project:
Take over the world
Plan:
Finish this book
```

The information regarding projects and plans originate from the files called **.project** and **.plan** in the users home directory. These are created by some users to give others an idea about their work.

The Short Form

A shorter form of **finger** output is obtained by using the **-s** (short) option.

```
$ finger -s alex
Login    Name                Tty   Idle  Login Time   Office       Office Phone
alex     Alexandra Matthew   p3    11:51 Dec 9 21:16  [ alex ]
```

Remote Users

finger can also be used to ask about users on remote machines, if you are connected to a network:

```
$ finger a.user@somehost.somecompany.co.uk
```

finger Services

Some host computers run information services accessed by the **finger** command. For example, to find out if there is mail waiting on a mail gateway machine, you might be able to use **finger** in this way:

```
$ finger mycomputer@postoffice.service-provider.co.uk
There are 3 messages for mycomputer on postoffice
```

Other uses of the **.plan** file include using it to present a public encryption key for use in secure communications. After a notorious virus in the late 1980s, a lot of commercial sites disabled the **finger** command, so don't be surprised if you can't use it.

Input and Output

So far, all the commands in this chapter have been fairly simple. You type them in and they respond with some output to the screen. By default this is what happens with most commands, but the output may be redirected as it can be in DOS.

Redirection Operators

To make the output from a command go to a file, use the output re-direct operator:

```
$ echo Hello Everyone > file1
```

The shell responds to the use of the output re-direct operator, **>** (pronounced 'onto'), by running the **echo** command with the arguments **Hello** and **Everyone**. Whatever data that command outputs is written to **file1**. To examine the contents of your newly created file, use the **cat** command:

73

```
$ cat file1
Hello Everyone
```

In the above example the contents of **file1** would have been replaced by **Hello Everyone**. In this way we can capture the output of most UNIX commands. To append output to the end of a file use **>>** instead of **>**.

```
$ echo Welcome to UNIX >> file1
$ cat file1
Hello Everyone
Welcome to UNIX
```

Streams

All commands write to their standard output. This is one of three input and output streams that all UNIX programs can use. The standard output is stream 1, often called **stdout**.

There is a second output stream called the standard error. This is stream 2, often called **stderr**. Typically, commands write error messages to this stream. By default both the standard output and standard error appear on the screen. The standard error stream can be redirected to a file.

For the Bourne and Korn shells, the operator **2>** is used to redirect the standard error stream to a file. As there are two output streams, you can separate them if you wish to do so. You can redirect the **stderr** to a separate file like this:

```
$ rm file-that-does-not-exist
rm: file-that-does-not-exist: No such file or directory
$ rm file-that-does-not-exist 2> file2
$ cat file2
rm: file-that-does-not-exist: No such file or directory
```

For the C shell, the operator **>&** sends both standard output and standard error streams to a file. For example:

```
$ diff one.file another.file >& file1
```

The **diff** command compares **one.file** with **another.file** and both the standard output and standard error streams are redirected to **file1**. However, the C shell does not supply a specific operator for redirecting the standard output to one file and the standard error stream to another, though it can be done using a command line as in the following example:

```
$ (diff one.file another.file > file1) >& file2
```

Input Flow

A lot of UNIX programs need input to function. Many will read their input directly from the user's terminal. For example, the **sort** command reads lines from the user and prints them out again in alphabetical order. To end the input, the user must type the end of file character, typically *Ctrl+D*. (The DOS equivalent is *Ctrl+Z*). Here we will show *Ctrl+D* as **^D**. Each line is terminated by pressing *Return*. Note that the shell is configured to recognise an end of file character, it does not itself form part of the input or file.

```
$ sort
the
cat
sat
on
the mat
^D
cat
on
sat
the
the mat
```

In this example the **sort** program is reading from its standard input, stream 0, often called **stdin**. We can use the shell to re-direct the standard input to come from a file by using **<** (pronounced as 'from').

Suppose **file3** contains a list of names. We can see the list in alphabetical order by using the file as the input to **sort**:

```
$ cat file3
john
bill
fred
ian
john
```

```
$ sort < file3
bill
fred
ian
john
john
```

Note that duplicates aren't removed by **sort**. The program **uniq** can remove repeated lines from sorted input. If we capture the output from the **sort** command into a temporary file, we can list the unique names.

```
$ sort < file3 > temporary-file
$ uniq < temporary-file
bill
fred
ian
john
```

There is a simpler way to achieve this result without having to create a temporary file. This is attained using what we call piping.

Pipes

We can run the **sort** and **uniq** programs at the same time, and make the output of the **sort** command become the input of the **uniq** command. This is called a pipeline and is created by the shell using the | character, sometimes called a 'pipe'. In a pipeline, command data is passed from left to right:

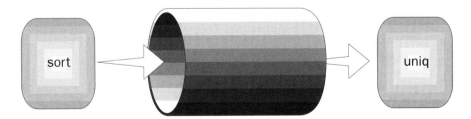

The standard error output will still appear on the screen:

```
$ sort < file3 | uniq
bill
fred
ian
john
```

Some people prefer not to mix input re-direction and pipes, and instead start the pipeline off with the **cat** command:

```
$ cat file3 | sort | uniq
bill
fred
ian
john
```

Here three programs are running at once, the output of one connected to the input of the next. This type of 'computer plumbing' is typical of how UNIX utilities are strung together to solve more complex problems.

tee

When the shell performs input and output redirection, it opens the files it will use before running the command. This means that the following attempt to sort **file3** and directly save it over **file3** will fail:

```
$ sort < file3 > file3
```

The file **file3** will be opened for writing by the shell as it is going to contain re-directed standard output. This has the effect of emptying the file before it can be read and sorted. Unfortunately, this means that the file will effectively be deleted.

A very useful program, **tee**, can be used to capture the data flowing in a pipeline. It is a simple program that copies its standard input to its standard output, but also writes it to a file.

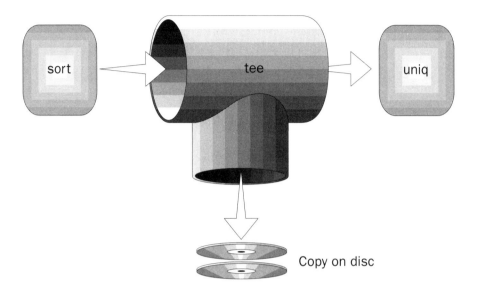

Copy on disc

We can capture the sorted, non-unique names to the file **allnames** with the pipeline:

```
$ cat file3 | sort | tee allnames | uniq
```

Note that in UNIX pipelines, unlike DOS, there is real concurrency. In a DOS pipeline, a temporary file is used to store the complete output of one command before the next command is run.

Of course in UNIX, we can save the sorted, unique list of names straight into a file if we wish.

> Finally, one small hint that you might find useful, which is also available in DOS (but which DOS pinched from UNIX); if you add | **more** to the end of any command that gives you output covering many screens, the information will be displayed one screen at a time.

Processes and Job Control

Up until now we have been running commands and waiting for the programs to finish. As UNIX is a multi-user, multitasking operating system, it's possible to run more than one program at the same time and independently of each other. To demonstrate this we will use a very simple command, **sleep**. It does nothing and does it for as long as you like.

```
$ sleep 10
```

After 10 seconds the next command prompt will appear. The **sleep** program waits for the given number of seconds, then it terminates. It produces no output, but can be useful for introducing delays, especially where timing is important.

Running Programs in the Background

We can run programs 'in the background' by using another special shell character, **&**, as the last character in the command. Hence:

```
$ sleep 100 &
[1] 1797
```

In this case, we get a shell prompt again immediately, but the **sleep** program continues to run. The shell tells us that this command is our job number 1, **[1]**, and that its process identifier is **1797**. Running a program in the background allows us to continue with other work. Although we'll illustrate the use of background processing with a simple program, it is more useful for long, time consuming jobs such as database reports or compiling large software systems. When time is important, having to wait for your terminal to finish would be very inefficient.

Process Identifiers

On UNIX systems, every program that is currently running is known as a process. Each process has a unique identifier, usually a number between 1 and approximately 32000. Every time a new process starts, it is given the next process identifier in sequence, as long as that identifier isn't in use. At roughly 32000 the process identifiers 'wrap' and start again from 1.

Job Control

We can see the processes that we are running by using the **jobs** command. This is actually a built-in function for those versions of the UNIX shell that support job control.

```
$ jobs
[1]+  Running                 sleep 100 &
```

Foreground and Background Management

We can bring a job into the foreground using the **fg** command:

```
$ fg %1
sleep 100
```

We'll now have to wait for the process to finish.

The syntax **%1** refers to job number 1. We could have used just **%** which refers to the current job (although there can be more than one background job). The current job is the job marked with a **+** in the jobs listing. All others are marked with a dash.

Now the **sleep** process is in the foreground we can terminate it with *Ctrl+C* (interrupt), or we can pause it with *Ctrl+Z* (suspend). Your shell may be set up to use different control characters for these functions. Check with your system administrator. For now, let us pause it:

```
^Z
[1]+  Stopped                 sleep 100
```

Now the **sleep** program isn't running. It will stay that way until we resume it. We can allow it to continue executing in the background by using **bg**:

```
$ bg %
[1]+ sleep 100 &
```

The **sleep** program will run until it has slept for 100 seconds, not including the time we stopped it. Note that you can also restore a suspended process into the foreground with the **fg** command.

When a background process finishes the shell notifies you, usually just before it issues the next prompt:

```
[1]+   Done                    sleep 100
$
```

If, however, a process running in the background requires input, it will stop. It will issue a message to the user, informing the user of the suspension. You can only continue the process by bringing it to the foreground and typing the required input.

If the user logs out and there are still jobs running in the background, they will all be terminated. There is a way of preventing this - the **nohup** command (short for no hangup). Take the following:

```
$ nohup sleep 999 &
[1] 15282
```

This process will continue after you log out, however, it won't be visible to you via the **jobs** command. This is because you have disconnected from the terminal.

nohup

If there are any errors that occur during the execution of the process, then they are logged into a file called **nohup.out**, located by default in the current directory. The output from the execution of a **nohup** process is also directed to this file.

You can use the **nohup** command to redirect output to another file and print the errors to standard output, via the **>** character. For example:

```
$ nohup sleep 500 > sleepfile &
[1] 15835
```

This command is useful if you want to run lengthy operations, such as the **find** command, and you don't wish to hang around for the result.

There are a number of options that you may use instead of job control. What is available will depend on your system. The X Window System, which is becoming increasingly popular, provides an alternative to job control. It allows the user to open several windows, each of which can run programs. This system is discussed in Chapter 7.

nice

Programs running in the background share the available CPU with programs running in the foreground. To maintain a good response to user commands, background processes automatically run at a lower priority. This means that they get a smaller share of the available CPU. You can explicitly request an even lower priority for particular processes by setting 'nice' values for them. Take this **weekly_report** program for example:

```
$ nice weekly_report weekly_data &
```

This runs the **weekly_report** program (together with its data) in the background at a lower than usual priority. We may wish to do this if we know that it is a very CPU intensive program and we don't wish to slow the computer down too much as it might affect other users.

nice values

Every running process has a 'nice' value attached, which controls how much CPU it is allocated. The range of values is -20 to 19. However the higher the nice value, the less time it gets to run. The superuser may use negative nice values. The **ps** (process status) command described below can be used to find the priority of a process. To change the priority of a process while it is running some UNIX systems have a **renice** command, which has the following syntax:

```
renice <priority> -p <process identifier>
```

ps

We can see more details about the processes that we have running by using the **ps** command. For example:

```
$ ps
  PID TTY STAT   TIME COMMAND
 1783 pp2 S     0:04 -sh
 1797 pp2 S     0:00 sleep 10
 1798 pp2 R     0:00 ps
```

Here we can see that we are, in fact, running three processes at once. The **PID** column shows the process identifier, the **TTY** column shows the terminal or window that started the process, and the **STAT** column shows the status of the process, which can contain one of many possible states, including:

PS State	Status	Description of Status
S	Sleeping	The process is currently suspended, waiting for a call to wake it up.
R	Running	Actually using the CPU at that instant.
T	Stopped	The process is runnable, but is temporarily stopped.
D	Uninterruptible	The process is waiting for the disk.
SW	Sleeping	Waiting for a kernel function to complete.

The **TIME** column shows how much CPU time has been used by each process, while the **COMMAND** column displays what the actual program and its arguments are.

The shell program is shown here as the **-sh** entry. The leading hyphen in **-sh** indicates that the shell is being used as a login shell, i.e. running as the primary interface to a user.

In the above output, we can see that the shell is sleeping, waiting for the **ps** command to finish. The **sleep** command we are running in the background is also sleeping, because that is its function. The **ps** command is currently running, producing the output we can see.

Options

There are many options that we can pass to the **ps** command, largely dependant upon your version of UNIX. Common options include:

-l   A long listing.

-a or -e   Show all the processes, even other users.

-u   User format, giving user name and start time.

-x   Shows all processes without a controlling terminal - if
                  you log out but leave a process running in the
                  background via the **nohup** command and then return, you
                  no longer control that process. It can only be seen via
                  the **-x** option, as the process no longer has a controlling
                  terminal.

Use the manual pages on **man ps** to find out about some of the other
options available on your system. By default **ps** only lists the processes you
have created. To get a full listing use the options **-a**, **-u** and **-x** together:

```
$ ps -aux
USER     PID %CPU %MEM SIZE  RSS TTY  STAT START    TIME COMMAND
neil      74  0.0  1.6  356  240 p 1  S    Dec 9    0:00 -bash
neil      89  0.0  1.7  365  256 p 1  S    Dec 9    0:00 sh startx
neil      90  0.0  1.9   64  288 p 1  S    Dec 9    0:00 xinit
neil      93  0.0  4.4  208  644 p 1  S    Dec 9    0:05 fvwm
neil      98  0.0  5.7  109  828 p 1  S    Dec 9    0:00 xconsole
neil     108  0.0  3.3  358  488 pp2  S    Dec 9    0:01 -bash
root       1  0.0  1.2   44  184 con  S    Dec 9    0:00 init
root       6  0.0  0.1   12   24 con  S    Dec 9    0:00 (update)
root      41  0.0  0.6   57   96 con  S    Dec 9    0:00 /usr/sbin/syslogd
root      43  0.0  0.0   36    0 con  SW   Dec 9    0:00 (klogd)
root      45  0.0  0.0   68    0 con  SW   Dec 9    0:00 (inetd)
root      47  0.0  0.0   68    0 con  SW   Dec 9    0:00 (lpd)
root      50  0.0  0.6   76   92 con  S    Dec 9    0:00 /usr/sbin/crond
root      73  0.0  1.1  288  160 con  S    Dec 9    0:00 /usr/lib/sendmail q10m
root      75  0.0  0.2   37   40 p 2  S    Dec 9    0:00 /sbin/agetty38400 tty2
root      76  0.0  0.3   37   44 p 3  S    Dec 9    0:00 /sbin/agetty 38400tty3
root      91  0.1 11.3 2729 1652 con  S    Dec 9    3:21 X :0
root     107  0.0  7.0  397 1028 p 1  S    Dec 9    0:03 xterm -ls
```

Output Information

The columns of output include:

Column Heading	Description
%CPU	The amount of available CPU time being used.
%MEM	The amount of available memory being used.
SIZE	The total process size (code, data and stack) in kilobytes.
RSS	The resident set size - kilobytes of program in memory.
USER	The user name of the owner of the process.
START or TIME	The time or date the process was started.

Other possible columns include:

Column Heading	Description
PRI	Priority - the number of times per time slice that the process will get a chance to run.
NI	The 'nice' value - the higher this value the less CPU time the process will be allocated.
WCHAN	The kernel function the process is waiting on.
PPID	The identifier of the parent process (the one that started this process).

Even on a single user UNIX computer there are often many processes running at once. Notable ones from the example output above are:

The init Process

The 'init' process is essentially the UNIX kernel itself:

```
root          1  0.0   1.2   44   184 con S    Dec  9    0:00 init
```

It is the first process started and always has the process identifier **1**. It is the ancestor of all other processes and is responsible for maintaining the 'run level' of the system. (The run level determines whether or not the system is in single or multiuser mode.)

The update Process

The **update** process runs every 30 seconds and writes any output buffers to disk:

```
root        6 0.0    0.1    12    24 con S    Dec  9    0:00 (update)
```

Because UNIX routinely uses disk buffering, it's possible for a large amount of data to remain in memory. To protect against loss in a power failure, **update** makes sure that this data is regularly written out.

Notice that the **update** process and some others are shown in parentheses. This indicates that the process has been 'swapped out', i.e. the program is no longer in memory, but has been written to the swap area. This is normally due to other processes needing the memory. When **update** needs to run again, it will be swapped back into memory and allowed to continue.

The X Window Server

```
root       91 0.1   11.3 2729 1652 con S    Dec  9    3:21 X :0
```

This is the X Window Server program. We'll look at it in more detail in Chapter 7.

The Line Printer Daemon

A daemon is a resource manager; there are several daemons on the system, each assigned to a specific individual task such as the mail. The line printer daemon is a program that controls the available printers allowing printing to be performed in the background:

```
root       47 0.0    0.0    68     0 con SW   Dec  9    0:00 (lpd)
```

It also controls all the queuing print requests to allow many users to share one or more printers.

> **We look at how to print files and standard output on the printer in Chapter 6.**

The cron Daemon

```
root        50  0.0   0.6   76   92 con S    Dec  9   0:00 /usr/sbin/crond
```

This is the **cron** daemon, a system for running programs automatically at regular intervals. We will meet **cron** again later on in this chapter.

The mail Daemon

```
root        73  0.0   1.1  288  160 con S    Dec  9   0:00 /usr/lib/sendmail
```

This is the mail daemon, responsible for ensuring that mail is delivered. There are many different versions each with their own features, for example, this one will check the mail queue every 10 minutes and try to deliver outstanding mail messages.

time

A program may be accurately timed with the shell equivalent of a stopwatch, the **time** command. Note that this is very different from the DOS program of the same name. Take a look at this example:

```
$ time backup
384.86 user 32.38 system 7:16.79 elapsed 95 %CPU
```

The output of the **time** command does vary between UNIX variants, but usually it will reveal at least the following:

user	Time spent executing the program itself.
system	Time spent by the system on behalf of the program; this would include time spent during input and output.
elapsed	Total time.
%CPU	Percentage of the available CPU consumed.

Times are given in hours, minutes and seconds in the form **hh:mm:ss.sss** where hours and minutes may be omitted. In the above example, the backup program spent about 10% of its time writing to the backup device and 95% of the CPU compressing the data.

Software Interrupts

We can control running or sleeping processes even further by sending them signals. These are software interrupts that cause processes to stop executing and perform one of a number of different actions. The signal numbers will vary depending on the UNIX variant you are using. A list of the codes can be obtained from the file **signal.h**. Common signals that you would find on the Linux system include:

Signal Number	Signal Name	Signal Action
1	SIGHUP	Hang up. This is the signal received by a process when its standard input is finished. It is usually the result of a user logging out.
2	SIGINT	Interrupt. The signal sent when you type *Ctrl+C* (interrupt). The process then usually terminates, but it is able to catch the signal and either ignore it, or perform some internal housekeeping, such as freeing resources and printing end messages, before finally exiting.
3	SIGQUIT	Quit is the signal that the shell sends to a process when you type *Ctrl+* (quit). It is similar to SIGINT, in that it terminates the process, but it also dumps a **core file** for that program (the core file being a file of output that is generated when a program terminates abnormally) and may be caught in a similar way.
9	SIGKILL	Kill a process (can't be ignored). SIGKILL causes the process to exit immediately. It can't be caught. It should only be used as a last resort.
15	SIGTERM	Terminate. This is a request to terminate. It is sent to processes on system shutdown. It asks them to exit quietly.
19	SIGSTOP	This may be sent to a process to cause it to stop. It is equivalent to typing *Ctrl+Z* (suspend) to a foreground process.

There are also other signals such as 11 SEGV (Segmentation Violation) which is the signal issued when you try to access illegal memory. Details about the different signals will vary according to the system you are using.

The kill Command

The **kill** command can send one of these signals to one or more processes. It takes as a signal to send and a list of process identifiers as its arguments. The signal can either be a number or a name (the name is as listed above but without the leading SIG). The process identifiers may include job references in shells that support job control. Take the following sequence of commands:

```
$ sleep 100 &
[1] 2956
$ kill -STOP %1
$ jobs
[1]+  Stopped (signal)         sleep 100
$ bg %1
[1]+ sleep 100 &
```

Here we have created a process and sent it a signal to stop it running (remember the process number is referenced by % beforehand which stands for job number). By typing jobs we can see that it is stopped. Use **man kill** to discover more details about your own system.

Running Programs Automatically

To run a program automatically at a given time in the future, the **at** command can be used. Reading commands from the standard input (or the specified file), **at** executes them at the specified time. For example:

```
$ at 1215
backup /usr
^D
Job a00c82e9f.00 will be executed using /bin/sh
```

> Note that the **at 1215** must be on a separate line from the **backup /usr**. This is because the **at** command requires its input separately.

At 12:15 p.m. (we are using the 24 hour clock) the system will run the backup program on the **usr** directory.

atq

To see the list of pending jobs use **atq**, or **at -1** (the **q** stands for queue in this option):

```
$ atq
Date                    Owner   Queue   Job#
12:15:00 12/11/94        neil     a      a00c82e9f.00
```

To remove a job from the queue use the **atrm** command, or **at -r** with the code:

```
$ atrm a00c82e9f.00
$ atq
$
```

The implementation of the **at** command differs from system to system. Some only allow **at** jobs to be queued up to 24 hours in advance, while others lack the ability to show or remove queued jobs. Some UNIX variants may restrict permission to use the **at** command for certain users.

cron

The **cron** utility provides the system administrator (and on some systems, users) with the ability to schedule tasks for automatic execution at regular intervals. In fact, behind the scenes, **cron** is usually responsible for starting jobs in the **at** queue as well.

The **cron** daemon, **crond**, runs in the background all the time, waiting until a command is due to be executed. It gets its information from a special file called the **crontab** file. On some systems there is a single **crontab** file, but on others there may be a **crontab** file for each user.

cron Schedule List

To see the list of scheduled commands, simply run **crontab -l**. This will print the list of commands that the user has scheduled. In the following example, the superuser examines the four scheduled system maintenance commands:

```
# crontab -l
# Run the 'atrun' program every 5 minutes
# This runs anything that's due to run from 'at'. See man 'at' or 'atrun'.
0,5,10,15,20,25,30,35,40,45,50,55 * * * * /usr/lib/atrun
# Expire C News
59 0 * * * su news -c /usr/local/lib/news/bin/expire/doexpire
# Manage news files and report if needed
10 8 * * * su news -c /usr/local/lib/news/bin/maint/newsdaily
00 5,13,21 * * * su news -c /usr/local/lib/news/bin/maint/newswatch
```

Amending cron Information

To change the **cron** information, you must create a **crontab** file with the task information in it and then run **crontab** on the file:

```
# crontab root.crontab
```

This replaces all existing entries with those in the file **root.crontab**. Therefore to add to existing entries we need to use **crontab -l** to list the tasks that are scheduled and edit the output of the file according to these tasks.

Entries in **crontab** files have a fixed format. Blank lines and those beginning with a **#** (comments) are ignored. Active lines in the **crontab** file consist of six fields::

Minute	0-59
Hour	0-23
Day of month	1-31
Month	1-12
Day of week	0-7 (0 and 7=Sunday)
Command	Task to be run

91

Each field, except command, may be an asterisk - five asterisks mean 'all'. The field may contain a range, like x-y, meaning all the values between x and y. It may also contain a list separated by commas. There can be more than one entry to run a given program. The entry below runs the command **example** at 8:00, 8:30, 9:00, 9:30, 10:00 and 10:30 on weekdays in July:

```
00,30 8-10 * 7 1,2,3,4,5  example
```

Some UNIX implementations offer another option that you can use with **crontab: -e**. This allows you to edit the contents of the **crontab** file and use the resulting output as the new **crontab** file. You can edit it using whichever editor you have specified. We will look at some of the different types of editors very shortly.

Regular Expressions

Many UNIX programs behave in a very similar manner. We have seen that utilities often treat options in a consistent fashion. There is another common task that UNIX utilities share and deal with in a unified way. This is searching and the specification of search strings.

The editors **ed**, **vi**, **sed** and **emacs**, and the search program **grep** all use wild card search patterns for locating or selecting data - usually lines in a file. They all use a common set of wild cards and conventions called regular expressions.

Shell Wild Card Expansion

We have already seen some wild cards in action in the selection of files. Shell wild card expansion, however, is a little different from the editors' regular expressions. The rules are given below:

^	Matches the beginning of the line.
$	Matches the end of the line.
.	Matches any single character.
[..]	Matches one of the characters in a range.

char	Any non-special character matches itself.
\char	Matches char, even if it is a special character.

Ranges may consist of a number of characters in square brackets, for example, **[abc]** matches either **a**, **b** or **c**. A range may contain a dash, in which case, all characters between those either side of the dash are included. For example, **[A-Za-z]** matches any alphabetic character of either upper or lower case. If the first character of the range is **^**, it denotes an excluded range, i.e. **[^abc]** matches any character that isn't **a**, **b** or **c**.

A regular expression, or pattern, may be denoted as optional by following it with a question mark. For example **A[BCD]?Z** matches **AZ, ABZ, ACZ, ADZ** and nothing else.

A pattern may also be repeated zero or more times by following it with an asterisk. For example, **A[BCD]*Z** matches **AZ, ACZ** and **ABDCCZ**, along with any other combination of **B**, **C** or **D** in between **A** and **Z**.

Note that the asterisk wild card is used very differently from the one used in shell file name expansion. It doesn't stand for any sequence of characters, but for the possibility of many occurrences of the preceding pattern. As a full stop matches any single character, the pattern **A.*B** matches all occurences of strings starting with **A** and ending with **B**. Anything may appear in between.

grep

To extract lines from a file that match a pattern, we use regular expressions with the **grep** utility. This can be very useful for simple searches. By default, **grep** performs sub-string searches; that is, it looks for any lines that contain the specified pattern. The **^** and **$** regular expression characters are known as anchors and restrict the search patterns to only the start or end of the line, respectively. Here we have an example list:

```
$ cat phonelist
 W. Johnson and Sons Telephone List
Bob        123    Robert Johnson
John       567    John Frederick
Bill       665    William Stiles
Chris      222    Christopher Jones
Christine  333    Christine Hickman
Mary       456    Mary Johnson
```

We can use **grep** to implement a simple telephone directory search. The file **phonelist** contains short form names, telephone extensions and employees' full names. It could, of course, contain many more details, and if they are all on one line per employee, then **grep** can be very useful.

Let's find the phone number for John:

```
$ grep John phonelist
  W. Johnson and Sons Telephone List
Bob         123     Robert Johnson
John        567     John Frederick
Mary        456     Mary Johnson
```

We have selected three lines from the phone list because the title line and the line for Bob also contain the match string, **John**.

To restrict the search to start at the beginning of the line where the short form name is, we can use ^ to anchor the matches:

```
$ grep ^John phonelist
John          567     John Frederick
```

That's better. Now let's try Chris:

```
$ grep ^Chris phonelist
Chris       222     Christopher Jones
Christine   333     Christine Hickman
```

Still not quite right. We need to match the whole of the short form name to distinguish Chris from Christine. We can match on the space or tab character that the **phonelist** file has between the short names and the telephone extension number:

```
$ grep '^Chris[<space><tab>]' phonelist
Chris       222     Christopher Jones
```

> Note that there has to be a space character and a tab character between the square brackets. This pattern has to be quoted to prevent the shell from passing two arguments to **grep**. If **tab** does not work, it is because the **tab** key has been assigned a special function on your system.

fgrep and egrep

There are two other variants of the **grep** utility that can be used: **fgrep** and **egrep**. The **fgrep** command is optimized to search for fixed strings without regular expressions. The **egrep** command contains support for extended regular expressions, which allows a number of expressions to be combined. Consult the **man** pages for further information on these two commands.

Options

Options to **grep** include:

-n	Print line numbers for matching lines.
-v	Print lines that don't match the pattern.

The nearest DOS equivalent to **grep** is **FIND**, but it's nowhere near as versatile.

Tip

A couple of useful commands using grep in conjunction with other commands might be:

**ls -l	grep /**	This will only list directories in a file listing.
**ps -aux	grep root**	This will display all the processes owned by root.

Substitution with sed

The **sed** (stream editor) program uses regular expressions to transform an input stream into an output stream, by substituting occurrences of one pattern with replacement text. It is often used as a filter, taking text from its standard input and writing the edited version to its standard output. It is often used as part of a pipeline command.

To replace the string 'Johnson' with 'Perkins' in the phonelist, use **sed** like this:

```
$ sed s/Johnson/Perkins/ phonelist
W. Perkins and Sons Telephone List
Bob         123    Robert Perkins
John        567    John Frederick
Bill        665    William Stiles
Chris       222    Christopher Jones
Christine   333    Christine Hickman
Mary        456    Mary Perkins
```

Notice that the company name has been changed as well.

Syntax

The general form of the **sed** command is:

sed   [address,[address]]<function>[arguments]

where the items in the square brackets are optional. Addresses can be input line numbers, **$** to indicate the end of input, or pattern matches to limit the range over which substitution takes place. To prevent the title line being altered we can try:

```
$ sed '2,$s/Johnson/Perkins/' phonelist
 W. Johnson and Sons Telephone List
Bob         123    Robert Perkins
John        567    John Frederick
Bill        665    William Stiles
Chris       222    Christopher Jones
Christine   333    Christine Hickman
Mary        456    Mary Perkins
```

In the above example, we specified line 2 in the first address as the line from which we wanted to make the substitutions onwards. To limit the substitution range more specifically to just Mary Johnson we can use:

```
$ sed '/Mary/s/Johnson/Perkins/' phonelist
 W. Johnson and Sons Telephone List
Bob         123    Robert Johnson
John        567    John Frederick
Bill        665    William Stiles
Chris       222    Christopher Jones
Christine   333    Christine Hickman
Mary        456    Mary Perkins
```

sed has many other functions that are documented in the manual page, but the **s** function (for substitution) is the most commonly used. Both the addresses and search strings may be regular expressions with extensions. Parts of the matched strings may be remembered and used in the replacement.

To add a leading 2 to all the telephone numbers we can use an ampersand in the replacement string to indicate the matched string. We search for the first occurence of a digit and add the number 2 to the front of the digits that have been found.

```
$ sed 's/[0-9][0-9]*/2&/' phonelist
W. Johnson and Sons Telephone List
Bob          2123   Robert Johnson
John         2567   John Frederick
Bill         2665   William Stiles
Chris        2222   Christopher Jones
Christine    2333   Christine Hickman
Mary         2456   Mary Johnson
```

Remembering Sub-Strings

At least nine sub-strings of a match can be remembered and reused. Wrapping parts of the search string in \(and \) causes them to be remembered. The strings are referred to by the number in the order they were matched, so \1 refers to the number 1, \2 refers to 2 and \3 refers to 3. In the replacement string the sequence \1, \2 and \3 is replaced by the third string, the second string and the first string respectively.

So, to reverse the order of the three digit telephone extension numbers we can use:

```
$ sed 's/\([0-9]\)\([0-9]\)\([0-9]\)/\3\2\1/' phonelist
 W. Johnson and Sons Telephone List
Bob          321   Robert Johnson
John         765   John Frederick
Bill         566   William Stiles
Chris        222   Christopher Jones
Christine    333   Christine Hickman
Mary         654   Mary Johnson
```

Data Manipulation with awk

awk is a pattern scanning and processing language and takes its name from its authors, Aho, Weinberger and Kernighan. There have been two versions of the **awk** program. Most modern UNIX variants contain the later version, previously known as both 'new **awk'** and 'System V **awk'**.

awk is sufficiently complex to warrant a book in its own right, but simple **awk** programs can solve many data manipulation problems. It uses regular expressions to extract records from files and has a programming language for manipulating and outputting the information in other formats.

awk can perform all the functions that **grep** and **sed** are able to and much more. It is beyond the scope of this book to explore **awk** in any great depth, but we'll have a quick look at how useful it can be.

An awk Example

Here is a simple **awk** program to print out our phone list in a different form:

```
$ cat > ph.awk
BEGIN      { print "Phone List" }
/[0-9]+/   { for (I = 3; I <= NF; I++)
             printf "%s ", $I;
             print $2
           }
END        { print NR, "records" }
```

The resulting output is:

```
$ awk -f ph.awk phonelist
Phone List
Johnson 123
Frederick 567
Stiles 665
Jones 222
Hickman 333
Johnson 456
6 records
```

Syntax

awk programs consist of program blocks (in braces) to execute when the input data matches given patterns. In this case, there are three such blocks. Special patterns, **BEGIN** and **END** are used to match the start and end of data. The **BEGIN** block is executed before any data is read, and the **END** block is executed after all data has been read. The other block is executed whenever an input record matches the regular expression **[0-9]+** (in this case a line). So, for each line that contains a sequence of one or more digits, awk will print out the full name and extension number of the employee.

Fields

Each input record is split into a number of fields that can be referred to as **$1**, **$2** and so on. The awk variable **NF** stands for the number of fields in the current record, and **NR** stands for the number of records in the entire input. Other awk variables are used to determine how the input is divided into records, how records are divided into fields and how fields are to be printed. Full details of these and other functions can be found under the manual entry for awk. Note that some versions of UNIX use the GNU implementation of awk - gawk, which is fully compliant with the POSIX 1003.2 standard.

Locating Files

It doesn't matter how careful you are or how well you manage your own data, there will always be moments when you can't find the file you want. To alleviate this problem, we have been given the **find** command.

find

find is a command that searches for files and can, in turn, run commands on the files that it finds. The parameters to **find** are a directory to search and a series of one or more operations. It searches the specified directory and all sub-directories in the tree below it. For each file that it finds, it runs the given commands, executing each one in turn until one of them returns false.

This sounds rather complicated, but in practice **find** is both easy to use and very useful. For example, suppose we have 'lost' a report file called **invent_424**. We know it was put somewhere in the **/usr** directory, but we just can't locate it. The command we need is:

```
find /usr -name invent_424 -print
```

This tells **find** to search all the directories below **/usr** (including **/usr**), and then for each file tested, if its name is **invent_424**, it prints out the full pathname of the file. Here we have used the options **-name** and **-print**.

Options

There are a large number of options associated with the **find** command, including:

-type	This tests the type of file found. It takes a single parameter which is the files type. The usual options are **f** for normal file and **d** for directories. To find just directories, we can use **-type d**.
-name	This tests the name of the file. Wild cards are accepted, but must be quoted so they are only expanded once a file has been found. To test for object files (files with the **.o** extension), we could use **name "*.o"**.
-user	This tests for a particular file owner. To find only files owned by the user Susan, we would use **-user susan**.
-perm	This tests for a particular set of file permissions, given in octal, so **-perm 755** will succeed for files that have **rwxr-xr-x** permissions.
-exec	This invokes a UNIX command on a file that has been found. The full pathname of the current file can be referred to by using **{}** in place of the file name in the command. Further parameters to the UNIX command may be given. The **-exec** is terminated with the sequence **\;** to mark the end of the command parameters. To invoke **ls -l** to give a long listing of the current file, we would use **-exec ls -l {} \;**.

-newer	This test succeeds if the file found has a more recent date and time than another file. This can be useful for finding files that need backing up.
-mtime	This test succeeds if the file found has a creation time that meets a specified criterion. For example, **-mtime 7** succeeds if the file has been modified in the last seven days.
-ctime	The same as **-mtime**, but the file has been modified or has had an attribute changed.
-atime	As **-mtime**, but the file has been accessed in the given time.
-print	Prints the file's name on the standard output.

A find Example

Now let's put all of these elements together. Suppose we are porting some code into our UNIX system. We create a new directory called **porting** and install the original source code in a set of sub-directories within that directory. Before we start porting the code into the system, we create a file called **TIMESTAMP** in the **porting** directory, then make our changes to the source code.

When we have finished we would like to discover which files we have changed, so that we may return them to the author of the code for reference. We don't want to return the object files, nor do we want to return the large number of files we didn't have to change. All we want is the new executable file and the modified source files. **find** is the ideal command to tidy up our **porting** directory. First we remove the object files by asking the command to delete all the object files in the **porting** directory:

```
$ find porting -name "*.o" -exec rm {} \;
```

This finds only those files with the extension **.o**, and then invokes the **rm** program with the full pathname of the file we want to remove.

We then use **find** to produce a list of modified files by finding files newer than our **TIMESTAMP** file, and save the list in a file called **changed_files**:

```
$ find porting -newer /usr/jim/porting/TIMESTAMP -print > changed_files
```

We can even use **find** to produce a list of files that need to be backed up and then use this with a backup program, such as **cpio**:

```
$ find porting -ctime 7 -print | cpio -oBcv >/dev/rmt0
```

You can see now how useful and easy to use **find** can be.

Editors

There are a large number of good editors available on the UNIX platform. They range from a remarkably powerful line editor based on regular expressions, to a complete user environment. We shall now take a brief look at three of the best.

ed

The editor called **ed** is available on all UNIX computers. In some senses it is therefore the lowest common denominator. It doesn't require any particular input devices as it's a line editor, and in some ways is like the DOS editor **EDLIN**. As a last resort, it's often worth knowing how to use **ed** if you are accessing a UNIX machine from a dumb terminal without any screen facilities.

Key Functions

ed uses regular expressions and addresses much in the same way as **sed**. The most useful functions are:

p	Print (to the screen)
s	Substitute
i	Insert text, up to a line containing just a full stop
a	Append text, up to a line containing just a full stop
w	Write (save) file
r	Read (insert) file
e	Edit (another) file

m	Move lines
j	Join lines
t	Copy lines
g	Globally perform a command
RET	Next line (carriage return)
q	Quit

Addressing Lines

Line addresses may include:

.	The current line
+n	The line n lines after the current line
-n	The line n lines before the current line
$	The last line
/.../	Next line containing ...
?...?	Previous line containing ...

An ed Example

We can edit the phonelist to change Mary Johnson to Mary Perkins as follows:

```
$ ed phonelist
194
```

ed tells us the size of the file we are editing or writing. Let's start by listing the file. We do this by specifying all the lines, 1 to the end, and the print command:

```
1,$p
  W. Johnson and Sons Telephone List
Bob        123    Robert Johnson
John       567    John Frederick
Bill       665    William Stiles
Chris      222    Christopher Jones
Christine  333    Christine Hickman
Mary       456    Mary Johnson
```

103

Now let's search for Johnson. We can do this by simply specifying the match in the address part of the command we give to **ed**. We can repeat the search 'by specifying a blank match:

```
/Johnson/
 W. Johnson and Sons Telephone List
 //
 Bob          123     Robert Johnson
 //
 Mary          456     Mary Johnson
```

We have searched on the string 'Johnson', and now we are at Mary's line, we can substitute the old string for the name 'Perkins' and print the result.

```
 s//Perkins/p
```

We can print all the lines that contain the string Johnson by globally performing the **p** command on all the lines that match:

```
 g/Johnson/p
  W. Johnson and Sons Telephone List
  Bob          123     Robert Johnson
```

Since the match string can be a regular expression (**re**) this command gives one explanation for the name of the **grep** command:

```
 g/re/p
```

Having made our change, let's add a couple more employees. We will go to the end of the list and append some more lines. We end the additions with a line containing just a dot. This line does not get added to the file:

```
 $
 Mary          456     Mary Perkins
 a
 Richard       292     Richard Belvedere
 Sue           761     Susan Wells
 .
 w
 246
 q
```

Although **ed** may appear quite cryptic, it can be used in shell scripts because it doesn't rely on any kind of display. There are programs, such as **diff** (find differences) and **patch**, that produce **ed** scripts to transform one input file into another.

vi

vi, or visual editor, is a screen based editor common to most UNIX systems. It's like the DOS **EDIT** program, but is a little idiosyncratic. It also has a lot in common with **ed** in that it has a command mode that accepts **ed** style commands and regular expressions.

vi runs full-screen and shows a page of the file at a single time:

```
$ vi phonelist
  W. Johnson and Sons Telephone List
Bob         123     Robert Johnson
John        567     John Frederick
Bill        665     William Stiles
Chris       222     Christopher Jones
Christine   333     Christine Hickman
Mary        456     Mary Perkins
Richard     292     Richard Belvedere
Sue         761     Susan Wells
~
~
~
~
~
~
~
~
~
~
~
~
~
~
~
~
~
~
~
 "phonelist"  9 lines, 246 chars
```

Lines on the screen that are not part of the file are shown as a tilde, ~. In this case, as the file is only 9 lines long, the rest of the screen is filled with these characters.

vi has two main screen modes, command mode and insertion mode. We start in command mode which allows us to navigate and perform operations on text. We can move around the file in command mode using cursor control keys.

vi Key Functions

Functions are performed by pressing one of the following keys:

Key	Function
↑ *or k*	Go up one line.
↓ *or j*	Go down one line.
→ *or l*	Go right one character.
← *or h*	Go left one character.
a	Append after cursor (enters insertion mode).
x	Delete the character under the cursor.
dw	Delete to the end of the current word.
dd	Delete line (into paste buffer).
cw	Change current word (end with ESC).
cc	Change to end of line (end with ESC).
G	Go to line (end default).
p	Paste from the paste buffer.
J	Join the current line with the next line.
r	Replace the current character with the next one typed.
u	Undo the last command.
i	Enter insertion mode.
b	Move back a word.
w	Move forward a word.
/	Search for a regular expression.
n	Repeat search using the previous regular expression.
ESC	Exit insertion mode, back to command mode.
:	Enter the extended command mode.

Other vi Functions and Commands

Many functions may be given an argument by typing a number before the function letter. For example **3dd** deletes three lines, whilst **120G** goes to line number 120.

Text can be inserted into the file by pressing *i* for insert, typing the required text and then pressing *ESC* to exit the insertion mode.

Extended commands are entered by using a colon when you are in command mode. This enters extended command mode and brings up a **:** prompt at the bottom of the screen. From this point, **ed** style commands are available. The most useful of these is probably **s** for substitute which works in the same way as it does in **ed**. The **w** command writes the file and the **q** command quits **vi**. Adding an exclamation mark to a command makes it unconditional, so to quit without saving changes, use **ESC : q !**.

It is as well to know how to exit **vi** even if you don't plan to use it, as it is often configured as the default editor for utilities that allow the user to edit files.

emacs

The original **emacs** was an editor written by Richard Stallman for the PDP-10. There are now a number of versions available for UNIX machines, including Stallman's own GNU **emacs**, part of a project to produce a complete development environment and to make it freely available.

emacs is a very capable full screen editor, supporting the display and editing of multiple files at once, sophisticated macros, and syntax directed editing for a large number of file types, such as C, Pascal and Lisp programs. It is extremely configurable and is often the editor of choice for systems capable of supporting it.

Tutorial

Control key sequences play a large part in navigating **emacs**, and learning these can seem a little daunting. Fortunately, **emacs** comes with a tutorial for beginners and an extensive on-line manual.

```
$ emacs
GNU Emacs 19.25.1 of Sun Jun 19 1994 on tilde (i486-unknown-linux)
Copyright (C) 1994 Free Software Foundation, Inc.

-----Emacs: *scratch*   (Lisp Interaction)--All------------------------
For information about the GNU Project and its goals, type C-h C-p.
```

To learn **emacs**, start by pressing *Ctrl+H*, followed by *t* for the tutorial. **emacs** has its entire manual available on-line - try *Ctrl+H*, and *i* for information.

emacs allows you to edit more than one file at a time, and to view them in their own windows. Each file that you edit is read into a buffer, and you use the buffer commands to navigate between them. **emacs** also allows you to use its windows to view part of a buffer. It's possible to view two parts of the same buffer in two different windows. This can be confusing for beginners, but can be a real boon to experienced users.

Common emacs Commands

Some of the more common **emacs** commands are listed below. Here the caret, ^, is used to indicate control characters:

`^@`	Set a mark.
`^A`	Go to the beginning of the current line.
`^D`	Delete a character.
`^E`	Go to the end of the current line.
`^H`	Help.
`^K`	Delete to the end of the current line.
`^V`	Page down.
`^W`	Delete the text between mark and cursor.
`^Y`	Paste text that has been previously deleted.
`^X^C`	Quit **emacs**, optionally saving files.
`^X^F`	Find and load a specified file; otherwise, if it doesn't exist create a new file with the specified name.
`^Xb`	Switch buffer.

ESC	**v**	Page up.
ESC	**<**	Go to the start of the file.
ESC	**>**	Go to the end of the file.

Summary

In this chapter we have learned about how UNIX programs can be run and manipulated. We have met a large number of utilities that most UNIX systems have as standard. We have also seen that the UNIX environment is a flexible one, allowing small programs to be used together to solve complex problems. We have looked at the use of pipes, whereby you can feed the output of one command straight into the input of another. We finally looked at some of the different editors available. You must decide which one you are most comfortable with and familiarise yourself with it, as you will need an editor to modify and create script files in the next chapter, when we look at programming scripts in UNIX.

Shell Programming

So far we've only been able to execute commands by individually typing them in at the shell prompt and pressing *Return*. Shells though, have more power than this - they have a full programming capability in their own right. Indeed, for some small tasks a shell program may be a more suitable choice than a traditional programming language.

In this chapter we will be learning a complete language. The shell script language behaves very much like any other traditional computer language, especially C and BASIC. We will be learning many variations on popular programming constructs as we progress through the following topics:

- What is a shell?
- Using standard and environmental variables
- How to integrate control structures
- How to make use of functions
- An examination of important commands
- Introducing arithmetic expressions
- How to debug your scripts

If you have experienced the limitations of DOS batch files, you will be pleasantly surprised by the power of the UNIX shell.

What is a Shell?

In the last chapter we defined exactly what a shell is: a command interpreter
- a program that enables the user to interact with the computer. There are
several different shells in common use, for example:

- The Bourne shell **sh**, written by Steven Bourne at AT&T's Bell
  Laboratories. It is possible to write good programs for this shell but,
  because of its lack of functions and because it has more than the odd
  quirk, it has been largely superseded. At the time of its creation,
  however, it was a significant innovation. It was originally shipped
  with many early versions of UNIX, making it widespread and very
  popular.

- The c-shell **csh**, originally written by Bill Joy at the University of
  California, Berkeley. This was designed for C programmers and
  includes many improvements for interactive use. It's different from the
  original Bourne shell and although it was initially only available on
  BSD derived systems, its distribution is improving.

- The updated Bourne shell also, confusingly, called **sh**. It has been
  shipped with all versions of UNIX from System V3 onwards. This
  modern version has added functions and is free of many of the
  oddities of the original Bourne shell.

- The Korn shell **ksh**, written by David Korn. This shell is similar to
  the original Bourne shell, but features improvements to aid interactive
  use. It also incorporates several improvements for programming, such
  as functions and greater execution speed.

- The Bourne Again Shell, **bash**, from the GNU project. This shares
  many features with the Korn shell and is evolving along the lines of
  the POSIX interpreter.

The POSIX 1003.2 command interpreter, which we will refer to as P1003.2. This is a standard shell and set of tools defined by an IEEE standards committee for a portable operating system.

Variants, such as the visual shell, the restricted shell, the tc-shell and others, which aren't very widely distributed, but deserve a mention.

The original Bourne shell has largely been superseded by the 'new' Bourne, Korn, Bourne Again and POSIX shells. Naturally they have many similarities, and with a great deal of care it is possible to write programs that will run on all of them, but for the remainder of this chapter we will concentrate on the Bourne shell, as this is universally available.

A Simple Example

Let us now take a look at a simple example. First we will issue the command **sh** which will ensure that we are using a Bourne style shell. We can always return to our original shell by typing **^D** when we have finished. For the first program, type the following:

```
$ sh
$ for i in 1 2 3 jim susan
> do
> echo $i
> done
```

The program creates a loop based around the variable **i**, and for each separate value of **i**, the program executes whatever is located in the **do** section. The output of this program is:

```
1
2
3
jim
susan
$
```

As you can see, the shell recognizes the start of a control structure and automatically issues a continuation prompt '**>**' for further lines, until the control structure is finished. The shell considers the variable **i** to be a string by default, so it can embrace the value **susan** just as easily as the value **1**.

Filename Expansion as Input

We don't need to type in the values **i** can take - they can just as easily originate from shell filename expansion, like this:

```
$ for i in *.c
> do
> cc -c $i
> done
Compiling file_a.c
Compiling file_b.c
Compiling file_f.c
Compiling file_z.c
$
```

This program takes all the files in the current directory that have **.c** extensions and compiles them using the UNIX C compiler, **cc**.

Scripts

What happens though if we want to run all that again? Surely we don't have to type it in again? No, we don't. We can store these commands in a file, commonly referred to as a shell script, and execute them without having to go through all the associated re-typing problems.

The following example shows how we can create scripts using the **cat** command:

```
$ cat > script1.sh
for i in *.c
do
cc -c $i
echo Compiling $i
done
^D
$ sh script1.sh
Compiling file_a.c
Compiling file_b.c
Compiling file_f.c
Compiling file_z.c
$
```

We use the **.sh** extension purely as a convenience.

Making Executable Scripts

If we make the script executable and ensure it's in our search path for commands, then it becomes a new command:

```
$ chmod +x script1.sh
$ script1.sh
Compiling file_a.c
Compiling file_b.c
Compiling file_f.c
Compiling file_z.c
$
```

Actually, using a makefile and the **make** command would be a more suitable solution in this instance, but this still serves as an example.

> **If you wish to execute a script file by just typing the file name, every time you create a new one, you will have to change that file's permissions to executable first. Otherwise you will be denied permission to execute the shell script. So make sure you type in**
>
> **chmod +x <script name>**
>
> **before you execute each script file.**

If this last example didn't work for you, it's probably because your default shell isn't a Bourne type shell, or your **PATH** environment variable did not include the directory where **script1.sh** is stored. Try the commands:

```
$ SHELL=/bin/sh; export SHELL
$ PATH=$PATH:.
```

before trying the command again.

The #! Prefix

You could also try prefixing the following line of code to your program:

```
#!/bin/sh
```

This is used to indicate which interpreter the file requires in order to run. Here we are indicating that we are using the **sh** interpreter. From now on, we will use this line of code in every shell script we create and it is good practice to do so. The **#!** prefix effectively indicates that the program following it is to be executed.

If the **#!** syntax is accepted on your system, you can use it for many other programs as well - not just for shells. For example, if you have written a script in the Perl language which can only be run by the program **/usr/bin/ perl**, then starting the script with:

```
#!/usr/bin/perl
```

will invoke the program **/usr/bin/perl** with the rest of your script as a parameter. This has the same effect as typing:

```
/usr/bin/perl script.pl
```

at the UNIX prompt. For our previous **script1** example, we would invoke the program as a parameter to **sh** in the following way:

```
sh script1.sh
```

This should always work, but it's not as elegant as making our script executable. Making a script executable effectively creates a new command, directly and conveniently available to us at the command prompt.

Extending Your Range of Commands

Script files are particularly useful for extending the number of commands available to your shell. Once you have created and tested a script it can be installed into a suitably accessible directory and made available to other users. Your script has extended the range of commands available and, for most practical purposes, a command implemented as a script is indistinguishable from one implemented in a language such as C. Using scripts to extend the range of user commands is an excellent way of customizing your UNIX installation. Indeed many versions of UNIX have several system utility commands implemented as shell scripts.

Overview

The advantages of using a script over a conventional, compiled language is that for many simple utilities, a script is a lot easier to write and maintain. The main disadvantage is that shell scripts normally execute much more slowly than a properly compiled program.

> It is wise to manage your own scripts carefully, because you don't want redundant commands filling up your system. This often happens when you begin experimenting and forget to delete the ones that don't work. A regular spring clean of your system does no harm whatsoever and will help you to streamline your system. You should now be able to find that script you've been looking for much more easily.

As we shall see later in the chapter, shell programs can utilize a wide range of control structures and comprise multiple source files. It is quite feasible to write and maintain complex shell scripts running to many hundreds of lines of code.

For the rest of this chapter we will present sample scripts and their sample dialog without repeating the stages involved. We will also be referencing an example file **myfile**, which can be created via your preferred editor. Just type in these two lines and save them under the name **myfile**:

```
This is the contents of myfile ...
...
```

Variables

You create variables in your scripts just by using them - you don't need any declarations beforehand. By default all variables are strings, so:

```
x="5"
```

makes the variable **x** contain the string 5, not the numeric value 5. The use of quotes isn't strictly necessary here, but we use them to emphasize that we are using a string, containing a single character, '5'.

Categorizing Variables

If we didn't include the quotes in the previous example, the shell would automatically assume that the variable was a string by default. This can lead to problems later when you're unsure of the exact type of a variable. Some newer shells allow you to specifically declare attributes for variables with the **typeset** command. You can display all the current types and their values by typing the **typeset** command without any parameters.

The main parameters are:

-u   Upper case

-l   Lower case

-i   Integer

-r   Read only

-L   Left justified

-R   Right justified

By using these concise specifiers, you can make the process of maintaining your shell scripts easier.

For example:

```
typeset -i x=5
```

declares **x** to be an integer and then sets its value to 5.

Sending Variables to Output

Variables can be output with the **echo** command. To refer to the value of a variable, precede its name with a **$**. For example, the following will print the contents of **x** to the screen:

```
echo $x
```

Normally, **echo** prints its arguments separated by a single space and followed by a new line. Different shells allow you to customize the format of your output in different ways. For example, if you wish to output data without a trailing new line, there are numerous choices, including:

```
echo -n "$x"
echo "$x\c"
print "$x\c"
print -n "$x"
printf "%s" $x
```

The **echo -n** method is the usual syntax for systems where **/bin/echo** exists, whilst the **echo \c** method should be used where **echo** is built into the shell. The **print** command is specific to the Korn shell and the **printf** command was subsequently introduced, although recent versions of Bourne Again also support it.

We will use the **echo -n** version throughout this chapter, but you should be aware of the possible compatibility difficulties of this command.

Reading Input Variables

Values can be entered into variables with the **read** command. For example, enter the following script:

```
#!/bin/sh
# script2.sh

for i in 1 2 3
do
        echo -n "Enter a string: "
        read x
        echo line $i was $x
done
```

This program asks for a string and then prints it out again to show you that your input was correctly digested by the variable. It does this three times, and if you execute it, you should get output like this:

```
$ script2.sh
Enter a string: hello
line 1 was hello
Enter a string: bye bye
line 2 was bye bye
Enter a string: this is the end
line 3 was this is the end
$
```

119

Note also that we have added indentation to the script to make it easier to read. The shell ignores all the white space.

Quoting Variables

It is usually a good idea to protect shell variables with "" when writing shell scripts. This allows the variables (linked to their intended values) to be expanded as normal by the shell.

Be careful though because quotes can cause problems, especially when they contain an empty string. Take the following example (we will be discussing **if/then/fi** structures later):

```
#!/bin/sh
# script3.sh

a="myfile"
if [ $a = myfile ]
then
        echo "is equal"
fi
b=""
if [ $b = myfile ]
then
        echo "is equal"
fi
```

This will result in a syntax error; the substituted line:

```
if [ $a = myfile ]
```

becomes:

```
if [ myfile = myfile ]
```

which is okay, but because **b** is an empty string, the line **if [$b = myfile]** becomes:

```
if [ = myfile ]
```

which is invalid, because you can't have an equality expression without two operands. This can make shell scripts abort with syntax errors on certain inputs, while working with other inputs. You should always take care to protect your variables against the possibility of them containing an empty string.

The script would be better written like this:

```
#!/bin/sh
# script3a.sh

a="myfile"
if [ "$a" = myfile ]
then
        echo "is equal"
fi
b=""
if [ "$b" = myfile ]
then
        echo "is equal"
fi
```

This method ensures that we always have an operand either side of the operator.

Shell Environment Variables

Some variables have special meanings that the shell recognizes as pertaining to the interface environment. We will be taking a closer look at these and many other environment variables in Chapter 5, but for now those in common usage are:

HOME   Contains the user's 'home' directory. If a user hasn't been assigned a home directory, the directory entered upon logging in will be used.

IFS   Stands for Internal Field Separator. The shell uses each of the characters in this variable to decide how to split commands and parameters. The default is Space-Tab-Newline.

PATH   Contains the full path to search for commands - multiple paths are separated by colons.

PS1   Is the primary prompt, used when the shell is waiting for a command.

PS2   Is the secondary prompt, used when the shell requires further input to complete a command.

SHELL   Contains the pathname of the shell currently in use.

Any of these may be set and displayed interactively. Examine and try to follow this series of modifications (your output may differ slightly depending upon your system):

```
$ PS1="yes sire "
yes sire PS1="$ "
$ echo $PATH
/bin:/usr/bin:/usr/local/bin:.
$ PATH=$PATH:/usr/local/admincmd
$ echo $PATH
/bin:/usr/bin:/usr/local/bin:.:/usr/local/admincmd
$
```

Exporting

Note that unlike DOS, the **PATH** variable can be appended to directly from the command prompt without having to re-type its existing value.

In addition to taking a value, each environment variable may be marked as exported, with the **export** command. This makes that variable available when a new shell, called a sub-shell, is invoked from the current shell. The current list of exported variables can be found either by typing **export** without any parameters, or by using the **export -p** command. Most of the standard environment variables will be marked exported by default.

When a new shell is invoked (which is what happens when you run a script), it takes a copy of all the exported variables, with a view to making them available to the sub-shell. Changes to these variables in the sub-shell, or the subsequent creation of new variables, doesn't affect the original shell. This means that you can't pass information back from a sub-shell to its parent shell by creating or setting variables in the sub-shell.

Once a variable has been exported with the **export** command, it remains exported - there is no unexport command. If you need to stop a variable being exported, you must destroy the existing variable with the **unset** command and create a new variable with the same name.

The following example creates a new variable, **FRED**, and shows how the **export** command makes it available in subsequent invocations of **sh**. Comment lines in *italics* have been added to guide you through the commands.

```
                first create and set the environment variable, FRED.
$ FRED=fred
$ echo $FRED
fred
                now start a sub-shell.
$ sh
$ echo $FRED


                FRED is null, since it wasn't exported. The sub-shell, therefore
                cannot recognize it.
                Type Ctrl+D to return to the previous shell, where FRED still
                exists.
$ ^D
$ echo $FRED
fred
                Thus the parent shell recognizes FRED and prints out its
contents.
```

C programmers will have noticed that this structure bears a resemblance to the local/global variable status that C provides.

We will now export **FRED** and see what happens when we enter the shell once more.

```
$ export FRED
$ sh
$ echo $FRED
fred
                We will now set FRED to a new value in the sub-shell.
$ FRED=bert
$ echo $FRED
bert
$ ^D
                We are now returning to the original shell.
$ echo $FRED
fred
```

You can see that any alterations to exported environment variables in sub-shells have no effect on the original values.

When a shell script is invoked as a command, a new shell is created to execute the script. This means that your parent shells can't be changed by the creation or modification of environment variables in shell scripts, because they are only being modified in a sub-shell. We will see how to use scripts to modify our current environment using dot scripts later in the chapter.

Control Structures

The main control structures available to us in scripts are **if**, **case**, **for** and **while**. These are important tools to aid the programmer, and mirror various other control structures in other languages. We will now discuss each of these in turn:

The if Statement

Most languages provide a decision-making statement, and shell scripts are no different since they make use of the popular **if** method. The syntax of the **if** statement is:

```
if <condition>
then
<statement -1>
else
<statement -2>
fi
```

The **if** statement executes the first statement if the value of the condition is true, otherwise statement two is executed. There can be multiple statements between the **then**, **else** and **fi** lines if you wish. (Most constructs are traditionally closed by the keyword being alphabetically reversed, hence **if** and **fi**, **case** and **esac**, etc.)

> The shell uses 0 (zero) to mean true, because this allows all other values to be used as error codes. Values above 128 are used to indicate program termination by a signal, so scripts should normally use the error codes 1-127 inclusive.

The test Command

The most common **if** condition is the **test** command, which is often written using [and]. For example, we can write a script that will print a message dependent upon the existence of a file called **a_test_file** in the current directory:

```
#!/bin/sh
# script4.sh
# example using '[' version

if [ -f a_test_file ]
then
        echo "file exists"
else
        echo "file does not exist"
fi
```

The following program produces exactly the same results but uses the **test** method instead:

```
#!/bin/sh
# script4a.sh
# The same as script4.sh, but using the 'test' notation rather than the
# '[' notation.

if test -f a_test_file
then
        echo "file exists"
else
        echo "file does not exist"
fi
```

File Operators

Both the [notation and **test** command use the same set of operators. The most useful file operators are:

-**f**   The file exists.

-**r**   The file is readable.

-**x**   The file is executable OR is a directory that may be searched.

-**d**   The file is a directory.

-**s**   The file exists and isn't of zero size.

Arithmetic Operators

In addition there are the following operators for arithmetic expressions:

`exp1  -gt  exp2`	True if exp1 is greater than exp2.
`exp1  -ge  exp2`	True if exp1 is greater than or equal to exp2.
`exp1  -lt  exp2`	True if exp1 is less than exp2.
`exp1  -le  exp2`	True if exp1 is less than or equal to exp2.

Group Operators

There are also a few other useful operators that can be used to group operators together:

`!`	Unary negation
`-a`	Binary AND
`-o`	Binary OR

Combining Multiple Operators

These enable us to write a script that can test many different attributes of a file in a single test:

```
#!/bin/sh
# script4b.sh

if [ -x a_test_file -a ! -d a_test_file ]
then
        echo "file has execute permission and is not a directory"
fi
```

This is often useful when complex combinations of **if** conditions are being tested.

Successions of decision statements can be made much easier to implement by introducing the **elif** (else if) statement. Here we perform a test on the existence of two files in the current directory:

```sh
#!/bin/sh
# script5.sh

if [ -f first_file ]
then
        echo "first file found"
elif [ -f second_file ]
then
        echo "second file exists,"
        echo "but the first does not"
else
        echo "neither file found"
fi
```

The case Statement

If we have to write a program to select one entry from a long list of possibilities, it becomes inconvenient to repeat reams of else-if statements. This is where the **case** statement comes in. Here is its syntax:

```
case   <variable>   in
    pattern1)   statement-1;;
    pattern2)   statement-2;;
esac
```

The case statement checks the variable against a series of patterns. If it matches one, it will execute the associated sequence of statements. Multiple patterns may be specified by separating them with |, and multiple statements are allowed between patterns. If no pattern is matched, no statement will be executed. The wildcard pattern * can be used to match a default case.

Here is a trivial word guesser script that demonstrates how pattern matching can be used in a **case** construct:

```sh
#!/bin/sh
# script6.sh

echo -n "Enter a word: "
read guessword

case "$guessword" in
        fred)       echo "guessword is fred" ;;
        bill | bert)    echo "guessword is either bill or bert" ;;
        [S,s]*)     echo "guessword starts with S or s" ;;
        xyzzy)          echo "You have been playing Adventure!" ;;
        *)          echo "guessword was not matched" ;;
esac
```

127

The use of patterns can significantly simplify **case** statements. Imagine how cumbersome this would have been if we had tried to implement it using **if** statements.

(For those who haven't come across **xyzzy** before, it was a password in an adventure game called The Colossal Cave Adventure - or simply Adventure.)

The while Statement

This statement allows a sequence of commands to be executed while a condition is true. The **while** statement syntax is:

```
while <condition>
do
<statement>
done
```

Suppose we require a simple script that waits for some other process to create a file. The script:

```
#!/bin/sh
# script7.sh

while [ -s test_file ]
do
        echo "File test_file is not of zero length"
        sleep 10
done
```

will loop whilst **test_file** is of a non-zero length. While this loop is running, **test_file** will never become of zero length. This means that the loop will be infinite and continue forever. You can stop the script prematurely by interrupting it, usually with **^C**.

There is a special command **true** which always returns a 'true' value. This is often used in conjunction with a **while** as a convenient notation for an infinite loop. For example, **while [true]**.

The break Command

The **break** command is used simply to break out of any enclosed **for**, **case** or **while** loop. If a program has loops within loops, then the flow of the program can become difficult to control. In most shells only a single enclosing level can be broken out of, but some newer shells allow the **break** command to take an optional parameter, the number of levels to break from. Below is a simple example showing the syntax of the **break** command:

```
#!/bin/sh
# script8.sh

fini="n"
while [ "$fini" = "n" ]
do
        echo "Sleeping for 10 seconds""
        sleep 10
        echo "sleep again (y/n) ?"
        read fini
        if [ "$fini" != "y" ]
        then
                break
        fi
        echo "going round while loop again"
done
echo "here after break"
```

Note how the unary negation operator (**!**) combines with **=** to form a not-equal-to operator. If you enter anything other than **y** at the **sleep again (y/n)** prompt, the loop will be terminated.

Command Line Parameters

When a shell script is invoked, it can have arguments, just like a conventional program. There are special shell variables that make the arguments available inside the program. These are:

$0	The name of the script being executed.
$1,$2,$3 etc.	The parameters. The command line is broken into separate parameters depending on the contents of the special environment variable **IFS** and the quotes in the command line.
$#	The number of parameters available.
$*	All the parameters together in a single string.

$$	The process identifier of the current shell. Since this is unique while the script is running, it can be used as a way of generating temporary filenames.
$?	The value returned by the last executed command. A zero indicates successful completion.
$!	The process identifier of the last background process invoked.

For example:

```
#!/bin/sh
# script9.sh

echo this script is $0
echo parameter 1 is $1
echo parameter 2 is $2
echo parameter 3 is $3
echo there are $# parameters
echo the parameters are $*
echo my PID is $$
```

This script shows how these special variables can be used within shells. If you invoke the program using the following line, you will see just how useful these variables can be:

```
$ script9.sh fred bloggs
this script is script9.sh
parameter 1 is fred
parameter 2 is bloggs
parameter 3 is
there are 2 parameters
the parameters are fred bloggs
my PID is 1542
$
```

Being able to pass parameters to scripts is a characteristic that enables you to increase the flexibility of your programs by specifying integral details to a general template. This is an attractive feature of script programming.

Functions

Although multiple scripts can be used to sub-divide a lengthy program, this method is rather clumsy and slow, since a new shell is created each time a script is invoked. A better way of doing this would be to use **functions**.

When the shell encounters a function, it leaves the main program and executes the function. When the function has been completed, control returns to the main program.

The shell is an interpreted language, so the definition of all functions must precede their use. Functions in the shell, like those in the C language, can take parameters and return a value. A function ends at its closing brace or when a return statement is executed. If you need to return a string from a function you must use a global variable.

The other difficulty (in most shells) is that the parameters to a function are passed in the same variables used when the script was invoked - overwriting the original parameters $*, $1, $2 etc. and $#.

Here is a simple example, that could be used as the basis for a delete command that always prompts before deleting:

```sh
#!/bin/sh
# script10.sh

# Function definition for yes_or_no
yes_or_no()
{
        echo $*
        while true
        do
                echo -n "Enter yes or no: "
                read x
                case "$x" in
                        y | yes | Y | Yes | YES) return 0;;
                        n | no | N | No | NO) return 1;;
                        *) echo "You must answer yes or no" ;;
                esac
        done
}

# Program starts here
echo Original parameters :- $*
```

```
myfile=$1
if yes_or_no "OK to delete file $myfile ?"
then
        rm $1
        echo "This file has already been deleted!"
fi
```

This creates the function **yes_or_no**, to which we pass the prompt string, "**OK to delete file $myfile ?**". The function loops until it gets a suitable answer to the question. Some sample dialog would be:

```
$ script10.sh junk.txt and random parameters passed here
Original parameters :- junk.txt and random parameters passed here
OK to delete file junk.txt ?
Enter yes or no: x
You must answer yes or no
Enter yes or no: fred
You must answer yes or no
Enter yes or no: yes
If there was file of this name then it has been deleted!
$
```

Notice how our programs are developing in sophistication as we progress. The simplicity of the script language allows us to grasp concepts quickly and use them effectively.

Commands

Some commands that you can use in shell scripts are commands that you could have used directly at the command prompt. Control structures and other commands are built-in to the shell and are only meaningful in a script. If a built-in command returns an error, the script will terminate. If an external command returns an error, it is up to the script to determine the action to be taken.

Here is a summary table that identifies many of the more commonly used script commands:

Command	Type	Meaning
$(())	built-in	Arithmetic operations (new form).
$()	built-in	Command result substitution (new form).

Continued

Command	Type	Meaning
`${}`	built-in	Pattern matching and parameter substitution.
`&&`	control	AND operator.
`.`	built-in	Dot operator, run in current shell.
`:`	built-in	Colon operator, always true.
`<<STRING`	built-in	Introduces HERE document.
`` `` ``	built-in	Command result substitution (old form).
`||`	control	OR operator.
`break`	control	Break from innermost construct.
`case`	control	`CASE` statement.
`echo`	normal	Output.
`exec`	built-in	Replaces the execution thread with a new program.
`exit`	built-in	Exits the script.
`export`	built-in	Makes environment variables available in sub-shells.
`expr`	normal	Arithmetic operations (old form).
`if`	control	`IF` statement.
`read`	built-in	Reads a value from the standard input.
`set`	built-in	Sets parameters.
`shift`	built-in	Shifts positional parameters.
`test or []`	normal	Test condition.
`trap`	built-in	Specifies signal handling.
`true`	normal	Always true.
`typeset`	built-in	Sets attributes of variables.
`wait`	built-in	Waits for process termination.

We will now take a look at some of these commands in a little more detail.

The : Command

This command does nothing, but it can be useful when you need to specify a command, but don't need an action to be performed. You will see an example of this when discussing the **trap** command. It takes as many parameters as you care to pass it and always returns 0.

The set Command

The environment variables **$1** through **$<n>**, **$#** and **$*** can all be altered while the script is running by using the **set** command. Variables are changed according to the parameters given to **set**. This is often used when a script needs to access a particular field of another command's output. The script below shows the **set** command and how to use it to extract the year information (field number 6) from the **date** command:

```
#!/bin/sh
# script11.sh

echo "$1 $2"
set par1 par2
echo "$1 $2"
set `date`
echo $6
```

If you type the following line, you will be able to see clearly how parameters are set.

```
$ script11.sh Hello World
Hello World
par1 par2
1995
```

The shift Command

A command often used in association with **set** is the **shift** command. This enables you to move all the positional parameters down by one, which is an easy way to access parameters in turn. The variable **$0** isn't affected by the **shift** command. For example:

```
#!/bin/sh
# script12.sh
```

```
while [ "$1" != "" ]
do
        echo Parameter 1 now :- $1
        shift
done
```

The `while` loop scrolls through all the command line parameters, checking them and printing each one out in turn. Thus the following dialog may occur:

```
$ script12.sh How are you today?
Parameter 1 now :- How
Parameter 1 now :- are
Parameter 1 now :- you
Parameter 1 now :- today?
$
```

Command Grouping

Commands are grouped with the `||` and `&&` operators. These allow us to perform logical operations, without having to work through complex combinations of `if` statements. The `||` operator means OR, whilst the `&&` operator stands for AND.

These operators behave just as they do in the C language. The `||` operator executes the conditions from the left until one returns true (it doesn't execute the remaining ones). The `&&` operator executes conditions from the left until one returns false, but doesn't execute the remaining conditions. Take the following script for example:

```
#!/bin/sh
# script13.sh

rm file1

if [ -f file1 ] || echo "Hi " || echo "there"
then
    echo condition1 is true
else
    echo condition2
fi
```

Of the 3 statements to the `if` command, the second is the one acted upon. This is because the `echo` command always returns true, so the final `echo` `"there"` is never invoked.

If you run the script you'll get the following output:

```
$ script13.sh
Hi
condition1 is true
$
```

Sub-shells and Grouping

When the shell executes commands, it sometimes invokes a separate shell process (a sub-shell). This is most commonly seen when executing a pipeline of commands (commands separated by |). As we saw earlier, changes to environment variables in a sub-shell don't affect the current shell. This isn't normally a problem, but if you create a script that works by calling other scripts, you should be aware that all the subsequently invoked scripts can't pass information back to the calling script via the environment variables. Even if the sub-shell changes to a different directory, the original shell will resume execution in its original directory.

Usually all that a sub-shell needs to pass back to its parent shell is an exit code to indicate success or failure. Temporary files are occasionally used for passing intermediate results, but usually only if it isn't possible to implement the sequence of commands with each 'piping' its output to the next command's input. If possible, you should try to 'pipe' output, rather than create a temporary file - because it is usually easier to read, more efficient to execute and you can't forget to delete the temporary file afterwards!

If commands need to be grouped for execution in a linear fashion, so that a single invocation of a new sub-shell executes each command in turn, this is done with parentheses. A sequence of commands in brackets is processed by the new sub-shell that it invokes.

Sometimes processing needs to be done in a different directory. You can neatly change directory and perform the required processing by enclosing a sequence of commands in parentheses. We saw an example of this in Chapter 2 where we used a pair of **tar** commands, running in different directories, to copy a directory tree. Here is a simpler example:

```
#!/bin/sh
# script14.sh

HERE=`pwd`
```

136

```
pwd
cd ..
pwd
cd $HERE
pwd
(cd .. ; pwd )
pwd
```

The **HERE=`pwd`** is a special syntax for command substitution which stores the current directory (the result of the command **pwd**) in the variable **HERE**.

If we run this script in **/home/jim** we get the following output:

```
$ script14.sh
/home/jim
/home
/home/jim
/home
/home/jim
```

Notice how the commands inside the sub-shell don't affect the parent shell's current directory.

Dot Scripts

When a shell script is invoked, a new shell is automatically created to run the script. This means that changes to environment variables in the script don't affect the current environment outside the shell. This is usually an advantage, but where we need the script to be run in the current shell, we use the dot command, which is simply a dot followed by the script name. For example:

```
#!/bin/sh
# script15.sh

FRED="billy"
export FRED
echo "$FRED"
```

If we set the variable **FRED** and then run the script in the following manner:

```
$ FRED=fred
$ export FRED
$ echo $FRED
fred
```

137

```
$ script15.sh
billy
$ echo $FRED
fred
$ . script15.sh
billy
$ echo $FRED
billy
$
```

we can see the dot command in action. This shows that the `. script15.sh` command has allowed the script to modify an environment variable in the current shell. This can be very useful when we want to execute a command to actually modify the current environment. This can be seen in scripts executed during login, when a user's environment is often initialized by a system-wide script and then modified and extended by one or more user-specific scripts, such as `.login` and `.profile`.

Here Documents

Often a shell script will use other commands to do most of the work, and the script is often little more than the 'glue' that assembles the parts together.

Sometimes difficulties arise when we want to use a command that is designed for interactive use, rather than a script. For example, we may wish to perform a sequence of simple edits on a file, which is relatively easy with **ed**, but more difficult to implement by other means.

The solution is often a 'here' document, which is a sequence of commands inside a script that act as though they were typed interactively. The following sample script contains a here document:

```
#!/bin/sh
# script16.sh

cat <<!FUNKYSTUFF!
hello world
Thanks for the fish
!FUNKYSTUFF!
```

The output from this script is simply:

```
$ script16.sh
hello world
Thanks for the fish
$
```

138

The here document is introduced with '<<', and the rest of the line is an arbitrary sequence, which will terminate the document. Subsequent lines of the script are read as though they are being input from the keyboard, until the special sequence that started the here document **!FUNKYSTUFF!** is repeated. The character sequence following the '<<' can't appear literally in the here document itself.

We can do quite complex tasks with here documents. Suppose we start with a file **junk** that contains:

```
Hello, this is line 1
Hello, this is line 2
Hello, this is line 3
Hello, this is line 4
Hello, this is line 5
```

We can modify this using a script that invokes the **ed** editor and passes commands to it:

```
#!/bin/sh
# script17.sh

echo "running ed on the file 'junk'"
ed junk <<ASILLYSEQUENCE
3
d
.,$s/this is/this was/
w
q
ASILLYSEQUENCE
echo "Finished"
```

After running **script17.sh** the third line is deleted and the remaining lines have been changed. The file **junk** now contains:

```
Hello, this is line 1
Hello, this is line 2
Hello, this was line 4
Hello, this was line 5
```

Command Substitution

Sometimes we would like the result (or output) of a command to be captured as a parameter to another command. Although this could be done by executing the command with the output redirected to a file, which is

139

subsequently read back, this would be very inefficient. A better method would be to use command substitution.

Syntax

Historically command substitution was done with back (grave) quotes, so `` `date` `` is replaced with the result of executing the **date** command. However, the use of quotes inside the grave quotes can lead to some difficult quoting requirements. To avoid this, the syntax **$(command)** was introduced to be the equivalent of `` `command` ``, and now the need for quoting is much reduced. Most newer shells will support the **$()** syntax.

Using the set Command

It is often useful to combine command substitution with the **set** command we met earlier. For example, to access different fields from the **date** command, we could use:

```
set $(date)
echo $6
```

which would print out just the year field. This is much more efficient than the `` `date` `` version we used in an earlier example.

Parameter Substitution

It's possible to use parameters in the substitution, so we can use:

```
ls -l $(echo "$1")
```

which gives a long listing of the filename in **$1** (assuming it exists!).

> Make sure there is a space between **echo** and **"$1"**, otherwise you will get an error message because the script will be unable to distinguish the **echo** from the **"$1"**.

Protecting Variables

So far we have only accessed the contents of a variable such as **i** by using **$i**, but there are cases where this is far too simplistic an approach. Consider trying to delete three files called **1file 2file 3file**. We could try:

```
$ for i in 1 2 3
do
            rm $ifile
done
$
```

but it wouldn't work because the shell is trying to replace the contents of the variable **ifile**, and not **1file**, **2file** or **3file**. Unless this variable exists, it will be substituted as the empty string and no file will be removed. What we need to do is protect the variable name **$i**. This is done using **{}**, for example:

```
#!/bin/sh
# script18.sh

for i in 1 2 3
do
            rm ${i}file
done
```

This ensures that the variable **i** is cycled through without conflict. But there are further substitutions we can do using curly braces. This line:

```
echo ${foo:-help}
```

will print the contents of **foo**, if **foo** is set, or the text "help" if it isn't. This line however:

```
echo ${foo:=bert}
```

will set **foo** to contain the string "bert", but only if **foo** isn't already set.

Pattern Matching

Some shells permit other substitutions, and the ones shown here (used for matching strings and obtaining the length of strings) are especially useful for processing directory paths:

`${foo#pattern}`	Match and remove small left pattern.
`${foo##pattern}`	Match and remove large left pattern.
`${foo%pattern}`	Match and remove small right pattern.
`$foo%%pattern}`	Match and remove large right pattern.
`${#foo}`	Give the string length of **foo**.

A small pattern is the least number of characters matching the pattern, whereas a large pattern is defined as the most number of characters matching the pattern.

The following example demonstrates the difference between small and large patterns (remember * matches any sequence of characters, so */ matches any sequence ending with a /).

```
#!/bin/sh
# script19.sh

# setup the variable HERE
HERE=/foo/bar/fud

# match and remove the short pattern
echo ${HERE#*/}

# match and remove the long pattern
echo ${HERE##*/}
```

If we run this script we get results such as the following:

```
$ script19.sh
bar/fud
fud
```

Notice how compact and simple the solution to this seemingly complex problem actually is.

The exit Command

This command stops further execution of the script and provides an exit status to the invoking process. All scripts should provide an exit status, because even if your script is just a simple sequence of commands intended for interactive use, it may be called later by another script that may need to determine if it is executed correctly. As we mentioned earlier, an exit code of 0 is used for success, and positive codes are used to return error values. It is a good idea to have different error exit codes to distinguish different types of failures.

The trap Command

The **trap** command enables us to perform actions when an executing script receives a signal, such as the user generating an interrupt.

By default, the script will simply exit when it receives a signal. If the script has created temporary files, or is in some critical section where we shouldn't exit immediately, we can modify the default behavior via the **trap** command.

If we wish to trap signals 1, 2 and 15 (these are normally SIGHUP, SIGINT and SIGTERM respectively), remove a file called **temp_file** and then exit with code 3, we would use:

```
trap 'rm -f temp_file;exit 3' 1 2 15
```

Note that the **trap** command must occur early in a program if it is to be used efficiently. There is no point in having a trap halfway through a program - you are effectively halving the chances of your trap being successful. We can restore the default behavior by using **trap** with no commands specified:

```
trap 1 2 15
```

This restores the default behavior of signals 1, 2 and 15. We can choose to ignore signals using the **:** command which does nothing:

```
trap : 2
```

This will ignore signal number 2.

Remember there are some signals that can't be caught or ignored, such as SIGKILL. Consult your manual for more details of your system's signals.

Invoking Programs from a Script

We have already seen that we can invoke other programs simply by using their name, but there are other ways of invoking programs. We can replace the execution thread of our program with another program, so that rather than our script waiting while the other program runs, it is replaced by it, and execution won't return to it. We do this with the **exec** command:

```
#!/bin/sh
#script21.sh

for i in 1 2 3
do
        echo $i
        exec cat myfile
done
```

If you run this script you should see the following output:

```
$ script21.sh
1
This is the contents of my file ...
...
$
```

The rest of the **for** loop will never be executed, because the thread of execution passes to the **cat** command, never to return.

As with interactive use, we can allow programs to execute in the background and wait for them to complete. (This example assumes the existence of a C program **hello.c**, so you will need to create this in order to run the example.)

```
#!/bin/sh
# script22.sh

echo "About to start compiling"
cc hello.c > /dev/null &
echo "cc is running now"
echo "it has PID $!"
wait
saveexit=$?
echo "It completed with code $saveexit"
```

Here the script starts the C compiler in the background (discarding the output), prints its process ID, waits for it to complete and then prints its exit code. We save the exit code **$?** into a new variable called **savexit**. This isn't really necessary in our simple script, but because **$?** is the result of the last command, it is updated for each command that is executed, so it's good practice to save it immediately.

Arithmetic Operations

There are two ways that you can perform arithmetic in a shell; your choice will largely depend on how flexible your shell is.

The expr Command

This is the only method available in older shells. Arithmetic must be done in the evaluation of the parameters of the **expr** command. For example:

```
#!/bin/sh
# script23.sh
x=0
for i in 1 2 3
do
        x=`expr $x + 10`
        echo $i $x
done
```

will create the following output:

```
$ script23.sh
1 10
2 20
3 30
```

Notice how we create the variable **x** before invoking **expr**. We must do this because if **x** doesn't exist, or is empty, then **$x + 10** becomes the incomplete **+ 10**, which would cause a syntax error, but the direct statement '**expr 0 + 10**' is valid.

This script is slow, since each time round the loop, it must invoke a new shell to evaluate the **expr** command.

The $(()) Command

The Korn shell introduced a new method of performing arithmetic operations, the **$(())** syntax. This should be available in the latest shells. It supports more operations than **expr** and executes faster than the **expr** version. The following example runs a **while** loop where the value of **x** decreases by one on each execution, until **x** equals zero and the loop terminates:

```
#!/bin/sh
# script24.sh

typeset -i x=3
while [ $x -gt 0 ]
do
        echo x is now $x
        x=$(($x-1))
done
```

Execution of this script will produce output like this:

```
$ script24.sh
x is now 3
x is now 2
x is now 1
$
```

The arithmetic is once again performed within the parameters - this time it is passed to the `$(())` command instead.

Arithmetic Operators

Here's a selection of the operations that can be performed within these parameters:

+	Addition
–	Subtraction
*	Multiplication
/	Division
%	Modulo
!	Negation
==	Equal to
!=	Not equal to
<	Less than
<=	Less than or equal to
>	Greater than
>=	Greater than or equal to

Commenting

There are two ways of writing commands. The first method uses the `#` character and has one special exception - when the first line of a script starts with `#!` (meaning it is an instruction that the specified file should be executed). The second way of commenting a script is to use the `:` command.

Take the following lines:

```
#!/bin/sh                    ` This isn't a comment
# This is a great script     ` This is a comment
: No - it really is          ` This is a comment too.
```

You may come across this convention in some older shell scripts, but it is inefficient because the command needs to be interpreted each time it occurs. New shell scripts should use the # style of commenting wherever possible.

Debugging Shell Scripts

When a script encounters an error it normally terminates with an error message including the line number on which the error occurred.

Since shell scripts are interpreted and not (normally) compiled, it is very easy to add additional debug code to scripts in order to trace the execution. There are two special parameters to the shell itself to aid debugging, these are **-v** and **-x**. The **-v** flag causes the shell to print each line before it is executed, and though similar, **-x** expands each argument before printing each line.

These flags are normally used when invoking a script:

```
sh -v bad-script.sh
```

You can change the state of these flags inside a script with the **set** command:

```
#!/bin/sh
# script24.sh
# Debugging aid
set -v
...
```

Summary

In this chapter we have shown that the UNIX shell isn't just a simple command parser. It is also a powerful and flexible command interpreter and programming language that you can (and should) use to customize your

UNIX installation. It is an ideal way to implement many programs, especially those that require pattern matching, and can be implemented by tying together some of the existing UNIX commands.

By reading this chapter not only have you learnt a whole new language, you've also learnt how to fully exploit the power of the shell script interface. So the next time you want to write a simple utility, don't just invoke a compiler - think about using the shell instead.

Chapter

The UNIX User

Each user of a UNIX system is to some extent able to treat the computer as if it was his or her own. Settings and system defaults can be customized, and every individual UNIX user has their own directory where they are able to keep personal files.

The facilities that allow this way of working are often collectively labeled under the user environment umbrella. This chapter will describe the way that UNIX provides access to many users at once, and how they are able to work independently and in a way that suits them. In this chapter we will be introducing the following topics:

- The user environment and how to log in
- Environment variables
- Shell aliasing
- Dot files and other initialization files

The User Environment

In Chapter 2, we looked at how to log in to the UNIX system; now we need to consider the whole login process and how the system verifies a login. To allow access for a number of users at the same time, UNIX uses the idea of access terminals, or **tty**s. The abbreviation **tty** stems from the early days of time sharing systems that allowed multiple users to access a single system from teletype machines. Such machines normally consisted of a keyboard and a printer, where you typed in your commands and the computer printed its response on a roll of paper - offering little scope for sophisticated user interaction.

Later, more sophisticated terminals became available - interactive use had become possible. Common terminal types included ADM-3A, Televideo and Digital VT-100, although the generic American National Standards Institute (ANSI) terminal type became far more prevalent.

The classic model of a UNIX multi-user system has a central computer and a number of terminals connected by wire (a serial connection), modem, or via a network with terminal concentrators. The terminals may even consist of other computers that have the ability to emulate a classic terminal type. As far as the UNIX system is concerned, regardless of the method of connection, it has to deal with a number of terminals each with a single user. Some variants even allow multiple 'virtual' terminals on one machine, switching between them using a keyboard sequence.

The login Procedure

For each possible access point, serial line, network connection or console, UNIX runs a program to control the process of logging in. The actual program differs depending on the type of connection; common ones are **getty** for serial lines and **telnetd** for network connections. Let's take the former of these as an example.

The getty Program

Consider a UNIX system with eight user terminals connected to eight serial ports on the UNIX computer. UNIX may refer to these ports as **/dev/tty00**, **/dev/tty01**, and so on, up to **/dev/tty07**. Typically, there will be eight **getty** programs running, each one controlling a terminal and prompting for a user login name. Each **getty** program will also ensure that the serial line is controlled properly and at the right speed, etc. If the terminal is connected via a modem, it also controls the answering of the telephone and hangs up at the end of a call. **getty** is configured to know the type of terminal that is used on each connection. Where this is unknown, such as in modem or network connections, **getty** will use a configured default.

When a connection is made, or a user activates a remote terminal, **getty** issues a welcome (a configured string or, for some variants, the contents of the file **/etc/issue**) and prompts the user for a login name. Often the prompt includes the computer name, in this case **tilde**:

```
Welcome to the UNIX System
tilde login:
```

The user types in a user name and **getty**'s job is finished - it hands control over to the **login** program.

The Logging In Process

If logins are allowed at this time and from this terminal, **login** prompts the user for a password and checks that it is valid. **login** usually allows a predetermined number of attempts to log in (usually 3), in case the user name or password is invalid. Typically, the response time is slowed as a security precaution against password-guessing intruders.

Assuming that a valid user name and password are given, **login** will then prepare the terminal session for use. This involves the setting up of user and group identities, setting the **HOME**, **PATH**, **SHELL**, **MAIL** and **LOGNAME** environment variables and printing a message of the day (the contents of the file **/etc/motd**). The message of the day is set up by the system administrator to pass on important information to users such as events, notices or warnings. **login** may also indicate whether the user has received any new mail since they last logged in.

The login Shell

A new shell is then started and subsequently takes control of the terminal session - the user is now logged in. This shell is a special one in that it was started by the login process; thus it is called a login shell. When you exit from a login shell, the user will be logged out and the terminal will be made available for the next user. This latter action is done by the operating system (**init**) starting a new **getty**.

How init, getty and login Relate

We can see the relationship between **init**, **getty**, **login** and login shells by examining the output of the **ps** command. This shows us the programs that UNIX is running, where each copy of a running program is a process. Each process has a process identifier (shown as **PID**) and a parent process (**PPID**) - the process that started it. Here is an extract from some **ps** output.

```
$ ps -al
F    UID    PID  PPID PRI NI SIZE  RSS WCHAN     STAT TTY  TIME COMMAND
0      0      1     0   0  0   44  204 10cee7     S    ?    0:16 init
0      0     76     1   0  0   37  540 10caed     S    v06  0:01 getty
0    501     75     1  13  0  428  164 10caed     S    pp1  0:00 -sh
0    501    254    75  26  0   68  220 0          S    pp1  0:00 ps -al
```

init has process identifier 1, the parent (or ancestor) of all other processes. It started the **getty** processes, so they all have a parent process identifier of 1 (**init**). Similarly, when **getty** hands over to **login**, and **login** hands control over to a shell (**-sh** above), these processes also have a **PPID** of 1. Programs run by a shell have the shell's identifier as their parent. When they exit, **init** re-starts a **getty** to control the terminal again.

The following annotated diagram shows the relationship between the various programs and files that are involved when a user logs in:

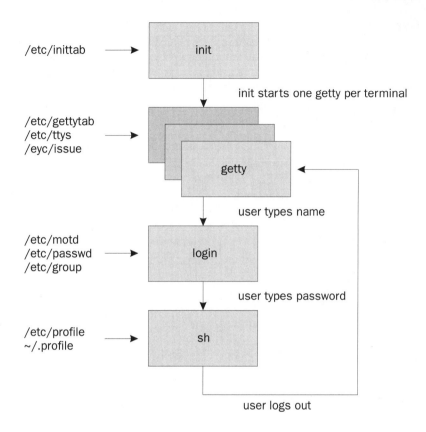

/etc/inittab → init

init starts one getty per terminal

/etc/gettytab
/etc/ttys
/eyc/issue → getty

user types name

/etc/motd
/etc/passwd
/etc/group → login

user types password

/etc/profile
~/.profile → sh

user logs out

Your Password

Each user has a password to protect his or her account from unauthorized access. As far as good security practices go, UNIX passwords tend to be very insecure. To offset the risk of unauthorized access to your system, you should follow the strict set of guidelines outlined in the chapter on security, Chapter 11.

To change your password use the **passwd** command:

```
$ passwd
Enter old password:
Enter new password:
Re-type new password:
The password must be at least 6 chars, try again
```

Note that the password isn't echoed as it is typed and a new password must be verified. Depending on your UNIX variant, the **passwd** command may enforce some minimum level of password security, in this case ensuring that the password is at least six characters long.

Your Home Directory

When you've logged into a UNIX system you can view and edit files, run programs and access information. To help you with these tasks you interact with a shell, a program that takes care of interpreting your input and running the programs required to execute your commands. To help with locating files, and navigating the UNIX filing system, the shell keeps a note of your 'current directory'. This is the directory you are in and where, by default, files will be created if you don't specify an absolute path. This is much the same as in DOS where the current directory is often part of the system prompt.

The starting point, or initial current directory, is typically different for each user. This directory is known as your 'home' directory, a private directory not usually accessible by others. All files in it are owned by you. Note that this is very different from DOS where, typically, all users start in the directory **c:** and have access to all files on that PC's hard disk.

Usually, users' home directories are kept on a separate file system, often called **/home**, sometimes **/usr**. So for users Jim and Susan, their home directories might well be **/home/jim** and **/home/susan**. The exact position is assigned by the system administrator and stored in the **/etc/passwd** file. See Chapter 2 on the UNIX file system for more details of home directory location, and take a look at Chapter 6 to see how to assign a home directory location.

Using a Different Account

The **su** (substitute user) command allows you to access the UNIX system using a different user identity. It creates a new shell that runs as the user that you specified, or the system administrator by default. **su** asks for the appropriate user password, just as if you were logging in as that user:

```
$ su susan
Password:
$
```

This new shell isn't a login shell, so all the relevant user's startup files, such as **.profile**, won't be read. You are effectively masquerading as that user, although you still have your previous environment (except for the variables **HOME** and **SHELL**) and current directory.

If the argument **-l** (or even just **-**) is given to the **su** command, then it performs a complete login for the specified user. The new shell will be a login shell and it will run in the new user's home directory. Your environment will be replaced by that of the new user, until you exit the new shell.

```
$ su - susan
Password:
$ pwd
/home/susan
```

umask

One important part of the user environment that is concerned with security is the **umask** (user file creation mask) value. **umask** is a variable that the system uses to set the permissions on the files that you create. Permissions and access control for files can be altered with the **chmod** command, but when a file is created, its initial set of permissions is determined by the value of the **umask** variable. The set of default permissions are assigned by whatever value is held within the **umask** variable.

When you first login, there will be a system-wide **umask** value that will act as your default value, until you change it. The permissions in the **umask** variable affect who can access the files that you create. This can become a security hole in lax systems. Examples are often found in universities or colleges where a relaxed **umask** value means that everyone can read each other's files. Of course, this means that students can read and copy each other's course work, until they change their **umask** variable! The **umask** variable may be viewed and changed by the built-in shell command **umask**:

```
$ umask
022
$ umask 002
$ umask
002
```

The **umask** value is an octal number that is used to automatically clear bits in the permissions flags for files that you create. The structure of this number's breakdown works just like the **chmod** command, as we discussed back in Chapter 2:

user	group	others
rwx	**rwx**	**rwx**
421	**421**	**421**

In the previous example where the **umask** is **022**, we are denying write permission for the 'others' group and for members of the same 'group'. So, when a file is created these users will have read permission (and execute permission on programs and search permission on directories), but not write access.

For further details on file permissions and the **chmod** command refer back to Chapter 2 on the UNIX file system.

User Account Information

Information about the accounts of users is held in two important system files that may be read by all users.

/etc/passwd

/etc/passwd is a file used by the system to record valid user names, an encrypted form of their passwords, and other information. Each line to the file consists of information about one particular user, and is split into a number of fields separated by colons, for example:

```
jim:xxxx:501:100:James Jameson:/home/jim:/bin/sh
```

The fields are as follows:

jim	The user name.
xxxx	The encrypted password (not shown, obviously).
501	Jim's user identifier, different for every user.

`100`	The primary user group that **jim** is a member of (this will also be the group identifier, **gid**, of all the files that this user creates).
`James   Jameson`	A full name, used by the **finger** program among others.
`/home/jim`	The home directory, **$HOME**.
`/bin/sh`	The shell that will be used for this account, **$SHELL**.

When **login** checks a password, it encrypts it first and then matches it against the value found in **/etc/passwd**. As this is a poor security method (see Chapter 11), many of today's systems don't rely on entries in **/etc/passwd** for password security (quite often they look in **/etc/shadow** instead), but the file remains to maintain compatibility with existing programs.

User Name Aliasing

It's possible to create user name aliases by creating more than one entry in the **/etc/passwd** file for a particular user identity. If **/etc/passwd** contains:

```
nm::501:100:A normal user:/home/nm:
neil::501:100:An alias for nm:/home/nm:
```

then logging in as either **nm** or **neil** refers to the same user identity. Different passwords may be set for each alias.

/etc/group

The file **/etc/group** defines user groups. Each line in this file lists which users are members of a specific group. It's also possible for a user to be a member of more than one group. If you browse the **/etc/group** file, a typical entry might look like this:

```
root::0:root
adm::4:root,adm,daemon
users::100:jim,susan,chris,neil,adrian
```

For more information about user groups, refer to Chapter 2 on UNIX file systems.

The id Command

The **id** command can be used to obtain the current user identity and group:

```
$ id
uid=501(neil) gid=100(users) groups=100(users)
```

Given an argument, the **id** program gives the identities of any user:

```
$ id chris
uid=502(chris) gid=100(users) groups=100(users)
```

Some older systems may not support the **id** command. If this is the case, the group command can be used to find which groups you belong to.

Environment Variables

Like DOS, UNIX makes use of shell variables to configure applications and the shell itself. Such environment variables are set in several places during the login process, including from special 'dot files' in your home directory. Some environment variables are set up automatically by the login programs, whilst others are set up by the invocation of the shell.

When you log in and use a Bourne shell (or derivative), the shell reads a standard file, **/etc/profile**, to set up variables for all users, and it reads a personal file called **.profile** in your home directory. This file isn't normally noticed since its name begins with a dot and is therefore ignored, by default, by the **ls** command. It is an example of a number of files which are used by different programs to store settings from one run to the next, or to set up initial behavior or options. We will meet some more 'dot files' later.

An Example : PATH

Possibly the most well known example of an environment variable is the **PATH** variable. If we type in this command:

```
$ edit file.txt
```

DOS will search for **EDIT.BAT**, **EDIT.COM** or **EDIT.EXE** in each of the directories specified in the **PATH** variable. UNIX will search for an executable file called **edit** in each of the directories specified in the **PATH** variable.

To see what the UNIX path is set to, we can use the **echo** command:

```
$ echo $PATH
/usr/local/bin:/usr/bin:/bin:.
```

As in DOS, some commands are integral to the command interpreter and can be used whatever the value of **PATH**. The shell expands such environment variables if we precede their names with a dollar sign. In this case, **echo** is executed with the value of the **PATH** variable as its argument.

In this case, the shell will first search in a local binaries directory (**/usr/local/bin**) and two standard directories (**/usr/bin**, **/bin**) for the specified command file. If it isn't found, then it will take a look in the current directory. Note that colons are used to separate directories in the UNIX **PATH** variable, whereas DOS makes use of semi-colons.

The env Command

There are many more environment variables used for configuring the environment you are working in, and we shall come across some of them later. To see a complete list of the environment variables in use, use the **env** command, the equivalent of the DOS **set** command:

```
$ env
LOGNAME=jim
HOME=/usr/jim
PATH=/usr/local/bin:/usr/bin:/bin:.
TERM=vt100
SHELL=/bin/sh
...
```

Setting and Creating Shell Variables

Each user is able to change the value of an environment variable, or even create a new one. The way to do this depends on which shell you are running. For the moment, we'll assume that you are using a Bourne, System V, Korn, POSIX or Bash shell.

To set the value of an environment variable, we type its name and an equals sign, followed by the new value. For example:

```
$ GREETING=Hello
$ echo $GREETING
Hello
```

Note that there are no spaces around the equals sign. If the new value contains spaces or characters that have special meaning to the shell, then they must be quoted:

```
$ GREETING='Hello Everyone!'
$ echo $GREETING
Hello Everyone!
```

We've now created a new shell variable called **GREETING**. This variable has been created in the shell we have been running, but isn't yet accessible to other shells or programs. It is like a local variable in programs. To make it an environment (global) variable available to all other shells, we must "export" it. We do this using the **export** function, which we discussed in detail back in the last chapter; refer to this if you're at all unsure about its usage.

Variables in the C-Shell

The variables in the C-Shell are considerably different, but facilities for accessing environment variables are still provided. To change the value of an environment variable, use the **setenv** command:

```
% setenv GREETING 'Hello People!'
% echo $GREETING
Hello People!
```

Common Environment Variables

There are a large number of environment variables for a wide variety of purposes. Here we shall be taking a look at some of the more common ones.

TERM

This is set to the terminal type for the login session; often VT100 is a common default as many terminals and software packages emulate this type of terminal. Systems consoles often have **TERM** set to **console**, a reduced facility terminal type, whilst **xterm** is a special terminal type used for sessions with the X Window System.

It's important that the **TERM** variable be set correctly so that programs that display forms or use the cursor keys use and expect the correct character sequences. Some UNIX variants will prompt for the correct terminal type during login. **TERM** is set by **getty**, during login, from an initial value configured in a system configuration file (usually **/etc/ttys** or **/etc/gettytab**).

The stty Command

There is a method of viewing the settings that are defined on your own particular terminal. The command **stty** (which stands for set teletype), suffixed by **-a** will show you which functions are mapped onto which key and other terminal settings:

```
$ stty -a
speed 9600 baud; rows 24; columns 80; line = 0;
intr = ^C; quit = ^\; erase = ^?; kill = ^U; eof = ^D; eol = <undef>;
eol2 = <undef>; start = ^Q; stop = ^S; susp = ^Z; rprnt = ^R; werase = ^W;
lnext = ^V; flush = ^O; min = 1; time = 0;
-parenb -parodd cs8 -hupcl -cstopb cread -clocal -crtscts
-ignbrk -brkint -ignpar -parmrk -inpck -istrip -inlcr -igncr icrnl ixon -
ixoff
-iuclc -ixany -imaxbel
opost -olcuc -ocrnl onlcr -onocr -onlret -ofill -ofdel nl0 cr0 tab0 bs0 vt0
ff0
isig icanon iexten echo echoe echok -echonl -noflsh -xcase -tostop -echoprt
echoctl echoke
```

If you want to change a particular setting and customize your working environment, then you use the **stty** command for this as well:

```
$ stty stop '^P'
```

This would redefine the **stop** signal to **control-P**. Be careful not to redefine a function to a key that has already been mapped to another function as this will cause a conflict. To reset the terminal to its default values, should you get into trouble, type **stty sane.**

TERMCAP

This variable is often used to convey the capabilities of the terminal being used, (hence **TERM**inal **CAP**abilities). It's usually set during the login sequence, and isn't normally changed by the user.

HOME

This is set to your home directory. This variable is expanded by shells and programs that support tilde in file names. So:

```
cd ~
```

and:

```
cd $HOME
```

have the same effect. Some other programs that prompt for a filename (for example, editors) also support the use of tilde to refer to home directories. Only system administrators are able to set **HOME** and we will be discussing the mechanics behind this in Chapter 6.

PATH

This is set to a list of directories that the shell will search in order for a program to run. This can be used to customize the behavior of the system and add new programs. You could, for example, maintain your own set of programs and have them run as well as, or in place of (if they have the same name) system commands. Suppose the user **jim** has a sub-directory called **bin**, where he keeps his own programs, including a special version of **ls**. He can set his **PATH** variable to include his directory before the system ones:

```
$ PATH=$HOME/bin:/usr/local/bin:/usr/bin:/bin:.
```

Now when Jim types an **ls** command, his version, stored in the **bin** sub-directory of his home directory (**$HOME/bin**), will be run instead of the system version. Any other programs in his **bin** directory will also be made available to his shell.

The **PATH** variable is often modified like this in **.profile** files to add additional directories, such as those used by applications (in a similar way to the use of **AUTOEXEC.BAT** under DOS).

> If **PATH** is long, place the directory where often executed programs are located at the beginning of the **PATH** statement and this will speed up the process of execution.

SHELL

The program to be used as the shell for executing shell scripts or commands in sub-shells is set in the **SHELL** variable. This is set up automatically during login and is rarely customized. Sometimes though, it might be used in interactive shells to specify a simpler shell that could be used for executing scripts.

LOGNAME and USER

LOGNAME is set to the user name given when you log in. It's usually set up automatically upon login (where supported) and isn't normally customized. Sometimes it's used by revision control systems to identify the intended author of revisions. The **USER** variable is utilized by the **telnet** program to attempt automatic logins.

MAIL

The variable that is set to the file where your mail is stored, is conveniently called by **MAIL**. This is used by some shells to tell you that new mail has arrived. It is usually set up automatically and not customized.

HOSTNAME

HOSTNAME is set to the name of the computer system you are working with. This is often set in **/etc/profile**, since it will be the same for all users.

PS1

This is the primary Bourne shell prompt, much like the DOS variable **PROMPT**. It's normally subjected to a great deal of customization. It gets set initially to a default value (often in **/etc/profile**), but you may wish to change it in your own **.profile**. The default is **$** for normal users and **#** for system administrators.

Escape Sequences

Some shells support certain escape sequences in prompts that are expanded to give additional information in the prompt. For example, the bash shell allows (amongst many others):

\t	The current time in HH:MM:SS format.
\w	The current working directory.
\u	The user name.
\h	The host name.
\$	This is either a **$** (a user) or a **#** (an administrator).

An Example

A useful and common setting for **PS1** is:

```
$ PS1="\u@\h:\w\$ "
jim@alex:~$
```

This sets the prompt to show the user, **jim**, using a computer called **alex**. Jim is currently in his home directory (shown as the tilde) and doesn't have system administrator access.

PS2

This is the Bourne shell secondary prompt and is used when the shell requires further input to complete a command. It defaults to > and is rarely customized, although it is possible to do so:

```
$ PS2='more> '
$ echo '
more> hello'

hello
$
```

CDPATH

Some shells support the use of a path for changing directories. The environment variable **CDPATH** can be set up as a list of directories. When the **cd** command is used and the directory given doesn't exist, the paths in the **CDPATH** variable are searched for a directory in which the specified target is a subdirectory. Then the shell changes to that subdirectory. For example:

```
$ CDPATH=/home:/usr/local:/usr/include
$ cd jim
/home/jim
$ cd lib
/usr/local/lib
$ cd sys
/usr/include/sys
```

The C-Shell uses a variable called **cdpath** to perform the same function. This variable requires a slightly different syntax and works in conjunction with the **set** command.

DISPLAY

This is used by X Windows clients to determine which screen and host to display on. This is usually set up automatically when the X Window System is started and defaults to `:0.0`, meaning the local console. For example:

```
$ DISPLAY=alex:0.0 ; xterm
```

will run an X terminal window on a different machine, called **alex**, assuming we are authorized to do so.

TZ

This variable sets the time zone for the user. It's often set by default, but can be customized to your particular time zone. UNIX machines run from a base time of GMT (Greenwich Mean Time) where all dates are recorded as seconds elapsed since midnight GMT on 1st January 1970. This means that files created at the same time will have the same date, regardless of time zone. To display a local time, the **TZ** variable is used to adjust GMT to your local time. A user calling in on a long distance modem line might be in a different time zone to other users, so they may set the **TZ** variable differently.

The **TZ** variable also controls the use of daylight saving time. The **TZ** setting of **GMT0BST** indicates that we are in the time zone GMT which is 0 hours west of Greenwich, and that daylight saving time is BST (British Summer Time).

```
$ TZ=GMT0BST
```

Daylight saving defaults to one hour time difference. The algorithms used for deciding times and dates to change differ between UNIX variants and countries. In Great Britain for example, there has been no one simple algorithm as daylight saving time is enacted by an Act of Parliament each year.

Some systems can also use the **TZ** variable to dictate the days of the year when daylight saving starts and ends. This can help overcome the difficulties of using a non-standard time zone.

UK and Eire Time Settings

The rules of the 1994 summertime directive, 94/21/EEC imply that the following **TZ** settings are correct for the UK and Eire. For 1995:

```
$ TZ=GMT0BST,M3.5.0,M10.4.0
```

From 1996 onwards the following **TZ** setting can be used:

```
$ TZ=GMT0BST,M3.5.0/01:00:00,M10.5.0
```

This setting means that daylight saving starts on the last Sunday in March and ends on the last Sunday in October. The change will now always be made at 01:00 GMT.

EDITOR and VISUAL

These environment variables are used by some programs for deciding which editor to run when required. For example, the **mail** program will use the program specified in the **EDITOR** variable when it edits messages with the **~e** command. It will use the **VISUAL** variable for the **~v** command. Other programs that start an editor (usually **ed** or **vi** by default) will often look for **EDITOR** and **VISUAL** entries for directories first. You can set these variables like this:

```
$ EDITOR=emacs
$ VISUAL=emacs
```

PRINTER and LPDEST

The **PRINTER** variable is used by some programs that support printing to specify the default printer. The **lpr** program has the integral **-p** option to specify the printer, otherwise it will use the printer identified in the **PRINTER** variable and, if that isn't set, it will accept a site-wide default instead. On the System V variant, the **LPDEST** function is the equivalent of the **PRINTER** variable.

MANPATH

This is used by the manual pages command, **man**, to specify the location of the manual pages on the system. **man** pages are notoriously split over many directories, making it a difficult task for the program to keep track of just where they are. The **MANPATH** variable acts as a search path for **man** in the same way that **PATH** acts for the shell:

```
$ MANPATH=/usr/local/man:/usr/X11/man:/usr/man
```

MORE

This is used by the file viewing program **more**. This variable can be used to set up options that **more** will use each time it is run. For example, to always override **more**'s treatment of form feed as a special character, you can specify the **-l** option. To have **more** act as if **-l** is always present, put it in the **MORE** environment variable like this:

```
$ MORE=-l
```

A lot of utilities use environment variables in just this way. Check their manual pages for details, then add and export the appropriate environment variable to your **.profile** file.

Shell Aliases

Most shells support the use of aliases for commands. These can be as simple as a replacement name for a command. They are often used to change the behavior of standard commands (they often take options) and some even implement a complete command.

The main advantage of using aliases over the shell scripts of replacement programs is that they are executed by the shell itself. There are none of the other additional overheads associated with running a script or another program.

The Alias Command

In Korn, C and Bash shells, aliases are introduced with the **alias** keyword. For the System V and POSIX P1003.2 shells, which don't support **alias**, functions must be used in their place. We shall consider the **alias** keyword first. Alias definitions are prime candidates for inclusion in shell initialization files, such as **.profile** and **.login**. A simple alias defines a new name for a command:

```
$ alias dir='ls -l'
$ dir t*
-rw-r--r--    1 jim      users      27804 Aug  8 21:27 tada.wav
-rw-r--r--    1 jim      users       3123 Dec  4 13:27 test.doc
```

Here **dir** is replaced by **ls -l**, so the command **dir t*** is expanded by the shell to be **ls -l t***.

System V Function Aliasing

In the System V shell we need to define a small function:

```
$ function svdir() { ls -l $* }
$ svdir t*
-rw-r--r--    1 jim      users      27804 Aug  8 21:27 tada.wav
-rw-r--r--    1 jim      users       3123 Dec  4 13:27 test.doc
```

Combining Aliases

Aliases may also refer to other aliases which in turn get expanded. They may be used to construct shorthand forms for complex commands. Here is another example for starting a network program in the background and redirecting the input and output:

```
$ alias net='term < /dev/modem > /dev/modem 2> /dev/null&'
```

From now on we can just type **net** to start a networked terminal session.

Listing All Your Aliases

All our defined aliases can be listed by typing **alias** without any parameters, while functions can be listed using the **set** command, which lists all shell variables and functions. Amongst the already defined functions you should find:

```
$ alias
.
.
dir='ls -1'
$ set
.
.
.
svdir=()
{
    ls -1 $*
}
```

> Some UNIX variants will automatically append **-F** to the **ls -1**. This is to make the output indicate whether a file is an executable, a link or a socket. An executable has * appended, a link has @ appended and a socket has = appended.

Alias Management

Note that excessive use of aliases, for example, to introduce new commands with the same names as DOS commands, can distance you from 'real' UNIX. If you customize popular commands and then move on to a different UNIX system, you have to re-create all your aliases in order to maintain a consistent environment. Thus, it's better to learn the appropriate UNIX command name thoroughly before you begin to simulate DOS with aliases.

Aliases can be removed with the **unalias** command, while the equivalent command for functions is **unset**:

```
$ unalias dir
$ dir
dir: command not found
$ unset svdir
$ svdir
svdir: command not found
```

Dot Files

Dot files are read by applications on startup to establish configuration details and user options from the outset. The chances are that your home directory will accumulate quite a number of these files over time. Some you will create and edit yourself, others will be created and maintained by the applications that use them.

Here we will take a look at some of the more common 'dot files'. By default, dot files are never displayed (likewise the contents of dot directories aren't listed) by the **ls** program.

Viewing Dot Files

To list all of the files in your home directory, enter it and run **ls** with the option **-a** (for all):

```
$ cd ~
$ ls -a
.Xdefaults
.emacs
.fvwmrc
.mailrc
.newsrc
.signature
...
```

This is a list of all the files in your directory. The dot files appear first because the list is in alphabetical order. To see just the dot files you can try:

```
$ ls -d .*
```

This limits the display to just those files beginning with a dot, but doesn't expand directories (**-d**), so that files in the current directory (**.**) and the parent directory (**..**) aren't listed.

The Life of a Dot File

Upon starting UNIX, the dot files are read in a special way because they need to affect the current environment. Although they may have a structure that would be allowed in shell programming languages, they aren't executed like normal scripts. They are executed not by a new sub-shell, but by the login shell itself. This means that any variables created, exported or modified in these files remain in the environment after the file has been read. They are said to be executed in the shell's environment, or 'sourced'. You can achieve the same result with your own scripts if you use the . command (or source in the C-Shell).

There are a whole host of initialization files that are accessed when you log on to UNIX. The file in which you should locate all of your initial setup commands is the **.profile** file. This way, you can customize your working environment.

The .profile File

This file is read (or sourced) by the Bourne shell (sh) when used as a login shell. It is used to set up environment variables, aliases and shell functions on a per user basis. This is only performed by login shells and isn't read when a sub-shell is started. This file is the closest UNIX equivalent to the DOS command **AUTOEXEC.BAT** for a given user:

```
$ cat .profile
stty sane
export TZ=GMT0BST
export EDITOR=emacs
...
```

Other Common Dot Files

The following table is a brief summary of some of the other dot files that you may find on a UNIX system. Changing these, or removing them may cause some applications to misbehave, so treat all unrecognized dot files with caution.

File	Function
`.article`	Some news programs use a file called `.article` for preparing postings. It's possible that you may find a file with this name left over from a session that was prematurely ended. It has no further function, so it may safely be deleted.
`.bash_logout`	This file is read when a login Bash shell exits.
`.bash_profile` `.bash_login`	Upon logging in, after `/etc/profile`, the Bash shell may read either one of these in place of `.profile`. If `.bash_profile` exists, it's sourced. If `.bash_profile` doesn't exist and `.bash_login` does, then `.bash_login` is sourced. If neither exist, `.profile` is sourced instead.
`.bashrc`	This file is sourced by every Bash shell each time it is started. This includes all shells used for scripts.
`.cshrc`	This dot file is read by every C-Shell each time it is started. This includes shells used for scripts. There isn't a Bourne shell equivalent.
`.elm/`	This directory contains files used by the `elm` mail program. It's created automatically and contains an options file (`elmrc`) and a mail alias database. Only `elmrc` should be changed, because aliases are maintained from within `elm` itself.
`.emacs`	The `.emacs` file is used by the GNU `emacs` for personalization of the editor. This dot file can be used to load `emacs` optional packages for every `emacs` session, or to add new key bindings for function keys.
`.emacsrc` `.joverc`	These files are read on startup by MicroEMACS and JOVE, two popular editors that are somewhat smaller than GNU `emacs`. They are used to set up key bindings, color schemes and menus.
`.gdbinit`	This file is used by the GNU debugger, `gdb`.

Continued

175

File	Function
.hushlogin	If this file is present, some UNIX variants suppress checking for new mail and the printing of a message of the day that normally happens on login. This enables the user to log in quietly.
.kermrc	This file is read on startup by the communications program, **kermit**. It is used to set a default serial line, baud rate and other options.
.login	This file is sourced by the C-Shell at login. It's similar in function to the Bourne shell **.profile** file.
.logout	This file is read when you exit a login C-Shell. file This is executed when the user types logout.
.mailrc	Some electronic mail programs make use of the variable **.mailrc**. It is used to set up user options and change the default behavior of the mailer. For example, to disable the carbon copy (Cc:) prompt, use **unset askcc**.
.MESSAGES/	This directory is used by the Andrew System mail program, **messages**.
.mosaic-global-history, .mosaic-hotlist-default .mosaic-personal-annotations/	These files are used by NCSA Mosaic, an Internet World Wide Web (WWW) browser program.
.netrc	This file is used by the file transfer program, **ftp**. It contains machine names, account names and passwords used for auto-login (login sessions without password or id). In order for **.netrc** to work properly, the permissions should be set to **rwx———**.

Continued

File	Function
.newsrc	This file is used by the Usenet news system to keep a record of the newsgroups that you subscribe to and the articles that you have read. It is usually maintained automatically by your newsreader, but can be modified if required. **.newsrc** consists of a number of lines, each of which details a newsgroup and the list of articles that you have read in the group. The file is read by a number of different newsreader programs such as **tin**, **trn**, **rn**, **nn**, and **tknews**.
.pinerc	This file is used by the **pine** mail program. It's automatically created by **pine**, but may be modified to change the configuration options.
.plan **.project**	These files are read by the **finger** program whenever anyone asks about your account. You can edit these files to provide information to others about your work or research. It isn't required that you keep these files up to date, or that you have them at all.
.signature	The **.signature** file is used by some mail and Usenet news programs. It's a text file appended to the end of each mail message or news article posted. In fact, this is a conventional name for a signature file, since most mail and news systems allow you to choose the file name to be used. Many signature files contain personal information and some can be quite amusing.

```
+ - - - - - - - - - - - - - - - - - - -+
|   Frank Sinatra    Compu$erve: 99999,999  |
|                                           |
|   Internet: fsinatra@blue.com             |
+ - - - - - - - - - - - - - - - - - - -+
|  Home Page: http://blue.eyes.com/         |
|                                           |
|            fsinatra/homepage.html         |
+ - - - - - - - - - - - - - - - - - - -+
```

Continued

File	Function
	It is, however, considered bad practice to have an awkwardly long signature file, or to divulge personal contact information (a home telephone number for example).
`.tin/`	This directory is created and maintained by the **tin** newsreader program. It contains files for customization and index files for speeding up access to news articles. The main files and directories are:
	tinrc Customizable options file.
	posted A file containing a list of postings you have made.
	replyto This file contains a string for the Reply-To: header.
	.index/ An index directory.

`.twmrc`
`.fvwmrc`
`.olwmrc`
`.openwin-init`
`.mwmrc`
	These files are used by the X Window System window manager programs. Most window managers use a file for storing definitions of menus, color schemes and the sizing and positioning of windows for programs.

`.Xdefaults` `.Xresources`	All dot files prefixed with X are used by the X Window System. User preferences for X programs are specified in either **.Xdefaults** or **.Xresources** depending on your version.
`.Xauthority`	The **.Xauthority** file is used for authenticating requests by other users to connect to your X server.
`.xinitrc`	The **.xinitrc** file is used to specify which applications are to be started when the X Window System is first run. Essentially, it's a shell script used to start an initial X terminal program, a clock, a console window and most importantly a window manager.

Continued

178

File	Function
`.Xmodmap`	The `.Xmodmap` file is used to modify the standard X Windows key map, specifying support for international keyboards or personal key preferences.

Environment Comparisons

To conclude this discussion of customizing the UNIX user environment, here is a quick table of rough correspondences between UNIX and DOS/Windows:

UNIX	DOS/MS-Windows	Purpose
`.profile`	`AUTOEXEC.BAT`	Contains a set of commands to be executed on startup of the system.
`PATH`	`PATH`	Contains a sequence of directories to be searched for when a command is to be executed.
`SHELL`	`SHELL`	Defines the shell to be used as default when one is initialized.
`.Xdefaults`	`WIN.INI`	User preferences for the chosen GUI operating system.
`.xinitrc`	Program Manager Startup Group	Contains a list of those applications to be automatically loaded upon GUI operating system startup.
`login`	Network Logon	Program that controls the process of a user logging in to the system.
`.mailrc`	`MSMAIL.INI`	Defines user preferences for their mail program.

Continued

UNIX	DOS/MS-Windows	Purpose
`alias`	**DOSKEY** <aliases>	A command for defining a substitute name for a command.

Summary

We have seen in this chapter that the user environment is characterized by a home directory, a number of special shell variables and a large number of initialization files for many application programs. All of these features ensure that the UNIX user environment is one of high versatility and is fully configurable. It is time to move on and take a look at the variety of responsibilities that the system administrator has to cope with.

Chapter

The System Administrator

Since UNIX is inherently a multi-user system, it needs a trustworthy person 'in charge'. This role is usually associated with the system administrator, internally referred to as the 'superuser' or sometimes the 'root' user.

In this chapter we will explore why every UNIX system needs a system administrator, as well as the variety of tasks and responsibilities involved. The running order is as follows:

- The need for a system administrator
- Configuring users
- Controlling the printers
- Starting and stopping the system
- Managing file systems and disk space
- Monitoring the system

The System Administrator

Because UNIX system administration and configuration hasn't been very well standardized, two main variants dominate. These are the systems derived from Berkeley UNIX (BSD) and AT&T UNIX (System V). In this chapter we'll take a look at these and show how they differ.

Because system administration can be a daunting task, some UNIX systems provide special administration shells or utilities to help with common tasks. For example, SCO UNIX has **sysadmsh** (a system administration shell), AIX has **smit** (the system management information tool) and Sun variants now offer **admintool**, arguably the most undeveloped front-end system administration tool available.

Who is the Superuser?

Conventionally, the system administrator has the user id of zero. A user is able to become the root or superuser either by logging in using the name **root**, or by logging in as a normal user and using the **su** (substitute user) command.

The Need for a System Administrator

All UNIX machines have an administrator's account, even stand-alone workstations with just a single screen and keyboard. If your UNIX machine is just for you, perhaps running Linux on a PC and not connected to any network, then you may wonder why there is a need for a superuser at all.

When a UNIX system is configured, many of the system files are protected so that normal users can't modify them. On multi-user systems this is a security feature, to prevent the accidental deletion or corruption of files that are important to the running of the operating system. Even on a PC the added protection of not being able to accidentally modify system files is still a very important feature.

All computer systems require some configuration, varying from incorporating a new peripheral, to providing a network connection. So there must be a means of configuring the system - and the superuser concept separates normal use from the power (and responsibility) of system management.

The Privileges of Root

Apart from being granted the right to run system configuration commands, root users also have additional privileges. They can:

- Read or delete any file.
- Change permissions on any file to any value.
- Change the ownership of files and directories.
- Create and modify disk partitions.
- Shut down the system and do other things not permitted to ordinary users.

In fact the only thing the root user can't usually do is determine the password of another user. This is because most UNIX systems use a 'one way' or 'trap door' algorithm for encrypting a plain text password. There simply is no decrypt routine. Even if there was a way, the security required to protect it from falling into the wrong hands would be stifling.

Every other restriction can be bypassed by the root user.

The Dangers of Root

The very considerable powers granted to the root user come at a price though. Mistakes made as root can prevent a UNIX system from operating. On a properly configured UNIX system it is all but impossible for a normal user to cause serious damage to the system. They may use a lot of disk space, delete their own files, delete other users' files (if someone has been generous with their permissions) or print reams of junk on the printer - but they can't stop the system from operating.

Accidental File Deletion

The most obvious danger while having root privileges is typing something like **rm *** (or even worse **rm -rf ***) in the root directory. Since the root user overrides normal file protection mechanisms, this can permanently erase a lot of very important files very quickly.

> Be very careful when you erase files. Always check which directory you are in and exactly which files you are deleting. And try to get into the habit of using the `rm -i *` command to confirm the deletion of each file you have specified.

The Home Directory of Root

On some versions of UNIX (mostly the older ones), if you log in as root, your home directory is set to `/`, the top level directory. This increases the danger of accidental damage, so many versions of UNIX have a special sub-directory, usually `/root`, that is allocated as the home directory of the superuser.

> Wherever possible you should try to avoid logging in as `root`. Even if you're the only user, create a 'normal' user login - and make sure you use it for all your everyday work. If you need root privileges then use the `su` command to temporarily grant yourself superuser status, then when you've finished, exit the `su` shell to return to your normal user id. Don't retain root privileges any longer than you absolutely have to.

File Recovery Procedure

If you, as the system administrator, ever do accidentally type `rm *` or one of its variants in the top level directory, there are three things to do:

1 Interrupt the command as quickly as possible to minimize the number of files deleted.

2 DO NOT SHUT THE SYSTEM DOWN. Your best hope of recovery is to keep the system running and attempt to recover the deleted files from a backup or original installation media.

3 Learn from your mistake!

Creating the Undelete Command

There is a method of effectively creating an undelete command. Firstly create an empty file called something like `.trash`:

```
$ cat > .trash
^D
```

Then you can alias the **rm** command, so that when you delete the file, it is simply moved into this new file. The syntax of this command might vary slightly from system to system; on Linux you would use this to accomplish it:

```
$ alias rm = 'mv $1 ~/.trash'
```

Whenever you delete something now, it's moved in to the 'invisible' dot file **.trash**. Bear in mind that this is a potential security hole, as someone could recover sensitive information from undeleted files. It must be left up to the system administrator to decide whether the danger of accidentally deleting your files is greater than the risk of leaving sensitive information hidden but not deleted.

Responsibilities

The duties that a system administrator is expected to perform are numerous and varied. This section gives a brief overview of some of the more important tasks that any UNIX system administrator must be responsible for.

Configuring Users

There are three distinct steps in adding new users to the system. These are creating a new user identity, establishing a home directory and setting up a default user environment.

Creating a New User

User identities are normally configured in the **/etc/passwd** and **/etc/group** files.

The User Information File

The **/etc/passwd** file consists of a number of lines, one per user. Each line contains seven fields separated by colons. An example is:

```
neil::10:100:Neil Matthew:/usr/neil:/bin/bash
```

187

The fields, in order, are login name, encrypted password (empty in this example), user identity, group, full name, home directory, and shell.

To incorporate a new user, the system administrator adds a new line with the appropriate fields completed. An unused user identity will be chosen, normally an increment from the last new user. A suitable group identity from the file **/etc/group** is also chosen. The password field is left blank by default so that the new user can complete it in privacy with the **passwd** command.

Shadow Password Configuration

As **/etc/passwd** needs to be readable by everyone, it is possible for someone to attempt to guess passwords, encrypt them and compare the results with the stored, encrypted version. Password encryption software is widely available, so to make the system more secure, some systems operate a shadow password scheme where an additional unreadable file, often **/etc/shadow** or **/etc/shadowfile**, is used to store the encrypted versions. Check the security chapter for more details on shadowing.

The Group Information File

The **/etc/group** file must be edited to include the new user in the appropriate group definition:

```
users:*:100:neil,chris
```

The fields, in order, are group name, password (often not included), group identity and group members. The new user's login name is simply appended to the end with a comma, like this:

```
users:*:100:neil,chris,bob
```

Tip

Placing an asterisk in the password position in **/etc/passwd** (when shadow passwording isn't used) effectively prevents the user from logging in. Adding a * to the front of a password string and removing it later can effectively disable an account temporarily.

Creating a Home Directory

The next step in adding a new user is to create a home directory, a normal directory usually situated in **/usr** or **/home** but may reside anywhere that the administrator chooses. It must be owned by the new user and you must remember to set the directory permissions appropriately - a common choice is **rwxr-xr-x** to allow read-only access by other users. This would be a good moment to set a password for the new user:

```
$ mkdir /usr/neil
$ chown neil /usr/neil
$ chgrp users /usr/neil
$ chmod 755 /usr/neil
$ passwd neil
```

Setting Up a Default User Environment

Many administrators maintain a set of default environment files for users to start with, mainly dot files. These will typically include **.profile**, but may also include other common application configuration files, such as **.emacs**. These will often be kept in a directory used solely for this purpose, **/etc/skel** and **/etc/default** are common choices. These startup files are copied into each new user's home directory to establish an initial user environment, display standard information for new users, or to enforce system policies.

Tools for Adding New Users

Many systems are shipped with a utility to help with adding new users, some of which perform all of the above steps automatically. Unfortunately there isn't one standard command for this. Look for commands with names like **adduser**, **useradd**, or **newuser**. If you use one of these utilities, you won't need to (and shouldn't) edit the configuration files concerned.

User Accounts on Networks

There are situations where it would be advantageous for a user to login to a system from any one of a number of interconnected computers. This is where the following technique is used:

- A user must have an account set up on each of the machines.

- A user must have a home directory with his or her files located on a single machine.

- Using an automounter (discussed later in Chapter 10), this directory is mounted via the network file system on all the other machines.

Now it doesn't matter what machine a user is logged in to, they have full access to their own files.

Solaris Admintools

Solaris GUI-based admintools operate a nice mechanism which implements this feature. The home directory for a user **foo** becomes **/export/home/foo** and is automounted to **/home/foo**. Therefore the entry in **/etc/passwd**, their home directory, should be **/home/foo**. The file that has to be updated with this information on each of the machines is **/etc/auto.master.**

Configuring Printers

The system administrator is responsible for managing all system-wide resources, though the main resource is primarily printers. In this section we'll see how to install a printer, enable printer management functions and manipulate printer queues. First though, we'll take a look at some of the options available to us when we print.

Preparing Files for Printing

The **pr** command is a useful utility that is available on all UNIX systems. It formats text files ready for printing, and can add page numbers, a header for each page, and line numbers. It operates purely as a prior filter to the system print command, **lpr** or **lp**. Some common options to **pr** are:

+ <page>	Starts printing at page number 'page'.
-h <header>	Replaces the file name in the header with the string 'header'.
-l <num>	Sets the page length as 'num' rows.
-m	Prints several files at the same time, one in each column.
-o <margin>	Prints text offset by 'margin' characters at the left.

| `-t` | Doesn't print the usual 5 line page header and trailer. |
| `-w <num>` | Sets the page width, in 'num' columns. |

The BSD Printing System

The BSD printer system is used on many UNIX systems, providing facilities for controlling printers connected via serial ports, parallel ports, and across networks. Specialized printers with their own proprietary interfaces can be accommodated as long as a device driver is provided. The system provides methods of querying the status of printer queues, starting and stopping the spooling of printer jobs, and removing jobs from the queues. In some ways this is similar to the way that the MS-DOS **PRINT** command prints files in the background.

Printer Devices

Each printer directly connected to a UNIX system is accessed by way of a device file, usually a special file in **/dev**. A common printer device is **/dev/lp**. If there's more than one printer, they might be called **/dev/lp0**, **/dev/lp1**, and so on. The printer device might even be a symbolic link to the special file used for the physical interface, i.e. **/dev/lp** might be an alias for a reserved serial port.

The Capabilities File

Printers are configured in a capabilities file, **/etc/printcap**. Each printer available on the system has an entry in this file, for example:

```
# HP Laser jet plus
lp|hplj:\
  :lp=/dev/lp1:\
  :sd=/usr/spool/lp1:\
  :mx#0:\
  :sh:\
  :of=/usr/spool/lp1/hpjlp:\
  :lf=/usr/spool/lp1/hp-log:
```

Each entry in the **printcap** file is a single logical line. To physically split it across several lines, you must place a backslash at the end of each line that is to be continued. The above example is such an entry.

Each **printcap** entry consists of a number of fields, separated by colons. The first field specifies the name of the printer, and any aliases for it. In this example a LaserJet printer is named **lp** (the default printer name), but may also be referred to as **hplj**.

In a **printcap** entry each field defines a capability, either Boolean, numeric, or string.

Boolean	Capabilities are set true if they appear in a field, or false if otherwise. In our example, the capability **sh** (standing for suppress headers), is a Boolean capability.
Numeric	Capabilities are specified by a hash mark, **#**, after the name, followed by a number. In this case the **mx** capability, for maximum job size, is set to zero.
String	Capabilities are specified by an equals sign, **=**, after the name, followed by a string value. In our example the log file is set to **/usr/spool/lp1/hp-log** by setting the **lf** capability.

The following table shows the common printer capabilities, their type and usage:

Capability	Type	Example	Usage
br	numeric	9600	Baud rate for serial devices
if	string	**/usr/lib/hpfilter**	Input filter
lf	string	**/usr/adm/lpd-errs**	Log file
lp	string	**/dev/lp1**	Printer device
mx	numeric	1024	Limit job size to 1024k -zero means unlimited
of	string	**/usr/lib/hpofilter**	Output filter
pl	numeric	64	Page length in lines
pw	numeric	80	Page width in characters
sd	string	**/usr/spool/lp1**	Spool directory
sh	Boolean		Suppress headers (banners)
tr	string	**\f**	Trailer, summary printed after job

Printer Filters

Filter capabilities can be used to specify programs that are run on the input to, or output from, the **lpr** command. These might, for example, set the font or paper orientation by inserting printer-specific escape codes into the data stream sent to the physical printer.

An advanced use of printer filters is to autodetect the type of data being sent to the printer and automatically run file conversion utilities. It's possible to insert a PostScript interpreter into the process (such as Ghostscript) to turn the output of a low-cost inkjet printer into the equivalent standard of a PostScript printer. Similarly, graphics filters make it possible to run **lpr** on graphics files such as TIFF and JPEG and produce good quality output without having to run any conversion utilities.

Printing with BSD

The **lpr** command is used to initiate a print job. It takes filenames as arguments and by default arranges for them to be printed on the default printer, **lp**. The value of the environment variable **PRINTER** can be used to override this behavior and set a different, preferred printer. With no filename arguments, **lpr** reads from the standard input. **lpr** has a number of options, including:

-P <printername>	Prints the files on the printer labeled 'printername'.
-p	Uses **pr** to format the files before printing.
-h	Suppresses the printing of a burst (header) page.
-m	Sends mail to the user when the job is complete.
-r	Removes the file after it has been spooled or printed (with **-s**).
-s	Uses symbolic links - don't copy the file to the spool area.
-# <number>	Prints 'number' copies.
-J <jobname>	Uses 'jobname' for the title on the burst page.
-C <class>	Uses 'class' for the job class on the burst page.
-U <user>	Sends 'user' as the user name on the burst page.
-T <title>	Uses 'title' as the header for the **pr** program (with **-p**).

`-i <columns>`	Indents the output by 'columns' number of columns.
`-w <number>`	Uses 'number' as the page width for the `pr` program (with `-p`).

The Line Printer Daemon

The `lpr` program communicates with a line printer daemon program, `lpd`, which is usually running all the time, and is started from the system startup scripts. It arranges for the selected files to be printed, or copied (or linked if the `-s` option is used) to the spool area defined for the destination printer. The line printer daemon takes responsibility for actually printing the files and deleting them from the spool area when done.

Errors that occur during printing are automatically recorded in the log file specified for that particular printer.

The Print Queue

The status of the printer queue can be seen by typing the `lpq` command, while jobs can be removed from it with `lprm`. Normal users can use these commands to view the progress and to cancel their own print jobs.

```
$ lpq
lp is ready and printing
Rank    Owner      Job  Files                              Total Size
1st     neil        288  chapter6.txt                       4796 bytes

$ lprm 288
dfA288tilde dequeued
cfA288tilde dequeued
```

Printer queues may be enabled or disabled using the `lpc` utility. This is a program that can be used to control printing, queuing of jobs, and even reorder jobs in the printer queues. It works in its own shell and a list of all commands can be seen by typing `?` or **help**:

```
# lpc
lpc> ?
Commands may be abbreviated.  Commands are:

abort    enable  disable help    restart status  topq    ?
clean    exit    down    quit    start   stop    up
lpc>
```

The System V Printing System

The System V scheme of printer management provides a similar set of functions, and from a user's viewpoint isn't much different - but the setup has significant differences.

Printer capabilities are defined in the **terminfo** database files. System V capabilities and even the capability strings are very similar to those found in the BSD system. For most common printers there should be an existing definition provided. If you do need to add a new capability, you will need to use the **tic** command to compile the definition and restart your printer service to load the new configuration.

The Interface

You also need to provide an interface program. These are short shell scripts that allow you to define how the printer is initialized, and customize the 'burst' page, that acts as a header to all printouts. By default, a 'dumb' interface is provided that makes an acceptable initial script that you can then copy and configure to your individual needs. The interface program is invoked with a set of parameters that allow it to process the request, such parameters include 'printer name', 'print job id', 'user name', 'title', 'copies', 'options', and 'filename to be printed'.

The lpadmin Command

Once you have a **terminfo** printer definition, an interface program and a printer device, you add the printer using the **lpadmin** command. The **lpadmin** command is the administrator's way of controlling the printer daemon program, **lpsched**, which operates a similar function to the BSD daemon, **lpd**.

The main parameters to **lpadmin** are:

-d <name>	Specifies 'name' as the system default destination.
-i <name>	Makes 'name' the interface program for the printer.
-p <name>	Specifies the printer as 'name'.
-T	Types from **terminfo**.
-v <name>	Specifies that printer output be appended to the file 'name'.

The default system printer is set with the command:

```
# lpadmin -d printer
```

Printer Controls

Printers can be set to accept or reject print jobs independently of the status of the physical printer. The **accept** and **reject** commands control the acceptance of spooling commands, and the **enable** and **disable** commands control the actual printing.

Printing with System V

With System V, the **lp** command is used to initiate a printer job. Its options are similar to the BSD **lpr** options, except that the destination is specified with the **-d printer** option.

When the printer is running, normal users can inspect the print queue with the **lpstat** command, and cancel their print jobs with the **cancel** command.

Starting and Stopping the System

Superficially, System V and BSD are both very similar in the way that they are started and shut down.

Flow during Systems Backup

When you turn the computer on, it boots UNIX automatically and can usually be made to stop in 'single user' mode - where no other users can login. This is very useful for performing stable administration tasks.

This single user state is required where tasks need to be performed when it's desirable for there to be as little system activity as possible. Earlier, we met the **fsck** command for repairing corrupted file systems. **fsck** is best run in the single user state, when it can be guaranteed that no other users or programs are accessing the disk.

Typically, the system will automatically go on to run in a 'multi-user' state, achieved from a single user state by either exiting the current shell (for BSD variants) or by executing the **telinit** command for System V variants (see later in this chapter).

Shutting Down

To shut down a UNIX system, the superuser can use the **shutdown** command. This normally accepts a delay parameter and a warning message text.

For System V the parameters are normally:

```
shutdown [-y] [-g <min>] -f "msg" [su]
```

-y	Doesn't ask any more questions, assumes yes.
-g <min>	Allows a grace period of 'min' minutes.
-f <msg>	Writes message 'msg' to all users terminals before shutdown.
su	Doesn't halt, just shuts down to single user mode.

For BSD systems the parameters are as follows:

```
shutdown [-t <secs>] [-rkhncf] time "message"
```

-t <secs>	Waits 'secs' seconds between warning and killing processes.
time	Shuts down at the specified time. Immediate shutdown can be expressed by the string 'now'.
-r	Reboots after shutdown.
-h	Halts after shutdown.
-n	Doesn't **sync** the disks before shutdown.
-f	Fast shutdown, doesn't check file systems on reboot.
-k	Doesn't really shut down, just warns users.
-c	Cancels a running shutdown.

shutdown arranges for the system to be halted or rebooted in an orderly fashion at the appropriate time. You should never power down a running UNIX system, except in the most serious of emergencies.

If Shutdown Fails

If the **shutdown** command fails, then the usual method is to tell all users to log off, manually kill any non-system processes that appear to be accessing the disk, then invoke the 'magic incantation':

```
# sync;sync;sync;halt
```

This uses the **sync** command, which forces the file system to write all 'dirty' disk buffers to the physical disk, and then the **halt** program physically halts the processor. The purpose of the two extra **sync** commands is to ensure that all disk buffers get written, as some systems limit the number of disk accesses for each **sync**. On some systems **halt** may have a different name, such as **haltsys**, whilst on others it might be assigned as an alias for **shutdown -h now**.

Shutdown Warnings

Remember, it's polite to give users as much warning as possible before shutting down. If you know a day or two in advance, then you can put a message in the **/etc/motd** file which is displayed to all users when they login. You can also use the **wall** command which writes a message to all users. It can be used interactively in which case it needs no arguments and will read a message from the standard input, otherwise it can be given a filename argument and will distribute a message from a file.

Tips

If users are in an editor or other full screen program at the time you use **wall**, it might just corrupt their screen, and they may not even be able to read the resulting message. Many editors have a screen redisplay command (often *Ctrl-L*) that can be used to clear up any resulting display problems.

One other command you may need as an administrator is the **reboot** command. This reboots the system, but doesn't issue any user warnings first. It would normally only be used from the single user state, and after a series of **sync** commands. On some systems, **reboot** is an alias for **shutdown -r now**. On System V, the command **telinit 6** (see later) provides similar functionality, but in a more elegant manner.

System Run Levels

Beneath the superficial similarity that the printing systems of the two main UNIX flavors have, there are significant differences:

BSD UNIX systems are generally run in one of two states, either single user or multi-user. On boot up, the **/etc/rc** script is invoked to get to the single user state, and the **/etc/rc.local** script is subsequently run when you want to move from single user to multi-user state.

System V UNIX systems are rather more complex, but have greater flexibility. These systems (and others such as Linux that have a System V compatible **init** system) use the concept of a 'run level'. The meaning may vary from machine to machine, but typical values used might be:

0	Not running, shutdown.
1,S,s	Single user state.
2	Multi-user, but without networking.
3	Multi-user with networking enabled.
4	Multi-user, allow terminal logins.
5	Multi-user, allow remote X sessions.
6	Reboot.

Note that in general, each run level builds on the previous one, adding system services.

The telinit Command

The run level is changed with the **telinit n** (or sometimes simply **init n**) command, where **n** is the new run level required. The facilities available are determined from the **/etc/inittab** file, which also has a special line for setting the default run level. When the system changes to a new run level, it automatically runs scripts placed in an appropriate directory, normally **/etc/rcN.d**, or **/etc/rc.d/rc.N**, where **N** is the new run level number. An important file to remember is **/etc/rc.d/rc.0**, which is where the shutdown scripts go. The shutdown scripts are created to help avoid problems caused by data corruption.

For systems with separate directories for each run level, scripts with names starting with an **S** are run when the new run level is entered, and scripts starting with **K** are run when a run level ends. If you place your own scripts in the appropriate directory, they will be run automatically.

Although this sounds as though the System V scheme is overly complex, it makes it much easier for programs being installed (or removed) to integrate themselves into the system in a clean way, without requiring the system administrator to manually edit scripts.

Managing File Systems and Disk Space

Resources on any multi-user system have to be shared and maintained. One of the most crucial resources is disk space. Errant users may quite easily be able to fill file systems up, to the detriment of others. In extreme cases, system performance can be adversely affected by a lack of disk space.

In this section we'll take a look at a few utilities that allow the system administrator to monitor and manage disk resources.

The Disk Free Command

The current state of UNIX file systems can be viewed using the disk free command, **df**. For each mounted file system (including networked ones) a summary of disk space usage is printed, for example:

```
$ df
Filesystem       1024-blocks   Used Available Capacity Mounted on
/dev/hda2            15860      13648     1388     91%   /
/dev/hda3           306284     281673     8792     97%   /usr
/dev/hda1           108664      97328    11336     90%   /dosc
/dev/sda2           508476     318374   184849     63%   /share
/dev/sbpcd          659246     659246        0    100%   /cdrom
```

Here we can see a system that's critically short of disk space, and possibly about to run into serious problems. (Note - on some systems the display will be in 512 blocks rather than the rather more familiar 1024 blocks or K for short. Use **df -k** if this is the case on your system.)

The temporary directory, **/tmp**, is not shown in the example as it has not been allocated its own disk partition. It is simply a directory in the root partition. There is less than 1.5Mb free space on the root partition, so users will be unable to create temporary files of any size. For example, mail programs and programming language compilers may create temporary files and if the disk fills up, these programs will be unable to run. Even programs that use an alternative temporary directory, **/usr/tmp**, may have problems as the **/usr** partition is also very nearly full.

UNIX typically reserves a proportion of the disk space for the system administrator's use. Often this is configurable, and it is normal for it to be set to 5%. This means that when the file system gets to be 95% full, users can't use more disk space on that partition. This helps to prevent excessive file system fragmentation, and also allows some room for manoeuver when resolving disk space problems. Bear in mind that overly large disk partitions with little data spread across them may result in a performance degradation due to excessive disk head movement in finding files. The percentage usage figures from **df** take this 'safety net' into account, so it is quite possible to see figures of 105% when a disk system is completely full.

In our example, the root file system was created a little too small, and so the administrator will probably have to create a new disk partition for a separate **/tmp** file system - a good idea as it will help separate user files from system files.

The Disk Used Command

The next step on the road to a well managed disk system is to find out where all the disk space is being used. The **du** command can be used to find out just how much disk space is being consumed by files and directories:

```
$ du /usr/chris
4      /usr/chris/.term
32     /usr/chris/.elm
42     /usr/chris/Mail
1      /usr/chris/.tin/.mailidx
1      /usr/chris/.tin/.index
11     /usr/chris/.tin
1      /usr/chris/News
7      /usr/chris/.xfm
145  /usr/chris
```

This user is consuming 145 blocks of disk space. Unfortunately, the block size units vary from system to system. Traditionally, BSD systems report blocks of 1024 bytes, while System V and POSIX variants report blocks of 512 bytes. Many **du** implementations have a **-k** option to force a 1024 byte reported block size.

A summary of disk space may be generated by specifying the **-s** option to **du**. This just reports a total for each directory (including sub-directories) rather than all files.

```
$ du -s /usr/neil
55054   /usr/neil
```

This user is consuming 55Mb of disk space in total.

Tip

To find the five largest sub-directories in a directory try:

```
$ du -s * | sort -n -r | head -5
20216   demon
7283    cgi
6362    wrox
4369    terryh
3196    internet
```

Limiting Disk Usage

To help manage disk space on multi-user systems, many UNIX variants have a quota or disk space accounting system. This allows the system administrator to set a limit for each user and for each file system. When a user exceeds this limit they are warned that they must reduce it the next time they log in. If they stay over their limit for too long, or their usage exceeds a 'hard' limit, they won't be able to create any more files at all. Some systems will refuse to allow the user to login until the disk usage has been reduced below the quota set.

The Quota Commands

Quotas are set with the **edquota** command. Typically, this will create a file in the top-level directory of a file system to record the limits set for each user in that file system. The administrator can set limits on total disk space usage, or number of files that may be created by a user, or both.

Quotas are enabled or disabled with the **quotaon** and **quotaoff** commands, usually at startup.

The current quota states may be determined by using the **repquota** command, a report that over time can provide the administrator with advance warning of future problems.

Monitoring the System

There are two aspects to monitoring the system: discovering what is happening, and discovering why it is happening. There is little point in knowing your memory appears to be full and your system is paging to and from the disk, unless you can also discover why. If it turns out that a user is running a very large and complex game, then it's going to be cheaper to ask them to refrain during busy periods than simply to go out and buy more memory.

Some commands that may be useful in gathering system performance and usage information are:

who	Tells you who is currently logged on.
ps	Lists current processes and information about them.
top	Animated process display.
date	Sets the date and time.
wall	Writes to all users.
w	Gives a system load report.

These commands are self-explanatory - try them out and you will soon become familiar with them.

BSD systems have a number of extra utilities for monitoring other system resources such as memory usage and input/output, including **iostat**, **vmstat** and **pstat**.

On some System V file systems there is a very useful set of performance monitoring options controlled by the **sar** command. The main ones are:

-b	Reports disk buffer activity.
-q	Number of processes waiting to execute.
-u	CPU utilization.
-w	Swapping activity.

These allow you to monitor the usage of your system, and more importantly enable you to determine where bottlenecks are occurring. You can record information over a long period of time and then sample the performance of the system at different times of the day. You can then extract that information and try to analyze it, looking for any trends - such as slower performance in the morning when everyone logs in to check their post. Unfortunately, the **sar** command isn't available on all systems.

Maintaining Root Security

All multi-user UNIX systems should protect their root account with great vigilance - we will show you just how to do this in Chapter 11.

Summary

In this chapter we have seen why a system administrator is needed and why they have their own special login, and we've looked at some of the tools a system administrator can use to configure and manage a UNIX system. We have also covered the need to monitor system resources and seen some utilities to help with this task.

This might seem at first like very brief coverage of a system administrator's duties, however some of the system administrator's commands are very powerful and could cause a lot of damage if misused. The remaining chapters in this book also fall broadly under a system administrator's brief.

Chapter

The X Window System

As we learned in Chapter 1, MIT set itself the task of solving the problem of presenting a common look-and-feel to all applications across diverse hardware platforms/operating systems. The fruit of all their hard work was the very popular X Window System, an elegant and simple method of communicating with UNIX. Refined and much improved from the original release, X Windows is still very much at the forefront of the UNIX interface world.

This chapter will be propaganda for X Windows, in the sense that we'd like you to get to know this graphical user interface intimately, as it greatly enhances the speed and usability of UNIX. Thankfully, X Windows removes the necessity of having to communicate with the unfriendly command line, a burden that has prevented UNIX from infiltrating the home. The itinerary is as follows:

- The graphic user interface
- The windows managers
- The X Windows application
- Configuring and initializing X Windows
- The X terminal

The Graphic User Interface

Until the advent of the X Window System, UNIX application software had traditionally been trapped within the confines of a character-based user interface. Athena's creation allows users of UNIX systems to enjoy the benefits of a **graphical user interface** (GUI) similar to the ones found on Apple Macintosh and Microsoft Windows-based personal computers. GUI-based applications bear the following attributes:

- They take advantage of bitmapped graphical displays.

- They make use of the 'desktop' metaphor, allowing users to arrange visual application elements in the way that they feel most comfortable.

- They share common elements and standards with other GUI applications, reducing the amount of training and documentation required.

- They provide immediate access to all application functionality through the mutual use of standard menuing systems.

In addition to these features, the X Window System also provides a mechanism for executing programs on one machine, whilst having the user interface appear on another. This **Client/Server** architecture allows powerful systems to execute calculation-intensive programs whose results can then be displayed on less powerful workstations with sophisticated graphic capabilities.

The X Windows Display

Developers have battled with changing display standards and VDU drivers. X windows is a GUI that is truly portable, thus removing the pain of proprietary screen addressing. This portability is made possible by a physical feature of X that is unique amongst GUI presentation management systems - it has a Client/Server architecture.

The X Windows Display is very reminiscent of MS-Windows in the way that it works. The X server allows client applications to display information to the user through one or more **windows**. Several X client applications may share the server's resources at once. However, only one particular window may receive the **focus** at any one time.

An X client application has the focus when it is the one chosen by the user (or a system event) to receive mouse and keyboard input. The window is highlighted by moving it into the 'foreground' - in front of any windows belonging to other client applications, or just highlighting its title bar in a different color:

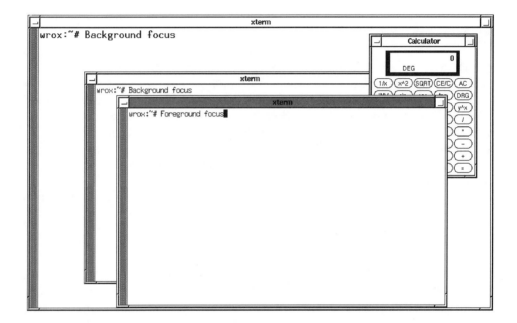

The user can shift the focus from client to client at will. This focusing mechanism allows multiple clients to share the display, one mouse and one keyboard harmoniously, without competing for attention or mistakenly receiving input meant for another program.

Getting Started

If you have X on your system, you can start it up by typing **startx**, **xinit** or **openwin** at the UNIX prompt.

Once you have done this, you will be greeted with a blank screen or whatever the initial setup of **xterms** and applications on your system is (an **xterm** being a simulation of a standard video terminal that you use to communicate with UNIX). To get around this system, use your mouse to select your application or call up a menu. Which mouse button it is will vary from system to system.

Widgets

The user interface window to an X application of any complexity is composed of a number of small building-blocks, predefined software components, called **widgets**. A widget is a part of the viewing window that is designed to behave in a certain way in response to user input. In addition to this, widgets may also display information back to the user. **Pushbuttons**, **menus** and **scrollbars** are all examples of X widgets. The analog clock face in the **xclock** application and the VT-100 terminal display in the **xterm** application are also widgets. Widgets make it easy for X programmers to reuse their user interface code and design by encapsulating standard functionality.

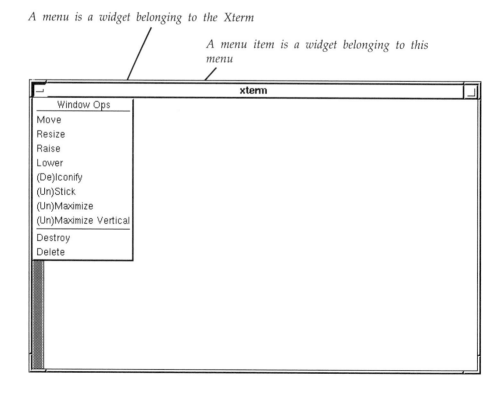

A menu is a widget belonging to the Xterm

A menu item is a widget belonging to this menu

Widgets in an X application can also be embedded in one another. The menu bar in a MOTIF application is a widget that belongs to the main window. The menu items in turn are widgets that belong to the menu bar. This 'tree' of widget ownership is called a **widget hierarchy**.

This will become important later in this chapter when we discuss the configuration of X programs.

Window Managers

Early in the development of the X Window System, its designers decided that the core of the system would "provide mechanism but not enforce policy". This means that the X Window System doesn't inherently look or act one particular way across all systems. Instead, these 'policy' decisions are left to third-party programs called window managers. Window managers are actually special X client applications that trap certain kinds of X server requests from other clients. Window managers can then impose their own look and feel on the system by augmenting the server behavior with their own functionality.

Window managers provide a variety of different schemes for resizing, moving and minimizing client windows. Some window managers add 'stretchable' borders for conveniently resizing windows, 'go-away boxes' that close windows when clicked by the mouse, 'minimize boxes' that shrink the window to an icon, or 'maximize boxes' that zoom the window to fill the entire display, to name but a few. These are all options that you can find within MS-Windows as well.

We'll look at three of the most popular window managers:

- **twm**, the basic window manager that everyone will have.
- **mwm**, an actual object-oriented layer which works in conjunction with MOTIF.
- **olwm**, the window manager of the Sun Microsystems workstation.

We'll look at how they perform basic window-management functions (like moving and resizing windows), how they employ icons and how to customize some of their common settings.

twm

The **twm** (Tab Window Manager - originally called Tom's Window Manager after its author) is included in the standard X software release. It is a basic, no-frills window manager.

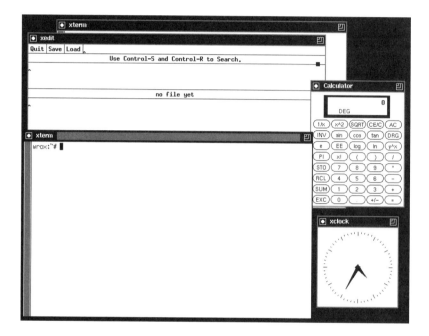

Window Decorations

The principal decoration that **twm** adds to your windows is a **title bar**. The title bar contains several important parts: command buttons, the application title, focus indicator and drag region. The default command buttons are the iconify (minimize) button on the left side of the title bar and the resize button on the right side.

The Root Menu

If you click on the root window when **twm** is running, it will display the root menu. The **twm** root menu contains all the basic window management operations. From the root menu you can control any other window on the display. You can generally perform the same kinds of functions that the window decorations provide (like moving and resizing a window), plus a few others. We say "generally" because the root menu is customizable by the user and the system administrator in the `.twmrc` and **system.twmrc** files respectively.

Manipulating twm Windows

There are four main ways to manipulate a window:

Moving a window   Clicking on the title bar (anywhere but the command buttons) and dragging the mouse around, while still holding the button down, moves the window.

Resizing a window   Clicking on the resize button and dragging the mouse around while still holding the button down, resizes the window.

Raising a window   A window is 'raised' when it is in front of all the other windows. Clicking once on the title bar of a window raises it. Remember that a window in 'focus' or use isn't necessarily in front of all of the others.

Lowering a window   Some **twm** configurations use a single click with the second mouse button to lower a window (send it to the back of the stack of displayed windows).

All of these functions are generally available on the root menu as well. To activate them from there, click on the root window and choose the appropriate function from the menu. Now select the window to which you wish to apply the function.

Working with Icons

Clicking on the iconify (minimize) button reduces the window to an **icon**. Iconifying lets you temporarily move some windows out of your way. This is the same as in MS-Windows. To get a window back to its full size once it has been iconified, simply click on the icon, or choose deiconify from the root menu.

Icons seem like a great idea at first, but on a large display with a lot of active windows, they can easily get lost. A better way to work with them is to use the **twm Icon Manager**. The Icon Manager 'corrals' all your wayward icons into a single centralized list, housed in its own window. The Icon Manager can be launched from the root menu, so it is easy to locate at all times.

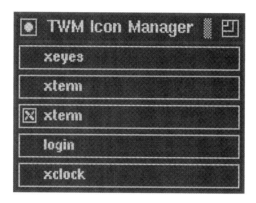

The Icon Manager automatically lists every application that is running on your display. It indicates iconified applications with a small X-logo.

Customizing twm

You can customize **twm** by changing the settings in your **.twmrc** file.

> If you don't have a **.twmrc** file, you are probably inheriting settings from a system-wide rc file called **system.twmrc**, which usually lives in the **/usr/lib/X11/twm** directory and is maintained by the system administrator.

If you create a **.twmrc** file in your home directory in order to customize your **twm** sessions, you should copy the **system.twmrc** file to start with. Your **.twmrc** will completely override **system.twmrc**.

Common Settings to Customize

The **.twmrc** file contains a set of statements that specify settings for **twm**. Here are some useful ones to add or edit:

AutoRaise
{application-
classes}

Adding this statement to **.twmrc** causes windows to be raised automatically when the focus is set to them. It only applies to those applications whose class names are listed within the brackets. For example:

AutoRaise { "Xclock" }

specifies that any **xclock** window will be raised automatically if the mouse pointer passes over it.

IconifyBy
Unmapping

If you get used to using the Icon Manager, you may want to further reduce your desktop clutter by getting rid of the actual icons for iconified programs. Putting this statement in your **.twmrc** will prevent icons from forming on your desktop. The only way you'll be able to find iconified programs will be from the Icon Manager.

NoTitle
{application-
classes}

This statement removes the title bar from instances of certain application classes. For instance, you may want your **xclock**s to always come up titleless (a common preference):

NoTitle { "Xclock" }

RandomPlacement

After using **twm** for a while, it may annoy you to have to keep using the mouse to place every window as new applications are started. This statement tells **twm** to find a place by itself to put each new window, without bothering you.

ShowIconManager

You can make the Icon Manager start automatically by putting the **ShowIconManager** statement in your **.twmrc** file. Then you won't have to always explicitly launch it from the root menu.

Color {item-list}

Your **.twmrc** (or **system.twmrc**) probably already has this statement in it. You may wish to edit it, however, and set the colors to match your bedroom curtains. Feel free to substitute any colors you like for the colors listed there.

Changing the Root Menu

The root menu itself is actually defined by a statement in your `.twmrc` file. You can rearrange the root menu if you like. Usually, it's a good idea to leave the basic window management functions where you find them within the root menu, otherwise you might accidentally disturb the placings of important files and cause yourself great problems.

There are all kinds of things you can do with menus in **twm**. Let's add a submenu onto an existing menu, by editing our `.twmrc` file:

```
menu "program_list"
{
"Cool Programs"         f.title
"Launch an xterm"       !"xterm &"
"What time is it?"      !"xclock &"
""                      f.nop
"Edit a text file"      !"xedit &"
}
```

The `f.title` statement gives the new menu a title when it is displayed. The `f.nop` statement creates a 'do-nothing' item for the sake of spacing (there really was no reason to put it in this menu except to show you that it can be done). The program commands are simply quoted text strings preceded by an exclamation mark and each will be executed when that menu item is selected by the user.

Next, you must integrate your new menu into the **twm** root menu. To do this, edit the root menu statement in your `.twmrc` file and add a new line to it:

```
"Cool Programs..."   f.menu   "program_list"
```

Now, restart **twm**. When you bring up the root menu, you'll see a new item. Select this item and drag off the right edge of the root menu. Your menu should pop down. When you select any of your programs, they should execute automatically.

OSF/MOTIF and mwm

MOTIF is a separate product from OSF/1. You can get it for virtually all versions of UNIX, including Linux. If you have OSF/MOTIF installed on your system, then you are using the **mwm** window manager. This window manager provides the standard MOTIF window decorations and behavior. MOTIF itself is more than just a window manager - it is an object-oriented layer on top of the X system, built using a set of widgets and libraries known as **xt** (the X Toolkit). It provides the **Xm** library for application development, including stand-alone systems. You don't need MOTIF or **mwm** to run MOTIF programs, but they will still retain the same MOTIF look and feel.

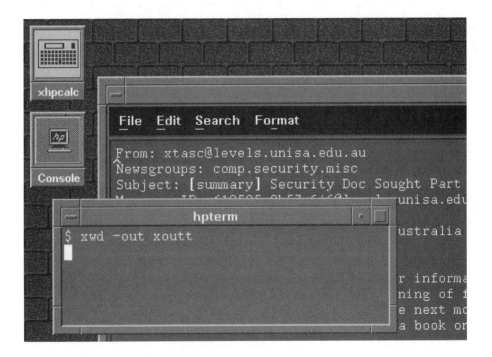

Window Decorations

MOTIF window decorations have a distinctive 3-D look, designed to complement the look of the **xt** widgets upon which the MOTIF system is based. This will be familiar if you are used to Microsoft Windows or IBM OS/2. There are five basic decorations on a MOTIF window:

Caption Bar	The caption bar displays the name of the application and allows the window to be moved using the mouse.
Border	MOTIF windows are given a thick border by **mwm**. This border can usually be used to resize the window. Some windows are programmed to be of a fixed size only, and their border can't be resized.
Window Menu Button	When you click on the Window Menu box, the Window Menu pops down. This menu lists the basic window management operations that can be applied to the window (like moving, resizing, etc.). Each item in the Window Menu has its keyboard shortcut key sequence listed alongside. You can type the key sequence instead of using the mouse to activate these operations.
Minimize Button	This button is used to reduce the window to an icon to get it temporarily out of your way without actually closing it.
Maximize Button	This button expands the window so that it fills the entire display.

The Root Menu

Since a lot of the window management functions are found in the Window Menu on each MOTIF window, the **mwm** Root Menu has fewer standard items in it than the **twm** Root Menu. The Root Menu doesn't see a lot of use in **mwm**, unless you customize it. You can do this in much the same way as you do the **twm** Root Menu (more on this later).

Manipulating MOTIF Windows

There are six main ways to manipulate a MOTIF window:

Moving a window	To move a MOTIF window using its caption bar, click in the caption bar and drag it to the position you want.
Resizing a window	Resize the window with the mouse by clicking on the border and dragging in the direction in which you would like to expand or contract the window.

Iconifying a window	Click on the Minimize button (the leftmost of the buttons in the upper-right corner of the window) to reduce the window temporarily to an icon.
Lowering a window	To lower a window, select Lower from the Window Menu.
Raising a window	To raise a window, simply click on the window.
Maximizing a window	Click on the Maximize button (the rightmost of the buttons in the upper-right corner of the window) to zoom the window to fill the entire display.

These functions are also available on the Window Menu (accessed by clicking on the Window Menu button in the upper-left corner of the window).

Working with Icons

Icons in **mwm** are larger and smarter than **twm** icons. When you click on an iconified **mwm** window, its Window Menu is displayed. Selecting the Restore item from the Window Menu (or double-clicking on the icon) restores the window back to its full size. This is a feature also found in MS-Windows.

Like the **twm** Icon Manager, **mwm** provides a more centralized way of working with icons, called the 'icon box'. To use the icon box, place the line

```
mwm*UseIconBox: True
```

in your **.Xdefaults** file.

Every running application shows up in the icon box, but icons representing iconified applications have a bevelled border.

Customizing mwm

Like **twm**, **mwm** has its own configuration file in your home directory, called **.mwmrc**. Unlike **twm**, however, **mwm** makes extensive use of resource definitions for all its customizable settings. We've already seen how to turn on the icon box using a resource setting. There are many other resource settings used by **mwm**.

219

Common Settings to Customize

Here are a few useful **mwm** resources to add to your **.Xdefaults**:

Focus Policy

Normally in **mwm** you must click on a window to give it the input focus. Some people prefer the focus to be set to whichever window currently contains the mouse cursor (which is the default behavior for **twm**). You can set this in your **.Xdefaults** for **twm**-style focusing as follows:

```
mwm*KeyboardFocusPolicy: pointer
```

or for the **mwm** default:

```
mwm*KeyboardFocusPolicy: explicit
```

Since this is the default, simply omitting this setting has the same effect.

Note that when pointer focus is used, windows won't jump to the foreground automatically when the focus is given to them. You can turn that behavior on, but generally it isn't a good idea.

Turning Off

If you wish to disable decorations such as **xclock,** you must add an **mwm** resource to your **.Xdefaults** file. For example, if you wish to disable all **xclock** decorations, insert the following resource (the minus sign instructs **mwm** to remove the specified decorations(s)):

```
mwm*XClock*clientDecoration: -all
```

Changing the Root Menu

It's as easy to customize the **mwm** Root Menu as it is to customize the **twm** Root Menu. Here's how you would add the Cool Programs menu from our **twm** example to your MOTIF Root Menu. First, define the new menu in your **.mwmrc** file as follows:

```
menu programList
[
"Cool  Programs"          f.title
```

```
{"Launch an xterm"      f.exec "xterm &"
"What time is it?"      f.exec "xclock &"
no-label            f.separator
"Edit a text file"      f.exec "xedit &"
}
```

Then, add the new menu to your root menu by adding the following line to the root menu definition in your **.mwmrc** file:

```
"Cool Programs"     f.menu programList
```

Now you'll be able to access your menu as a cascading submenu of the Root Menu.

OpenLook and olwm

If you have a Sun Microsystems workstation using OpenWindows, or other platforms where OpenLook is installed, then you will probably use the **olwm** window manager. Like MOTIF, OpenLook is a set of extensions to the basic X environment, based on the Xview toolkit.

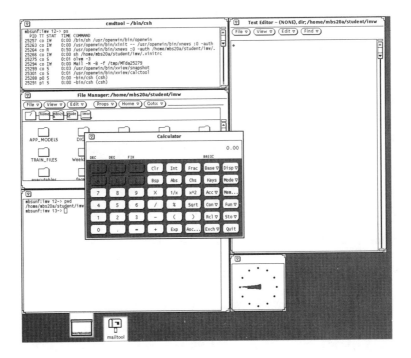

Window Decorations

The **olwm** window manager adds its own set of decorations to the windows it manages:

Caption Bar The caption bar displays the name of the application. It also provides a means of moving the window with the mouse. The Window Menu is accessed by clicking the rightmost mouse button over the caption bar.

Border Around the edge of the window is a thin border. This border can be used to move the window using the mouse. The Window Menu can be accessed by clicking the rightmost mouse button anywhere along the border frame.

Resize Corners At each of the four corners of the window is an L-shaped decoration that can be used to resize the window using the mouse.

Iconify Button In the upper-left corner of the caption bar is a small command button that can be used to iconify the window.

The Root Menu

The **olwm** Root Menu is called the **Workspace Menu** and is accessed by clicking the rightmost mouse button over the background of the OpenLook display. It contains a set of useful utility functions as well as a submenu where you can place launch points for commonly-used applications. In fact, under OpenWindows the entire Workspace Menu can be redefined.

Manipulating OpenLook Windows

Moving a window To move an **olwm** window using its caption bar or thin border frame, click in the relevant region (but not on a resize corner) and drag in the direction you wish the window to move.

Resizing a window Resize the window with the mouse by clicking on any resize corner and dragging in the direction in which you would like to expand or contract the window.

Iconifying a window	Click on the Iconify button to reduce the window temporarily to an icon.
Lowering a window	To lower a window, select Back from the Window Menu.
Raising a window	To raise a window, simply click on it.
Maximizing a window	Select Full Size from the Window Menu to zoom the window to fill the entire display.

These functions are also available on the Window Menu (accessed by clicking on the Window Menu button in the upper-left corner of the window).

Working with Icons

OpenLook icons work similarly to MOTIF icons, except that there is no icon box. Double-clicking on an **olwm** icon restores the icon to a full-size window.

Customizing olwm

OpenLook is much more rigidly standardized than the other window manager environments we've looked at so far. Therefore, there's not a whole lot you can customize. There is a useful program called **props** that lets you set a number of configurable properties. It can either be run from the Workspace Menu (Properties... item) or from an **xterm** or **xconsole** by typing:

```
props &
```

Changing the Root Menu

The main thing that you can change about your OpenLook environment is the contents of the Workspace Menu. The best way to do this is to copy the predefined menu files from **/usr/openwin/lib** to your home directory and edit them from there. That way your changes won't affect the rest of the system. The relevant files have names starting with **.openwin-menu**. A good one to experiment with is **.openwin-menu-programs**. We can make this look like our Cool Programs menu in **twm** by changing the lines not commented out with **#**'s to:

```
"Cool Programs" TITLE PIN

"Launch an xterm..."     exec xterm
"What time is it?..."    exec xclock
""                       SEPARATOR
"Edit a text file"       exec xedit
```

You'll probably want to add the **exec** lines to the existing menu code rather than wiping it all out. You can arrange these applications and customize the menu according to your own personal preferences.

Simple X Applications

In this section, we'll get better acquainted with, and customize some of the most commonly supplied X applications. You can start all these from any **xterm** or **xconsole** window. Be sure to include the ampersand at the end of the command line when running X clients so that they will run as independent tasks.

xterm

```
■ xterm                                                          ▣
wrox:~# ps
  PID TTY STAT   TIME COMMAND
   66 v02 S     0:00 /sbin/agetty 38400 tty2
   67 v03 S     0:00 /sbin/agetty 38400 tty3
   68 v04 S     0:00 /sbin/agetty 38400 tty4
   69 v05 S     0:00 /sbin/agetty 38400 tty5
   70 v06 S     0:00 /sbin/agetty 38400 tty6
   76 v01 S     0:01 -bash
  129 v01 S     0:00 sh /usr/X11/bin/startx
  130 v01 S     0:00 xinit /usr/X386/lib/X11/xinit/xinitrc --
  132 v01 S     0:00 sh /usr/X386/lib/X11/xinit/xinitrc
  135 v01 S     0:04 fvwm
  137 v01 S     0:00 /usr/bin/X11/xterm -sb -sl 500 -j -ls -fn 7x14
  138 pp0 S     0:00 -bash
  144 pp0 S     0:00 xclock
  146 v01 S     0:00 xcalc
  148 v01 S     0:00 xedit
  151 v01 S     0:00 /usr/bin/X11/xterm -sb -sl 500 -j -ls -fn 7x14
  152 pp1 S     0:00 -bash
  159 v01 S     0:00 xgrab
  167 v01 S     0:00 xgrabsc -sleep 3 -post 0 -brighten 100 -bdrs --reverse -k
  169 pp1 R     0:00 ps
wrox:~# ■
```

If you've got X up and running, you're probably already somewhat familiar with the **xterm** application. It's the X command shell window. You can have as many **xterm**s running as your system resources permit, and it's often quite useful to have several up and running all at once. Again, the 'standard' command-line options apply. There are other options available to **xterm**, but most of them are rarely necessary. Check the **man** pages under **xterm** on your system to see the additional options that your version of **xterm** supports.

From a running **xterm** or **xconsole**, type:

```
xterm -sb -bg Blue -fg White &
```

Now you should have created an **xterm** with a scrollbar, a blue background and white text.

xclock

It's always nice to have a clock handy on your desktop, so let's look at the **xclock** application. This simple program displays either an analog or digital clock face that automatically updates as the system time changes.

In addition to the 'standard' command-line options for X client applications we've previously discussed in this chapter, **xclock** takes a few special ones of its own:

-help   Displays a quick reference for the command-line options.

-analog   (Default). Runs the clock as a graphic representation of a conventional analog clock (with a circular face, minute, hour and second hands).

225

-digital	Runs the clock in digital (text) mode. Hours are displayed in 24-hour format.
-chime	Causes the clock to chime every half-hour and chime twice on the hour.
-update *seconds*	(Default = 60). Specifies the time interval between updates of the clock display. If the clock is in analog mode, and this value is set to anything less than 30, a second hand will be displayed.
-hd *color*	(Default = Black). Specifies the color with which to draw the hands when in analog mode.
-hl *color*	(Default = Black). Specifies the color with which to draw the edges of the hands when in analog mode.

From a running **xconsole** or **xterm**, type the following:

```
xclock -bg Pink -hd Green -hl Red -update 1 &
```

Now you have a rather garish clock with a sweep second hand.

xedit

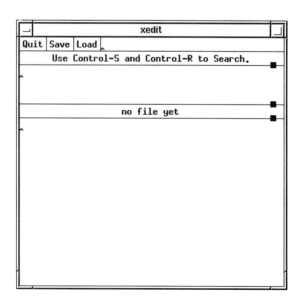

xedit is a very rudimentary text editor. You can use it to create and modify text files. It is neither very powerful nor particularly stable, but it is very handy to know how to use in case of an emergency. There are four parts to the **xedit** main window:

Commands   This section contains three pushbuttons for exiting **xedit**, loading a file for editing and saving a file.

Filename   Displays the name of the file loaded for editing. Also indicates whether the file is writable or read-only.

Messages   Displays any messages from **xedit** to the user during the session. May also be used as a simple scratchpad.

Edit   Holds the text of the file being edited. This is the main workspace in **xedit**.

There are a number of key commands you can use while editing files in **xedit**. Some useful ones are:

Key	*Effect*
Ctrl-A	Move cursor to start of line
Ctrl-B	Move cursor back one character
Ctrl-D	Delete next character
Ctrl-E	Move cursor to end of current line
Ctrl-F	Move cursor forward one character
Ctrl-K	Delete to end of current line
Ctrl-N	Move cursor to next line
Ctrl-P	Move cursor to previous line
Ctrl-S	Search/Replace forward
Ctrl-Y	Undelete

From a running **xterm** or **xconsole**, type:

```
xedit &
```

227

Move the cursor over the large editing space in the lower portion of the **xedit** window and type away. When you want to save your text, move the cursor to the box next to the command buttons and type a file name. Now click on Save. You can also pass **xedit** a file name to edit on the command line.

There are many other applications and utilities available to the user. If you aren't satisfied with the ones available in the menu, there are plenty more available from ftp sites and X Windows libraries.

The Concepts of X Windows

Now we've had a look at the front-end of X Windows, let's take a look at the basic ideas that underlay the X Window System. Here we will be discussing some of the fundamental features of X Windows' structure, operation and configuration.

The X Architecture

X application software plays the client role in this architecture, and hardware and platform-dependent 'display servers' form the other half. X clients and servers communicate with each other using the **X protocol**, a special digital language based on a generic set of instructions. The X protocol allows servers to communicate user actions, such as keystrokes and mouse movements, to the client applications, and allows client applications to return display manipulation instructions back to the server. Since the instructions are generic (not specific to any display type or operating system), the client application needn't know any particulars about the server upon which it is executing. However, it is advantageous for clients to know about color depth and screen size from the servers. In fact, the client application and the X server need not even be running on the same physical machine, since X protocol commands are transportable over a network (more on this later).

All X client application programs are written using a special library of program code (**xlib**) that provides a standardized API for issuing X protocol instructions. This library provides routines for establishing connections to X servers, issuing X protocol requests and managing the queue of requests currently in process. Since this library is well-established and standardized, X applications can be ported to new platforms with relative ease by simply recompiling on the new target platform and linking them with a native version of **xlib**.

The X Server Program

The purpose of the X server program is to manage the available console and display resources on a particular machine, and allocate them to the X clients that request them. The principal resources are the display, the mouse and the keyboard. X servers read the incoming streams of X protocol requests from their client applications and translate them into the appropriate display information. X servers also translate user actions, received via the user input into X protocol messages, back to the client applications.

Since the X server program has to directly control the local display, you must make sure that you install the correct version of server for your particular type of display adapter hardware. The X Window System software is packaged with a variety of different X server versions for commonly-used display types for your particular platform. The documentation accompanying your X software should tell you which server to use with your particular configuration.

Before we continue, let's make sure that we understand this situation with the X Client/Server. The X Client/Server architecture may seem backwards with respect to other typical Client/Server arrangements, like those used with databases. In the typical Client/Server model, there is a server which distributes a particular resource to the multiple clients who need it. In X, the resource being shared on the server machine is the console, not the processor. Client applications are *display* clients. One X display server can run many display clients from the local machine or from a remote network connection.

For instance, if you have the applications **xclock**, two **xterms**, and a supersonic turbulence visualization X application running remotely on a Cray and X-Fighter on your display, you're servicing five clients. The 'work' being done by the server in this case is all user interface related. A file server manages disk space, a database server distributes data records and a display server doles out display real estate.

Starting and Exiting the X Server

To use the X Window System on your UNIX host, you will first need to get an X server running. There are several ways to do this, and which one you use partly depends on which methods are supported by your version and how you wish to administer X.

The xinit and startx Commands

The most common way to get an X server running from a UNIX shell command line is by running **xinit** or **startx**. These are essentially equivalent operations (**startx** is slightly smarter) that initialize the console for X use by reading an **.xinitrc** file, if available, to determine the current configuration. These commands can be placed in your **.login** or **.profile** script in order to start X immediately upon logging in. Be aware though, that if your X installation should become corrupted or if a console hardware problem arises, you may not be able to login.

Upon exiting the X session, the system returns you to the character-mode UNIX shell prompt.

The xdm Command

The X Display Manager (**xdm**) is a two-part system designed to facilitate 'full-time' X servers, which allows UNIX users to log in and out entirely from within the X environment. Its principal use is in supporting X terminals, although it sees use on UNIX workstations as well. To use **xdm**, you must run an **xdm daemon** on the local host or on a networked remote host. To start an X server on an X terminal or workstation that will use **xdm** services, you must execute the **xdm** command. It will then request a 'login box' from the host running the **xdm daemon**. The host can be running **xdm** for local use and serve X terminals at the same time.

Once **xdm** is running, users will be presented with an X display containing a login box. When they login to the system, their **.xsession** script (analogous to **.xinitrc**) will be processed and they will begin an X session. Upon exiting the X session, instead of being dropped to a character-mode shell prompt, the system will re-display the login box ready for the next user to login. This way, the system never needs to leave the X environment, even when no user is logged in. For most X terminals, where it is impossible to exit the X environment, this is essential to their continuing operation.

> Please note that **xdm** takes additional resources from the server, so if there aren't any X terminals, don't run it.

The xdm Xservers File

This configuration file, found in **xdm**'s configuration directory, tells **xdm** where to find the X server on your system. Generally, you won't need to modify this file if you have correctly installed **xdm**. If you want **xdm** to function on the machine you are running it on (for example, if you are running it on a stand-alone workstation), make sure there is a line in the file that starts with **:0**. This line tells **xdm** where to find the local X server on your machine. If this line is commented out with a hash, you won't be able to use **xdm** locally. Whether or not you use **xdm** locally, this setting won't affect your ability to serve X terminals when **xdm** is running.

> In order for this to work, the **xhost** command (which controls server access) has to be executed on the server. Type **man xhost** for further details.

Configuring and Initializing X

A key feature of the X Window System is that it is highly configurable by the user, almost to a fault. Nearly all aspects that contribute to the look and feel of X applications can be modified. You can make such modifications on a run-by-run basis with command-line options. Or you could store the settings instead in file format, to be used by one, some, or all of the X applications on a regular basis.

The Xconfig File

On some systems, when you install X, you must tell it what kinds of hardware devices the X server can expect to find - including the display adapter, monitor, mouse and keyboard. You usually only need do this on systems that aren't 'native' UNIX/X Window systems, like IBM-compatible PCs running Linux or FreeBSD with the XFree86 X Window package. These systems can have a wide variety of different configurations of their display and input hardware. X needs to know some detailed technical information about these devices to control them properly. This information is stored in a file called **Xconfig** (or **XF86config** if you are using Xfree86) in your X installation. In the old days, you had to go into the **Xconfig** file and edit all of this by hand. More recent XFree86 releases include a program called **ConfigXF86** that handles the setup of **Xconfig** for you.

Here are the steps you should use if you are installing XFree86 version 3.1.1, or later versions:

- Carefully read the caveats and disclaimers in the XFree86 documentation about damaging your display hardware before proceeding. These are usually found in the **README.Config** file in the **/usr/X386/lib/X11/etc** directory.

- Immediately after unpacking XFree86 from the distribution, run the program called **SuperProbe**. This program will attempt to automatically identify the display adapter hardware you are using. It has knowledge of an astounding number of different display configurations and will detect most systems. If **SuperProbe** fails to identify your display hardware, you're probably not going to be able to run X at all. If your adapter uses a programmable dot clock (an information file that adjusts the resolution of your screen, via the refresh rate of the video card. Beware as an unsuitable refresh rate can actually **destroy** your monitor), it may not be detected properly and you'll have to set it up by hand. The **Xconfig** manual page will tell you if your adapter's programmable dot clock is supported and what to do to set it up by hand.

- There is more than one X server in the XFree86 installation. The XFree86 documentation will tell you which server goes with which adapter or video chipset. This information changes with just about every release of SuperProbe.

- Look up the video modes and scan rates for your monitor in the documentation that came with it. This information is needed for **ConfigXF86.**

- Determine the serial port to which your mouse is connected and the UNIX device that handles that port.

● Determine the kind of mouse you have (Microsoft, Logitech, PS/2, etc.). We don't mean the name of the actual manufacturer, but what kind of mouse it appears to be to the computer (a third-party mouse that emulates a Logitech *is* a Logitech).

● Run **ConfigXF86** which has a large database of display adapters that it knows how to correctly configure for X. It uses logic similar to **SuperProbe** to automatically choose the **Xconfig** settings for your particular system. It will also ask you for the monitor, mouse and keyboard layout you wish to use, and will update **Xconfig** accordingly.

Resources and the Resource Database

Let us now take a look at the stored settings called **resources** that are situated in a series of files which successively merge together to form the **X resource database**. Applications consult this database when they need to get resource definitions at run-time. The most significant of the resource files is called **.Xdefaults** (or sometimes **.Xdefaults-*hostname***, where ***hostname*** is the system name of your machine). Also, you may have a series of files in the directory **/usr/lib/X11/app-defaults** whose names correspond to various X applications. These contain application-specific resources for each type of application and are part of the resource database.

Resource Formats

Resources in X are organized by **application class**. All running instances of a particular X client application belong to the same class. For example, if you run three **xclocks**, they will all belong to the application class, **xclock**. When you set your resources for **xclock**, any **xclock** you run will read those same resources.

To set most resources, you specify the application class, followed by an asterisk, then the resource to be set, a colon and the value. An example would be:

```
xclock*background:Green
```

The .Xdefaults File

The easiest way to configure your resource preferences is to put them in a file called **.Xdefaults** in your home directory. This file is automatically queried by running X client applications when they read the resource definitions upon starting.

Setting Resources in the .Xdefaults File

To give all your **xclocks** a green background, you'll need to add the following line to the **.xdefaults** file in your home directory (if this file doesn't exist, create it):

```
xclock*background:Green
```

Now, from a running **xterm** or **xconsole**, type:

```
xclock &
```

The **xclock** should now have a rather fetching green background.

Resources in X applications are actually set at the widget level via the menus. The syntax discussed earlier actually uses a wildcard (*****) to set the background property for all widgets in the application. You can actually spell out exactly which widget or widgets you want to affect, instead of blanketing all of them like we have just done. However, you would need to know more about the widget hierarchy in your specific application, and that is beyond the scope of this discussion. For most common resource settings, the wildcard approach works fine.

> **Different applications require different resources. Check the man pages for the applications available on your system to see which resources they support.**

The xrdb Program

An alternative to using the **.Xdefaults** file is to run the program **xrdb** (the X Resource Database Manager) upon starting your X session. The **xrdb** program installs your resources in the X server where all clients will have access to them without hitting the disk space. It also allows you to make dynamic changes to your resources without editing your more permanent resource files. If you run **xrdb**, your **.Xdefaults** file will be ignored. You place your resources in a file, just like **.Xdefaults**, but then you pass this file into **xrdb** with the **-merge** option. For example, let's say that you put your resources in a file called **.my-resources**. You would install this by typing:

```
xrdb -merge .my-resources
```

You probably wouldn't want to type this every time you start X. Instead, you would add this line to the beginning of your **.xinitrc** or **.xsession** script, so that it would automatically run every time you start up X (more on these files later).

To see what resources you currently have installed with **xrdb**, type:

```
xrdb -q
```

You will see a list of all the installed resources of **xrdb** (the **-q** option being short for query). If you see nothing, then **xrdb** hasn't got any installed resources.

The .xinitrc and .xsession Files

The **.xinitrc** and **.xsession** files are scripts that are used to set up your X desktop upon the startup of the X server. The **.xinitrc** file is used when running X with **xinit** or **startx**, and the **.xsession** file is used when you start X with **xdm**. These dot files can be found in your home directory.

Client Command-line Options

Another way to configure the resource settings for X client applications is to use command-line options. There are some fairly standard options that you can use to set some basic run-time properties for an application. When these properties are configured using command-line options, they remain in effect for the current session only. If you discover settings you like by using command-line options, you may want to set those properties using resources instead, so you won't have to type in the command-line options every time you run the application. Also, you can use as many of these options as you wish. So, if you want a purple and green **xterm** with a 24-point Lucida Sans bold italic font in the lower-right corner of your screen, with the caption 'The World's Greatest xterm', you should be able to do it.

Here are some commonly-used command-line options that set basic properties for applications at run-time. Note that not all X client applications support these options, but many do. Check your application's documentation to see which options it supports.

The Foreground and Background Options

-fg <color>   This sets the foreground color to be used by the application. This mainly affects the display of text characters. It determines the color to be used to actually draw the characters.

-bg <color>   This sets the background color to be used by the application. It determines the color to be used to draw the space 'behind' each character.

From a running **xconsole** or **xterm** window, type:

```
xterm -fg SpringGreen -bg Pink &
```

Luckily, these settings won't be permanent!

A note about X colors - all the common names for colors you can think of are supported. X uses a database of names and RGB (red-green-blue) color values to decode the name of a color into values that X programs can understand. If you want to see the entire list of entries in the X color database on your system, type:

```
showrgb | more
```

The list will usually be quite long, so be sure to use **more** (or your favorite pager) when running **showrgb**.

For applications that optionally use a scrollbar to allow the display of more information than will fit in a window at one time (such as **xterm**), the **-sb** option allows the user to enable the scrollbar control.

From a running **xconsole** or **xterm** window, type:

```
xterm -sb &
```

Now, when your typing runs off the bottom edge of the window, you can scroll it back.

The Geometry Option

This option allows the user to configure the initial size and position of the application window on the display. The format of the **-geometry** option is:

-geometry   <widthxheight>   +/-xoffset+/-yoffset

You typically specify these values in pixels, although the **xterm** application requires that you specify the width and height in rows and columns of text characters. Therefore, the actual pixel dimensions of an **xterm** window are dependent upon the size of the font that the **xterm** window will use.

Let's look at the following examples:

-geometry 200x100	This creates a window 200 pixels wide by 100 pixels tall, in the initial (default) position. For an **xterm**, dimensions would be interpreted as characters rather than pixels. The x and y offsets aren't specified so they are taken from the default position (0,0), in the top left-hand corner of the screen.
-geometry +50-100	This creates a window of default size, 50 pixels from left and 100 pixels from the bottom of the terminal screen display.
-geometry 300x200-50-20	This creates a window 300 pixels wide and 200 pixels tall, 50 pixels from the right edge of the display and 20 pixels from the bottom. Again, for an **xterm** the width and height would be interpreted as characters rather than pixels, but the position would still be interpreted as pixels.

From a running **xconsole** or **xterm** window, type:

```
xterm -geometry 40x40 &
```

Now, as you have specified small width and length dimensions, you will have a tall, skinny **xterm**. From a running **xconsole** or **xterm**, type:

```
xlogo -geometry 100x100-0-0 &
```

You should now have a 100-pixel-square X logo in the lower right corner of your display.

You don't have to specify any parameters to these commands, the system can supply its own defaults. So if you were to just type the **xlogo** command without any parameters, you would get the following display:

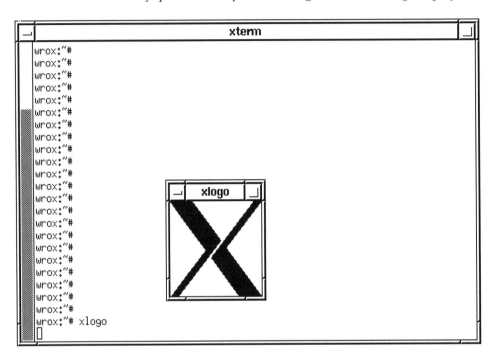

The Title Option

You can change the window caption of an X application with the **-title** option. This option takes as an argument the text string to be used as the windows caption.

-title *string*

Don't forget to properly quote multi-word caption strings! For example, from a running **xconsole** or **xterm**, type:

```
xterm -title "Bill and Ted's Excellent xterm" &
```

You now have an **xterm** with a personalized caption.

The Name Option

The **-name** option is similar to the **-title** option, except it makes a more serious change to the way the application runs.

-name *<string>*

The **-title** option only sets the caption of the application's main window. The **-name** option, however, changes the caption and the name by which the entire X system sees the application. This is significant because the name of an application is used as an index in the resource database. If you set the name of an application to something other than its actual name, any resources defined under the actual name won't be applied to the application during a run in which the name has been altered.

Conversely, if you set the name to another name that happens to have resources defined for it in the resource database, those resources will be used instead of those defined for the application's actual name. For example, let's say that you wanted to run an **xterm** using the resource settings defined in the resource database for **xclock**. You could type:

```
xterm -name xclock &
```

You would wind up with an **xterm** with the caption xclock, and it would be using the **xclock** resources instead of the **xterm** resources. Of course, it probably isn't a good idea to muddle resources like this.

The Font Option

You can set the font to be used by an X client application by using the **-fn** option. It takes one argument, which is the font name:

-fn   *font-name*

The format of the font name option is:

```
-fn -foundry -type -weight -slant -width -additional style  -pixel
size -point size -resolution X -resolution Y -spacing -average width
-registry -encoding
```

There is a program that usually accompanies X installations called **xlsfonts**. When you run this, it lists all the font names that are available on your machine. You give the full text of a font name as displayed by **xlsfonts** when passing it into the **-fn** option. The font names can be quite long as you can probably deduce from the format (although there are some short forms of these). Take the following example:

```
-b&h-lucidabright-demibold-i-normal--19-190-75-75-p-114-iso8859-1
```

To save your fingers, you can use wildcards when specifying font names. Place asterisks wherever you wish to wildcard text in a name. Be sure to quote the font name on the command line to stop the shell from getting confused. Here are some examples of the **-fn** option:

```
xterm -fn -adobe-helvetica-bold-r-normal-12-120-75-75-p-70-iso8859-1 &
```

This launches an **xterm** with a 12-point Adobe Helvetica bold font.

```
xterm -fn '*helvetica-bold*-12*' &
```

This launches an **xterm** with the first 12-point bold Helvetica font found on the system.

Remote the Display Option

There is another standard X client command-line option that you can use to take advantage of the Client/Server nature of the X Window System. The **-display** option allows you to specify a display, other than your local one, upon which to post the windows for your X client application. There are two parts to the argument you supply to this command-line option. You must specify the network name and the number of the remote display to be used. The display number is usually 0 (the primary display on most systems). So, for instance, if you wanted to make an **xlogo** pop up on the display of another machine on your network (we'll call that machine andromeda), you might type:

```
xlogo -display andromeda:0 &
```

This completes our look at initializing and configuring the X Window system. You should be able to customize your system to meet your own preferences. However we have one final loose end to tie up - a user workstation that doesn't usually run a full operating system - the X terminal.

The X Terminal

An X terminal is a user workstation that doesn't generally run a fully-fledged operating system, but rather runs just the necessary software to be a networked X display server. It's as close as you can get to a 'dumb' terminal in the X world. X terminals are much smarter than conventional dumb terminals, though, because they have to have all the hardware and software to run high-performance X displays. Some of them even have their own on-board mass-storage, and a few are even convertible to fully-fledged UNIX workstations with optional upgrades.

X terminals generally make extensive use of **xdm**. A remote networked host machine acts as an **xdm** server, and X terminals on the network request login services from it using a special protocol called **XDMCP**. Because they use **xdm**, X terminals can stay in the X environment full-time, even when no user is actually logged on through them.

The Pros and Cons of X Terminals

X terminals provide an alternative to purchasing separate, fully-outfitted UNIX workstations for everyone in a workgroup, but they may not be suited to everybody.

There are several advantages to using X terminals:

● They tend to be slightly cheaper than fully-configured UNIX workstations.

● They tend to be easier to administer because most of the work they do actually happens on a remote server, which can be a single point of administration for a whole workgroup.

● They are usually physically smaller than full workstations and therefore take up less office space.

● Because each one doesn't contain its own high-horsepower CPU or hard disk, but uses those resources on a remote server instead, a carefully-designed network consists of one or more UNIX servers. A group of X terminals can also make much more efficient use of standard computing resources for light-duty applications.

● X terminals generally arrive preconfigured to boot directly into a built-in X server program. Once you've got **xdm** set up on your server, a few simple settings on each X terminal will get it up and running.

● Because of their greater reliance on hardware and embedded software, X terminals tend to be more 'bulletproof' for unattended environments (like terminal laboratories) and more resistant to hacking and other tampering.

● Since processor power tends to evolve more quickly than display technology in the computing world, X terminals have a longer practical life than workstations. Remote hosts used as application servers can be upgraded independently of X terminals at more frequent intervals, as processor speeds increase.

● X Terminals are often equipped with a lot of RAM, video memory and their own graphics processor. This makes processing very efficient.

There are, however, some disadvantages to using X terminals for certain applications:

● Since they rely on a remote host to execute the bulk of an application's code and they frequently share the remote host's resources with other X terminals, they may exhibit sluggish performance when the remote host's resources are limited.

- With a few exceptions, X terminals are not upgradable to workstation machines. This means that if you decide that you need the power and independence of a workstation after using an X terminal for a while, you may have to completely replace it.

- If the remote application host is down, your X terminal is essentially useless until the remote host comes back on-line. In that sense, X terminal computing is a throwback to the days of centralized mainframe computing. In a workstation environment you at least stand a chance of continuing to work as long as your work is resident on the workstation.

- If your users are reasonably sophisticated and don't need super-high performance from their workstations, you may find that the price difference between X terminals and low-end workstations isn't enough to worry about.

Summary

Just as Microsoft Windows became the nice user-friendly front for DOS, UNIX has welcomed the introduction of a similar but quite distinct graphical user interface of its own. X Windows has become such an important factor in the development of UNIX applications that it is imperative that we understand how it integrates into UNIX.

We have discussed the concepts, components and commands of the X Window System as well as examining how we can edit configuration files to our advantage. We took a peek at three Window Managers, **twm**, OSF/MOTIF with **mwm** and OPENLOOK with **olwm**. Then we examined some simple X applications including **xclock**, **xterm** and **xedit**, followed by an introduction to X Terminals and how they fit into the scheme of things.

Now after playing with your pretty windows, you should be ready to dip into the technical maelstrom that is networking under UNIX.

Chapter

Networking

Nowadays, few UNIX systems stand alone - instead, they are most frequently interconnected with other UNIX systems (or with machines running other operating systems) via various types of computer networks. To understand how to set up a network, it's important first to look at the physical and logical structures of UNIX networking systems, before we consider what it takes to configure a UNIX system to operate successfully on a network. This chapter's main subject areas are:

- Network topologies
- An introduction to the Ethernet
- The protocol stack
- Interconnecting networks
- Client/Server networking
- Configuring network software
- Basic TCP/IP network applications
- Remote operations

Network Topologies

The arrangement by which a network is wired is known as a topology. Topology actually refers to how the various elements in a network are interconnected. You will probably be familiar with this, but before we race into the particulars of the Ethernet, we'll give a quick reminder of the three main types of network topology. A diagram illustrates the differences between them most efficiently:

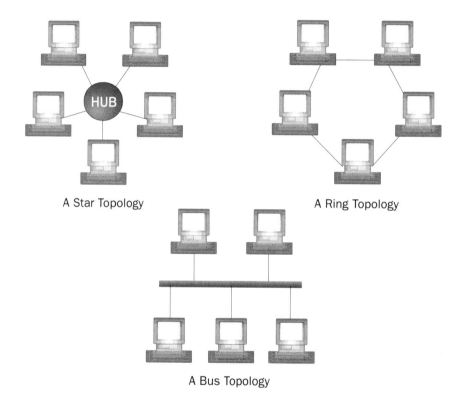

A Star Topology   A Ring Topology

A Bus Topology

Networking Media

In order for computers to communicate with each other over a network, they must be connected through some sort of physical **networking medium**. This domain represents a shared communications space, through which all networking information travels. Commonly, this is achieved via some form of electrical cabling to which all network machines are connected, but connection can also be accomplished with just about any path along which information can travel. The most important networking media are all cable-based, and that's what we'll be concentrating on here.

Ethernet

Ethernet is a networking system designed to connect computers that are relatively close together (physically in the same department or locality), at very high data rates. Networking schemes of this type are typically referred to as **local-area networks** (**LANs**) - by contrast, schemes that link up geographically isolated computers are referred to as **wide-area networks** (**WANs**). Here are the main aspects of Ethernet:

- Ethernet is today's foremost LAN technology.

- Nearly every vendor of computer hardware provides some sort of Ethernet connectivity solution.

- Ethernet is covered by the IEEE 802.3 standard which specifies the precise method that machines must use to access the medium.

- The Ethernet specification defines a physical connection as well as the very low-level formatting of transmitted data.

- By itself, Ethernet isn't a complete networking system - other software, such as Novell IPX or TCP/IP, runs on top of Ethernet to provide high-level networking services to application software.

- Essentially, Ethernet is a **broadcast** medium; since all machines are connected to the same wire, when one machine transmits data, all the others 'hear' it. This scheme makes it unnecessary to have lots of cables connecting each machine to all the others - there's just one wire and they all tap into it using a device called a **media-access unit** (**MAU**).

Ethernet and 802.3

The IEEE picked up the Ethernet scheme as the basis for its emerging LAN specification, labeled 802.3. Since Ethernet was a registered trademark belonging to Xerox, the IEEE specification is simply referred to as 802.3, although 802.3 and Ethernet are interchangeable terms in popular parlance. New Ethernet equipment usually adheres to the 802.3 specification. In this chapter, we'll assume that Ethernet and 802.3 mean the same thing, although you must be aware that there are slight differences.

Ethernet Addressing

Every computer is assigned a unique Ethernet address, which is a 48-bit number directly encoded into the machine's hardware. This is known as a **MAC (Media-Access Control)** address - manufacturers are allocated suitably large blocks of these addresses to use on their machines.

Ethernet data is transmitted in small bursts, called **packets** or **frames**. Each packet is 'stamped' with the Ethernet address of the sender and that of the intended receiver. Each machine on the LAN looks at each frame and determines whether or not the frame is intended for them. If it is, then a copy of the data is taken and the frame is passed on to the next node in the network.

Collision Detection

If two or more machines try to send data over the wire at the same time, they'll garble each other's transmissions. It's just like trying to have a conversation when several people are trying to talk all at once - information gets lost. To prevent this, Ethernet uses a scheme called **Carrier-Sense Multiple Access / Collision Detection (CSMA/CD)** where machines 'listen' for a quiet moment on the wire before trying to transmit. If two machines do accidentally try to transmit at the same time, they both stop and wait for a small random interval of time before retrying, decreasing the likelihood that they will collide again. This is the basic mode of operation for all Ethernet media.

Thick, Thin and Twisted Pair

While all Ethernet systems function in basically the same way, there are several different physical wiring schemes for Ethernet that have gained widespread popularity and acceptance. These all have different capabilities and liabilities, which we'll outline here.

Thick Ethernet

The earliest Ethernet cabling scheme is the so-called 'thick' Ethernet, which is based on 0.5 inch diameter coaxial cable, running up to 500 meters in length and servicing up to 1024 machines on a single cable. This kind of Ethernet is sometimes referred to by the designation **10Base5** (10Base5 = 10 Mbps over 500 meters).

A Thick Ethernet Connection

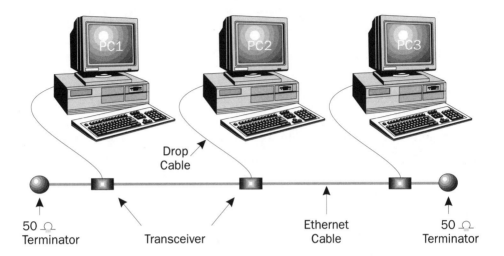

50 Ω
Terminator

Transceiver

Drop
Cable

Ethernet
Cable

50 Ω
Terminator

The thick Ethernet cable is marked with black stripes every 2.5 meters, indicating where MAU (Media Access Unit) taps can be placed - the half-wavelength of the Ethernet signal is 2.5 meters. There is also a minimum radius through which a cable can be bent without data corruption - the same applies to fiber-optic cables.

Vampire Taps

The most common kind of MAU tap used with thick Ethernet is the **vampire tap** - so named because of the sharp point that pierces into the center of the cable to make contact with the 'hot' conductor. Tapping into a thick Ethernet cable requires a special tool called a **tap corer** which is used to bore a hole at the tap point to allow the point to penetrate.

Vampire Tap

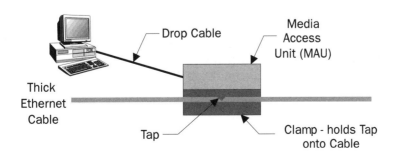

Thick
Ethernet
Cable

Drop Cable

Media
Access
Unit (MAU)

Tap

Clamp - holds Tap
onto Cable

249

Vampire taps are particularly useful in situations where a thick-wire network is regularly being reconfigured as they can be added and removed quickly, quietly and easily, without disturbing network activity. On the downside, vampire taps don't always make a reliable connection and, if they are installed incorrectly, the contact point can bend or break, rendering the tap useless.

Intrusive Taps

There is another, less common tap type, called the **intrusive tap**, which requires that the cable be broken at the tap point and the tap be inserted between the two ends.

Intrusive Tap

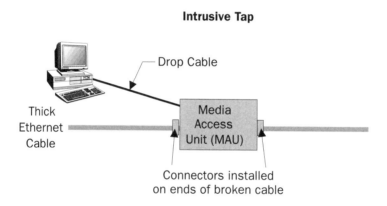

All in all, thick Ethernet is expensive and inconvenient to use for many applications - it's best used to run **backbones**, or sections of a network that connect one part to another (like links between floors in a building or long runs through conduits).

Thin Ethernet

Thin Ethernet is sometimes referred to as Cheapernet, because it evolved partly as a backlash against the expense of thick Ethernet cabling. It's also referred to by the **10Base2** designation.

T-connectors

Thin Ethernet is based on inexpensive 0.25 inch RG-58 coaxial cable, and tapping is accomplished with T-connectors placed between cable segments rather than by core tapping. The T-connector is connected directly to the thin Ethernet MAU to make the network connection.

A Thin Ethernet Connection

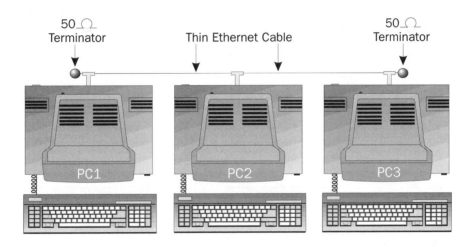

Thin Ethernet, however, isn't designed to support large networks by itself - the total segment length is limited to only 185 meters maximum and can only support up to 30 machines. Thus it's frequently used with hubs connected to thick Ethernet backbones. A hub is a feature of star topology and is a central ring where all circuits meet.

Twisted Pair Access Unit Ethernet

A popular network medium for large organizations is the twisted pair copper wiring used for office telephone connections. It already has an established infrastructure and the organization's telecommunications staff know how to handle it, too. It's extremely inexpensive and easy to work with. The **10BaseT** Ethernet scheme makes this possible - it uses a hub that has individual twisted pair connections to each machine's MAU. In this sense, 10BaseT differs from the other Ethernet cabling schemes, which allow multiple machines to tap into the same physical cable segment.

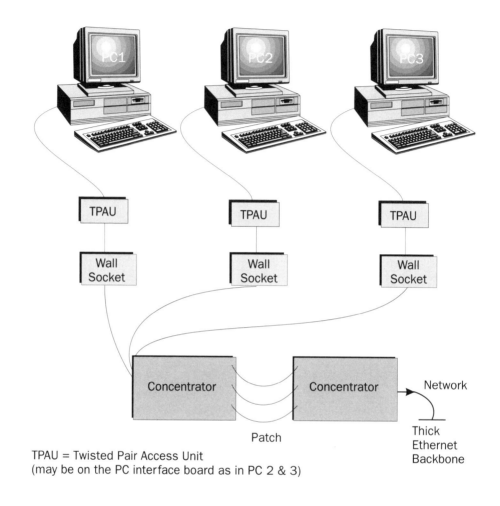

TPAU = Twisted Pair Access Unit
(may be on the PC interface board as in PC 2 & 3)

The actual 'network' really resides inside the 10BaseT hub. 10BaseT segments must be 100 meters or less in length, meaning that all machines must be located within that distance of a hub box.

High-Speed Ethernet

Ethernet is an evolving standard and, recently, moves have been made to establish a new higher-speed Ethernet specification. The current Ethernet standard supports 10Mbps data transfer rates, while the new proposed Ethernet will be able to support rates of up to 100Mbps. Manufacturers are now producing Ethernet MAU chipsets that support both the 10Mbps and the 100Mbps Ethernets, maintaining backward compatibility with earlier Ethernet equipment.

FDDI and Token Rings

The **Fiber Distributed Data Interface (FDDI)** defines a method for moving 100Mbps over fiber-optic cable. Due to its prohibitive cost, FDDI is typically used to connect very large machines, departmental network concentrators, etc., rather than individual workstations. FDDI uses **token-ring** technology to move data.

FDDI Ring

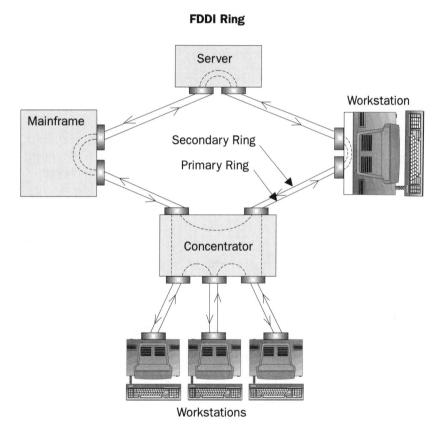

Workstations

A token ring operates very differently from a CSMA/CD network like Ethernet. In a token ring, the member machines are connected point-to-point to form a loop. Thus each machine is connected to two neighboring machines. Rather than allowing each machine to broadcast at will, the token ring passes data around the loop in one direction. A special packet is circulated, called the **token**, which grants each machine permission to transmit when it receives it. FDDI is implemented as a kind of counter-rotating double token-ring, with one ring used solely for error recovery.

253

Network Connections

There are two kinds of network connections in a FDDI network - **single-attached** and **dual-attached**. Single-attached machines are connected only to the main FDDI ring through a concentrator, and therefore can't take advantage of the error recovery mechanism provided by the second ring. Dual-attached machines are connected to both rings. If a neighboring machine breaks the ring integrity, its adjacent dual-attached neighbors can loop the main ring back onto the error ring, thus re-establishing the connection. Single-attached machines connect to the network through a dual-attached concentrator to protect the network should one of the single-attached machines go down.

CDDI

The **Copper Distributed Data Interface (CDDI)** implements the FDDI protocols over twisted pair cabling. It provides the superior error-recovery of FDDI without the expense (and speed) of fiber-optic cabling. CDDI arose mainly from proprietary implementations and is very loosely defined.

ATM

The explosive growth of multimedia technology has created demand for a low-cost, high-bandwidth networking technology. For instance, in order to facilitate the transmission of real-time digital video and high-quality audio, telecommunications providers need such a networking technology. The rising star in this field is **Asynchronous Transfer Mode (ATM)**, which is based on switching technology and represents the convergence of both telephony and computer networking technologies.

ATM was developed as a way for telecommunications companies to increase the efficiency of gigabit bandwidth long-haul fiber-optics, but it's rapidly gaining acceptance for other uses as well. ATM resides principally at the physical and data-link layers of the ISO/OSI model (see later in this chapter) and thus can serve as the basis for other networking services, like TCP/IP. The equipment and standards of ATM are still evolving.

The Protocol Stack

As network technology has evolved, its designers have come to realize that the various parts of a networking system break out into layers of functionality that build logically upon one another. The lowest-level layers are closest to the physical network connection while the highest layers are closest to the application software using the data that's transmitted and received.

The ISO/OSI Model

In 1977, the International Standards Organization (ISO) set out to define a model for open systems networking. Their conclusions spawned the **Open Systems Interconnection (OSI) Model**, which represents a theoretical framework for understanding how all the parts of a data communications network logically fit together. This model consists of seven layers, each of which defines a set of related network functions. In a practical implementation, more than one layer may be embodied in one particular piece of equipment or software.

Layer	Name	Function
7	Application	Consists of application software that requires network services.
6	Presentation	Handles standard data presentation to ensure that data is in a uniform format across co-operating software applications.
5	Session	Manages network data communication sessions between co-operating software applications.
4	Transport	Provides guaranteed data delivery and data integrity.
3	Network	Manages host-to-host connections across the network. Handles addressing and the delivery of data.
2	Data-Link	Provides the low-level data transfer protocol, data packeting/framing, error and flow control, and synchronization.
1	Physical Link	Embodies the actual physical, electrical connection between the equipment and the network.

TCP/IP

The most important networking architecture in the UNIX world is the **TCP/IP** network. TCP/IP was originally developed by the U.S. Department of Defense (DOD) for use on the ARPANET, which formed the basis for what eventually became the Internet. The Internet uses TCP/IP, and most implementations of UNIX now ship with TCP/IP networking capability built in.

The DOD needed a network architecture that was reasonably open and could accommodate a wide variety of hardware, software and telecommunications media from a wide variety of vendors. The network would be patched together with many different kinds of connections - some local, some remote. The network had to be very flexible, easily expandable and fault-tolerant. Legend has it that it had to be resistant enough to work around the devastation caused by nuclear blasts.

TCP/IP is also a layered protocol stack, like the ISO/OSI model. The ISO/OSI model is another model, but this hasn't been widely adopted and doesn't map exactly onto many real-world network architectures. TCP/IP really only defines four of the ISO layers, with some overlapping.

TCP/IP Layer	Equivalent OSI Layer	Function
Application	Application	Application software requiring network services.
TCP	Transport	Reliable data delivery with error-handling.
IP	Network	Non-guaranteed, connectionless datagram delivery.
Data-Link (ARP/RARP, kernel)	Data-Link	Physical network device control, IP-to-Ethernet address resolution.

TCP/IP doesn't define the Physical layer while Session and Presentation are all incorporated in the Application layer.

ARP

TCP/IP doesn't define the Physical layer of the network model and therefore can't make assumptions about it. If we assume that there is a network over which broadcasts can be made, then, in order for a device on a TCP/IP network to talk to another device, it must be able to refer to it by its **IP address** only (explained later), and let the Data-Link layer somehow resolve the IP address into a physical network address.

In TCP/IP networks the **Address Resolution Protocol (ARP)** handles this. When a device wishes to make contact with another device, it broadcasts an ARP request containing the destination device's IP address. The destination device sees its IP address in the request and responds with its physical address; in an Ethernet environment, this is its raw 48-bit Ethernet address.

RARP

The **Reverse Address Resolution Protocol (RARP)** was designed to facilitate IP address resolution for diskless workstations and X terminals, for which it's either impossible or inconvenient to locally store the IP address configuration. RARP allows a central server to map physical addresses to IP addresses on behalf of other systems. When a diskless workstation boots, for instance, it sends out a RARP request to find out its IP address. The RARP server checks to see if the requesting machine is listed in its client table and, if it is, it responds with the client's IP address.

This also makes administering IP addresses on a large network much simpler - when address changes need to be made, rather than having to go around to each machine and change each individual IP address, the network administrator can make all the changes at the central server. The next time the machines boot, they'll receive the new IP address through RARP. RARP has some problems, however, and a newer protocol with similar functionality, called **bootp** does its own RARP in some situations.

IP Addressing

As we've just seen, the IP address is central to TCP/IP communication. A device must know another device's IP address if it hopes to communicate with it. The device's Ethernet address is the physical address and is essentially fixed, while the IP address is the device's logical network address and is usually software defined. This logical address definition makes IP addressing highly flexible and configurable, and it makes the physically highly heterogeneous Internet look like one big logical network.

The IP address is a four-byte number and, by convention, it's expressed as four decimal values separated by full stops. For example, 128.8.14.92 might be a valid IP address. As you read from left to right, the bytes get more specific about the machine the address is referencing. The rightmost number identifies the machine, and the numbers to the left specify larger and larger subnetworks of the Internet.

Class A, B and C Addresses

The Internet Network Information Center, or INTERNIC, allocates IP addresses, normally in blocks. Anyone can request IP addresses for their network by contacting the INTERNIC. Small networks can request a **Class C** IP address allocation, which assigns the first three bytes of the IP address. The rightmost byte can then be used to specify up to 254 individual machines on your own network. Larger organizations can request a **Class B** IP address allocation, which leaves the rightmost two bytes for machine assignments, allowing for up to 65,536 individual machines on the network. Really large organizations can request a **Class A** IP address allocation, which leaves room for an awesome 16,777,216 individual machine assignments.

Internet Addressing

x = can be 0 or 1

Class A distributions are nearly impossible to attain nowadays and are generally used for international networks, governments, etc. Most large corporations now use multiple Class C addresses.

Subnetting

Class A and Class B IP address allocations make it possible for an organization to assign thousands or even millions of individual IP addresses. The assignable portion of the address can be thought of as one big pool of addresses. However, it's more popular to split up the bytes of the assignable portion of the address and use them to specify your own subnetworks in order to better organize your pool of assignable addresses.

For instance, let's say an organization registers the Class B network 128.8.*.* with INTERNIC. The last two bytes are now available to specify individual machines. Instead, the network administrator decides to use the first available byte to indicate the department where the machine is located, and the last byte to indicate the individual machine. It is decided that the machine IP addresses are organized into 256 pools of 254 addresses each, divided up by department.

Class B Address	◄——— Network ———►		◄——— Host ———►	
	10 x x x x x x	x x x x x x x x	x x x x x x x x	x x x x x x x x
Subnet Mask	8FF	8FF	8FF	800
	11111111	11111111	11111111	00000000

Subnet Mask to Treat a Class B Address as if 256 Separate Networks

This makes the IP addresses much more readable and manageable for network administrators. It also makes it easier to route network traffic across an enterprise-wide network backbone.

Interconnecting Networks

As the networking requirements for an organization grow, the need quickly develops to link several smaller networks together to form one big network. Typically, the organization will have a backbone network connecting smaller departmental networks. There are three main ways to connect networks: repeaters, bridges and routers.

Repeaters

When two networks simply need to be physically connected to each other, and doing so would exceed the maximum cable length or permitted number of nodes on each segment, a **repeater** can then be used. Repeaters provide signal amplification and timing correction - they serve to isolate the segments on either side of the repeater from each other. This isolation prevents a cable break on one segment from bringing the whole network down.

When laying out a network that will use repeaters, bear in mind that they must be figured into the total node count for each segment, as if they were another workstation or server. Repeaters also come in handy for connecting together segments of different media types, like 10BaseT to thinwire Ethernet. Repeaters are pretty basic devices and, as such, don't make any attempt to interpret the packet information carried by the network. For more sophisticated handling of network traffic, you need a bridge or a router.

Bridges

Bridges are principally hardware-based devices that operate at the data-link level to pass packets from one network to another. The bridge is connected to both networks and as the packets come through on one side, it forwards them to the other. Some bridges contain firmware learning algorithms that figure out which addresses are on which side of the bridge, so that the bridge only forwards packets destined for addresses across the bridge. Bridges are a very effective way to connect two Ethernets, but they can be quite expensive and are generally not as configurable as routers. Two remote bridges can connect two networks via a high speed link such as microwave or laser.

Routers

Routers are principally software-based and operate at the network level. As such, they are protocol-specific (an IP router won't route IPX, for example). A router can be as simple as a UNIX machine with an extra Ethernet adapter and the proper software configuration (UNIX networking has built-in routing capability). Servers and workstations can therefore act as routers on a LAN.

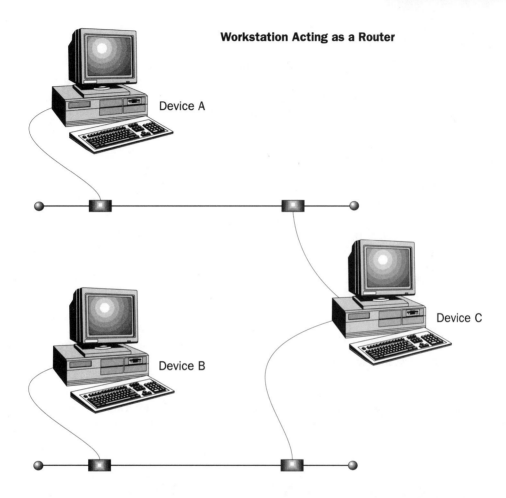

Workstation Acting as a Router

Device A

Device C

Device B

When using a non-dedicated machine as a router, be advised that routing can be a highly intensive resource activity and many organizations find that they have to use dedicated routers to maintain performance. Dedicated routers tend to make more use of advanced features, including improved security and more intelligent routing.

There are two kinds of routing that a UNIX machine can perform: static and dynamic.

Static Routing

Static routing is only appropriate for small, isolated networks where the network topology is known and doesn't change frequently. Static routing is accomplished by adding **route** commands to the system startup files, which add specific routes directly into the routing tables.

Dynamic Routing

Dynamic routing, despite being more resource-intensive, is the way to go if your system is connected to a large, changing network or is directly connected to the Internet. Since the topology of the Internet is constantly changing, static routing is totally impractical and dynamic routing must be used.

Dynamic routing is accomplished by running **routed**, or the more powerful **gated** from your startup file. The **routed** and **gated** daemons communicate with dynamic routing daemons on other systems to build a picture of the current network topology and automatically handle any changes. The **/etc/gated** daemon isn't available on all systems - check your system documentation for further details.

Static and dynamic routing can be used together to optimize the routing within a large network. Machines that don't gate out of the local network can route statically, letting a dynamic router handle traffic to the outside world.

Client/Server Networking

The advent of the LAN has made it possible to factor some essential services out of desktop workstations and centralize them on the network as shared resources. UNIX machines can act as servers for files, databases and even application execution - other machines can then share these services. Sharing resources allows multiple users to collaborate on the same data, and server equipment and software can be optimized for top performance. Client/Server computing uses the LAN to introduce the best aspects of mainframe computing to the desktop environment.

In a typical Client/Server environment, a department will supply servers on the LAN for those services required by the users in that department (files, databases, etc.). The servers provide centralized repositories for departmental data, where it can be accessed from all workstations whilst easily and centrally maintained (for instance, the servers can be centrally backed up to tape).

In a large organization, servers can be made available across the backbone for inter-departmental use. For instance, your Sales and Accounts departments may want to share the same customer database, even though they are in different buildings, cities or even countries. As long as the routing and network interconnection is established, users in the two departments should be able to access the same database server just as if it were on their local machine.

Disk versus Diskless Clients

Diskless workstations enjoyed brief popularity as a way to control the cost of placing a fully-configured workstation on everyone's desk. This concept evolved from the idea that since diskless workstations could boot from firmware, they could boot without a disk and attach to a server's file resources to obtain storage.

Diskless workstations aren't as common now since hard disk prices are so low. Most of the uses for diskless workstations have been largely superseded by cheap disk-based systems or by X terminals. Centralized administrative tools and services like **bootp** allow disk-based workstations to take advantage of many of the same things that originally made diskless workstations so attractive.

X Terminals

For applications that must be run on a remote machine (extremely intensive tasks), or for light-duty applications where several workstations can share resources, X terminals can be a highly effective solution. They don't require the kind of system maintenance demanded by fully-fledged UNIX workstations, yet they can provide users with all they need to get their work done. X terminals frequently deliver high-performance graphics for considerably less expense than buying a full-blown UNIX-based graphics workstation.

The success of the LAN has made it possible for technologies like the X terminal to flourish. It has its own basic built-in TCP/IP implementation that allows it to communicate over the network.

Configuring Network Software

Let's look at the basic steps involved in getting TCP/IP networking up and running on a UNIX system. Since most UNIX implementations inherited networking from the BSD variant, we'll concentrate on a typical BSD setup. UNIX system administration procedures vary considerably from implementation to implementation, so you'll need to consult your system documentation carefully to find out how all of this applies to your specific system.

Here are some of the things you'll need to do to get your BSD system on the network:

1   Install the physical network interface hardware.

2   If not already done, build a kernel that includes the networking system and any device drivers for your network hardware.

3   Choose a name for your host and find out what your domain name is.

4   Find out what your numeric IP address will be (unless you're going to get it dynamically via RARP or **bootp**).

5   Set up the **/etc/hosts** file with the domain names and hosts you'll want to access even if Domain Name Services aren't functioning (DNS overrides **/etc/hosts**).

6   Set up the **/etc/services** file.

7   Set up the **/etc/protocols** file.

8   Add networking initialization and routing commands to **/etc/ rc.local** or **/etc/rc.boot** (we'll discuss this later).

9   Set up the **/etc/inetd.conf** file (we'll discuss this later, too).

10   Add pseudo-terminals (**pty**s) to allow network logins.

264

The above procedure applies to BSD machines - System V machines are different. Commercial System V variants provide administrative software to automate the network configuration process.

Startup Files

In order to get networking running, you'll need to modify some of your system startup files:

The Boot Up File

The file **/etc/rc.local** (or sometimes **/etc/rc.boot**) contains those system-specific commands that are run when your machine is booted. This is the file where you place the commands to start up your network interface or interfaces, and it's also where you can set up routing across interfaces if your machine spans more than one network.

Editing

To bring up your network interface, add a line like this (with your own information substituted) to your **/etc/rc.local** file:

```
/etc/ifconfig ne00 128.8.72.2 up netmask 255.255.0.0 arp broadcast
128.8.72.255 > /dev/console
```

where **ne00** is the interface device, **128.8.72.2** is the interface's IP address, **255.255.0.0** is the Class B network's subnet mask and **128.8.72.255** is the address to use for network broadcasts (interface IP address with the host portion set to 255, or binary 1's).

Incorporating Routing

If you wish to perform routing, you can add static routes to your routing tables with a command like this:

```
/etc/route add 128.8.56 shipping-router 1
```

This says that all traffic for the **128.8.56** subnet is to be sent to the machine called **shipping-router**, which is **1** hop away. You need to add lines for each router you want to be able to cross. To use dynamic routing instead, simply run the **/etc/routed** or **/etc/gated** daemon here.

The inetd Initialization File

`/etc/inetd.conf` is used to initialize the Internet network daemon process (`inetd`). The `inetd` daemon is the master network daemon, responsible for initializing and managing the other principal network daemons that oversee the basic network services.

The `/etc/inetd.conf` file contains a line for each subordinate network daemon, telling `inetd` how to handle it. This file is usually configured for you during the installation of your network software. Here's an excerpt from an example file:

```
#
#   Internet server configuration database
#
ftp      stream tcp   nowait root    /usr/libexec/ftpd      ftpd -l
telnet   stream tcp   nowait root    /usr/libexec/telnetd   telnetd
shell    stream tcp   nowait root    /usr/libexec/rshd      rshd
login    stream tcp   nowait root    /usr/libexec/rlogind   rlogind
finger   stream tcp   nowait nobody  /usr/libexec/fingerd   fingerd
```

Each line lists respectively a service, its socket type, the transport protocol to use (for datagram sockets), whether to wait for the current service instance to exit before commencing another, the user to setuid to when running the service (notice that finger is nobody), the path to the service and the command-line arguments to execute the service.

Starting and Stopping Network Interfaces

The `ifconfig` command is used to start, initialize and stop the network interfaces. It's used within the network startup files and is often invoked more than once for each interface in order to configure different settings. The superuser can also issue the `ifconfig` command manually in order to change the status of a network interface. Issuing the `ifconfig` command with just a network interface device name as an argument will report the current settings for all the options to the device. The `ifconfig` command can be used to bring a network adapter up or down as well.

The format for the command looks something like this:

```
/etc/ifconfig ne00 128.8.72.2 up netmask 255.255.0.0 arp broadcast
128.8.72.255
```

The first argument is the network adapter device name. The second argument is the IP address to use with the adapter, followed by a flag that specifies that the interface is to be brought up. The next argument (**netmask**) sets the subnet mask for the adapter to use and the next argument specifies that ARP is to be turned on. The last argument sets the broadcast mask for the interface.

Network Monitoring

Here are some basic tools that you can use to troubleshoot and monitor your network:

ping

The **ping** command is one of the simplest tests you can use to see if your system can make contact with another over the network. If you can't **ping** the remote machine, then it's unlikely you'll be able to reach it with anything else either. It uses a datagram broadcast request to force a response out of the remote machine.

You can run **ping** by simply invoking it with the name of the remote system or its IP address as an argument. It then launches into an infinite loop, sending datagrams and printing the response. On some systems you can stop it with *Ctrl-C*, however you can't on Sun's, so you must use a different method.

There is an option for ping, **-c** (count) which allows you specify how many times you want to **ping** the connection:

```
wrox:~# ping www.wrox.com -c 10
PING www.wrox.com (192.168.1.101): 56 data bytes
64 bytes from 192.168.1.101: icmp_seq=0 ttl=32 time=1.5 ms
64 bytes from 192.168.1.101: icmp_seq=1 ttl=32 time=1.4 ms
64 bytes from 192.168.1.101: icmp_seq=2 ttl=32 time=1.4 ms
64 bytes from 192.168.1.101: icmp_seq=3 ttl=32 time=1.4 ms
64 bytes from 192.168.1.101: icmp_seq=4 ttl=32 time=1.4 ms
64 bytes from 192.168.1.101: icmp_seq=5 ttl=32 time=1.5 ms
64 bytes from 192.168.1.101: icmp_seq=6 ttl=32 time=1.4 ms
64 bytes from 192.168.1.101: icmp_seq=7 ttl=32 time=1.4 ms
64 bytes from 192.168.1.101: icmp_seq=8 ttl=32 time=1.4 ms
64 bytes from 192.168.1.101: icmp_seq=9 ttl=32 time=1.5 ms
```

```
— www.wrox.com ping statistics —
10 packets transmitted, 10 packets received, 0% packet loss
round-trip min/avg/max = 1.4/1.4/1.5 ms
wrox:~#
```

The netstat Command

The **netstat** command can be used to show the status of the network relative to your machine.

Options

Various command-line options can be used with **netstat** to display different information about the network status:

-a	Displays the status of active TCP connections.
-i	Displays statistics for the network interfaces.
-m	Shows the current memory buffer usage.
-n	Forces the numeric display of addresses.
-p	Filters the information for just one protocol.
-r	Displays information from the current routing table.
-s	Shows packet summaries broken out by protocol (IP, TCP, UDP, for example).

Examples of netstat

Here's a sample of **netstat**'s output:

```
$ netstat -i
Name  Mtu   Network       Address      Ipkts   Ierrs   Opkts  Oerrs  Coll
ef0   1500  net.cais.co   cais.com    7635751   2386  6135312    1  1368453
ef1   1500  internal.ca   cais        1241410      2   802475    1  52073
lo0   1536  loopback-ne   localhost    592066      0   592066    0     0
```

In this example, there are three network interfaces and for each one the following information is displayed:

- The device name of the interface.
- The packet size.
- The external network to which the interface is connected.
- The address of the interface.
- The number of input and output packets processed by the interface and the input/output errors.
- The number of packet collisions that have occurred on the interface.

The Routing Tables

When invoked with the **-r** option, the **netstat** command can also be used to display the currently active routing tables, which can be very useful. Frequently, the **-n** option is added as well to force a numeric display of addresses; this is most useful for troubleshooting:

```
$ netstat -nr
Routing tables
Destination      Gateway          Flags    Refs      Use   Interface
default          199.0.216.201    UG         37  1584089   ef0
127.0.0.1        127.0.0.1        UH          1    58631   lo0
128.9            199.0.216.3      UGD         0     2010   ef0
128.35           199.0.216.3      UGD         0       30   ef0
128.42           199.0.216.3      UGD         0     1539   ef0
128.63           199.0.216.3      UGD         0     2981   ef0
128.83           199.0.216.3      UGD         0     2020   ef0
128.96           199.0.216.3      UGD         0      343   ef0
```

The routing tables tell the system how to reach networks other than the one to which it is directly connected. Each route entry in the above listing shows a destination network number, the address of the gateway on the local network through which it can be reached, the status of that gateway, the number of times the route has been used to make a connection, the packet count across that route and the interface device to use to get to that route.

269

The **Flags** column, which indicates the gateway status, can have several different entries:

U   The gateway is up and running.

G   The route is through a gateway - if the **G** flag isn't set, then the route is probably a direct connection to a network through the interface.

H   The route is to an individual host rather than to a network.

D   The route is the result of a redirection - another gateway has rerouted traffic through this route.

There are two entries of special interest in the above routing table excerpt - the default gateway entry and the loopback entry. The entry that has **default** in the **Destination** column indicates the gateway through which all the traffic to networks not explicitly listed will be routed. If your system is having trouble reaching remote networks, then this is an entry to check. In this case, all default traffic is routed through 199.0.216.201, while most of the explicit routes seem to be through the gateway at 199.0.216.3.

The entry whose **Destination** is listed as 127.0.0.1 is a route to the local loopback adapter - interface device lo0. Notice that it is an 'H' type route - directly to a specific host (back to the local system, in this case).

Other Tools

Sun system administrators have some additional tools at their disposal - etherfind and traffic. Etherfind acts like a network analyzer, providing tracking for specific kinds of packets, while traffic provides a sort of graphical, dynamic version of **netstat**.

NIS

The Network Information Services (NIS) system was created by Sun Microsystems around 1985 in order to make the Network File System (NFS) easier to configure and administer. In NFS, it is important that user and group ID definitions are consistent across hosts for file-sharing permissions to work correctly. However, administrators found that they had to copy system files from machine to machine to accomplish this, which was very tedious and complex for a large network.

Keeping everything consistent in a changing network environment could become quite a hassle. Sun initially called the system Yellow Pages, or YP, but had to change the name to avoid trademark conflicts. The YP designation still lives on in the command names, however, many of which are still prefixed with **yp**.

NIS consists of a collection of Client/Server processes and administrative tools, together with their associated databases of system administration information. The server and client process components are **ypserve** and **ypbind** respectively. Here are some NIS administrative tools:

ypcat	Lists the contents of the NIS map databases.
ypmatch	Looks up values of keys in the NIS map databases.
yppoll	Reports on the version of NIS maps on the NIS server.
yppush	Moves new map information out to slave servers.
ypwhich	Reports on the NIS server that serves a specified system.

NIS+

NIS+ is a new, expanded version of NIS that's only available for Sun's Solaris operating system - it isn't likely that other UNIX vendors will pick it up.

NIS Features

An NIS 'domain' consists of a master server, slave servers and clients that use NIS services. NIS centralizes user and group name databases for an entire domain, allowing it to be administered as if it were a single system. Instead of storing user and group information in **/etc/passwd** and **/etc/group** files on individual systems, it stores it in special database files, called **DBM files** or **maps** which reside on NIS servers. The system libraries on the client UNIX systems are actually modified so that all system calls that would normally read the local information make RPC calls to the NIS servers instead.

NIS takes over many of the local network configuration functions on the client machine. NIS centralizes the following:

- Hostname lookup
- Userid and password lookup
- Groupid lookup
- Broadcast and subnet mask information
- Protocol names and numbers
- Network service names and port numbers

In conjunction with NFS, NIS really integrates a network into one centralized system, both from a user's and administrative point of view.

Master and Slave Servers

Each NIS domain has one master server which holds all the ASCII source for the maps. Any updates to the maps are always made on the master server and then the maps are rebuilt and 'pushed' to the slave servers.

Slave servers can act as backup NIS servers when the master server goes down, and they can also help to distribute the NIS server load in a large domain. Slave servers are required for NIS domains that span multiple IP subnets due to a limitation that requires NIS clients to be on the same subnet as the NIS server. Therefore, there must be at least one slave server on every IP subnet in the domain.

Disadvantages

The centralization of NIS administration has a downside - if the server goes down, it takes all NIS functionality with it, i.e. passwords, etc. While this can be somewhat mitigated by implementing slave servers, it still has to be taken into account.

NIS is very powerful and it's also very complex, requiring a large dose of careful planning upfront. If you are converting an existing system to NIS, you have a lot of work ahead of you. One last point - since administrative changes can propagate quickly through a NIS system, errors will spread just as quickly - be careful and pay attention to what you are doing when performing NIS administration!

Remote Operations

Finally, let's take a look at some UNIX remote network operations and the concept of **trust**. When two or more UNIX machines are used by the same group of people, it's sometimes desirable to be able to configure them to allow users on one machine to trigger operations on another machine. These operations include copying files from one machine to another, executing programs on a remote machine and logging onto a remote machine without the bother of re-authenticating. In order to accomplish this, the machines must be listed in each other's **/etc/hosts.equiv** files or in the **.rhosts** files for individual users. Machines listed in these files are said to be **trusted**.

While remote operations can really improve the productivity of users within a close-knit group of machines, they also present some serious security weaknesses for systems connected to the Internet. Many sites disallow trust relationships entirely for this reason.

The /etc/hosts.equiv File

If you wish to establish global trust with another system (so that all users can gain access to your system without supplying a password), place the name of the trusted system in your **/etc/hosts.equiv** file. You can see what a serious security risk this can pose - make sure you feel comfortable with the security on the remote system.

The **/etc/hosts.equiv** file is simply a text listing of the names of the hosts that are to be trusted on a system-wide basis. If a host is listed in this file, users on that system can log into accounts with the same name on the local system without authentication. This is convenient for users who have multiple accounts on different systems and who frequently move from machine to machine to get their work done. However, it also allows an intruder to do exactly the same thing.

The ~/.rhosts File

Users who wish to trust individual users on a remote system can create a **.rhosts** file in their home directory. They simply add a line to the file for each system they want to trust, and optionally specify a user on the trusted system. If a user isn't specified, then the local userid is used on the remote system. Again this allows users with accounts on more than one system to move freely between systems across the net, but also allows intruders who compromise such an account on one system to gain trusted access to the other.

The **.rhosts** file controls access to that user's account for remote operations. It's like **/etc/hosts.equiv**, except it only applies to the account of the owner. It consists of a text listing of hosts and userids, one pair per line, that are trusted to remotely access that account. For example, the entry:

```
andromeda   aevans
```

would indicate that the user **aevans** on the system **andromeda** is granted trusted access to the account owning the **.rhosts** file.

The Remote Commands

Once trust has been established between two machines, there are several remote operations that users can perform. Here are some of the most useful ones:

The rlogin Command

The **rlogin** command allows a user on a trusted system to log into a remote system without authenticating. For example, if the system **andromeda** trusts the local system or the current user,

```
$ rlogin andromeda
```

allows the user to jump over to an equivalent account on **andromeda** without supplying a password.

The rcp Command

This command operates much like the standard UNIX file system **cp** command, except that the syntax has been expanded to allow host-to-host copying. Placing the hostname and a colon in front of a file path tells **rcp** that the file resides on a remote host. For example:

```
%rcp andromeda:/usr/tmp/userguide.doc usergd.doc
```

copies the file **userguide.doc** from the directory **/usr/tmp** on the **andromeda** system to the current directory on the local machine as the file **usergd.doc**.

The rsh Command

The **rsh** command allows users on trusted systems to execute programs on a remote host. For example:

```
%rsh andromeda cat /usr/aevans/txtfile
```

lists the contents of the file **txtfile** in the directory **/usr/aevans** on the system **andromeda**.

Summary

In this chapter we've looked at the available physical networking media, the structure of network protocols, IP addressing, network interconnection schemes and Client/Server networking. We also reviewed the basic steps for configuring a UNIX machine for TCP/IP networking, and we looked at some useful network monitoring tools and basic network applications. Finally we looked at NIS as a solution to centralized network management.

Chapter

Network File System

Network file systems allow data to be shared across a network so that users don't need to know which system it resides on. They help to create the user perception of the network as one universal system, particularly when used in conjunction with services like NIS (discussed in the previous chapter). We'll be focusing on NFS, which is currently the most widespread and popular network file system and exploring its configuration, operation and associated utilities. We'll be taking a look at the following topics:

- Past and present network file system schemes
- Configuring NFS
- Mounting a file system
- Monitoring NFS
- The automounter
- AMD configuration

The Concept

With the proliferation of local-area networking and workgroup computing, the file-sharing needs of computer users have escalated. The need has arisen for a virtual file system that spans multiple systems. Such a file system offers several key advantages to users. Primarily, it eliminates the need to use complex network tools to move data around the workgroup; instead, files can be accessed as if they resided in local directories on the user's system and can be manipulated with conventional UNIX file commands. They can also be accessed from DOS clients, as additional drives.

Network file systems are vital to the operation of diskless workstations and they also simplify many administration tasks. Programs and configuration files that would normally be duplicated can effectively be centralized with a network file system. This eliminates the need to repeat changes to these files by hand on all systems in the workgroup. For example, manual pages can be stored on one host and then the source directory can be read by all the other machines in the workgroup, rather than having each system unnecessarily maintain its own set.

Network file systems generally operate on the **Client/Server** model - one system acts as a file server and client systems connect into it in order to gain access to the server's files. One system can also act as both a client and a server, using its own directories whilst accessing others from remote systems. A server directory that is made accessible to remote systems is referred to as an **export**, while a client connection to an exported server directory is a **mount**.

Types of UNIX Network File Systems

Over the years, various schemes have been developed for sharing UNIX file systems over a network. Let's now take a look at some of the more important ones.

RFS

Remote File Sharing (RFS) is a network file system developed by AT&T for use with UNIX System V. It is similar in many respects to NFS, but is now outdated and not widely used.

NFS

The Network File System (NFS) is by far the most widely-used network file system protocol on hundreds of thousands of sites world-wide. Originally introduced by Sun in 1985, NFS is part of the public domain. The public nature of this standard led to a large number of implementations (including Macintosh and DOS/Windows versions) from a wide variety of vendors. Now, just about every UNIX variant has NFS support. Since it is the clear market leader and the network file system you're most likely to encounter and use, NFS will be the focus of our discussion. It is defined by an Internet RFC (1094).

AFS

The Andrew File System (AFS) was originally developed at Carnegie-Mellon University as part of the Andrew Project. Subsequently, it has been distributed commercially by Transarc Corporation. AFS was designed to pick up where NFS left off, since NFS doesn't handle large-scale networks too well and is weak in security. AFS addresses these issues, but is still quite new and hasn't yet set the commercial marketplace alight (there are only several hundred AFS sites to date).

DFS

The Distributed File System (DFS) is an emerging standard being pushed by the Open Systems Foundation (OSF) as part of their Distributed Computing Environment (DCE). DFS is the most likely successor to NFS because of the improvements it has inherited from AFS and the backing of the OSF, but it too, is still in its adolescence.

279

Configuring NFS

Since NFS is the most widely-used network file system, let's take a look at how to get it up and running.

Setting Up NFS

NFS makes use of a number of daemon processes that must be running on the client and server machines in order for NFS to operate. Both client and server machines must be running the remote procedure call (RPC) daemon, **portmap**, and the block I/O daemon, **biod**. On the server side, the **mountd** remote mounting daemon and the NFS daemon, **nfsd**, must also be running. All of these daemons, except **mountd,** are usually run from **rc.local** or **rc.boot**. The **mountd** daemon is normally handled by **inetd**.

Most new systems either ship with NFS already installed (Solaris even has the automounter pre-configured and running, by default) or have scripts to help with the installation and configuration of NFS. Check your system documentation for specific details on installing NFS.

Exporting a File System

Once you've got an NFS server up and running, you'll need to specify which file systems you want to make visible to remote systems. This process is referred to as **exporting**. The terminology is particularly specific to BSD variants - if you are using a System V variant, then you will have to use the command **share** instead of **exportfs**. The commands are very similar, but you'll have to consult the manual pages for any specific differences that might be encountered with **share**.

Exporting shouldn't be done haphazardly - plan all your exports carefully beforehand. Only export file systems for which the client has a definable and substantial need and only export those parts of a file system that are necessary to the client, rather than exporting the entire file system. Be especially thorough when you set access limits on NFS servers that are connected to the Internet - one poorly administered NFS server can quickly compromise the security of your entire network. Finally, don't export root privileges to an NFS client unless it's absolutely necessary.

exportfs

The **exportfs** program is used to manage the exported file systems on an NFS server. It's usually invoked by boot scripts, but it can also be invoked by the superuser to make on-the-fly changes to the export settings. When run at boot time, **exportfs** is usually invoked with the **-a** option. **-a** instructs the system to consult the file **/etc/exports** to obtain the list of directories to export with their associated options. The file **/etc/xtab** lists the current state of all exported directories on your system.

Unexporting

The **exportfs** program can also be used to unexport (remove export) directories by invoking it with the **-u** option. If both the **-u** and **-a** options are used together, **exportfs** unexports all exported directories on the system.

The /etc/exports File

The **exportfs** program is rarely explicitly used to export fixed-disk file systems. The usual method is to put those parts of the file system that are available for mounting into the **/etc/exports** file. There is an entry in this text file for each file system to be exported, and they can be changed by hand by the superuser. Whenever changes are made to the **/etc/exports** file, **exportfs** must be rerun. Each entry in the file contains several possible elements:

- The directory path to be exported.
- A list of remote client systems (or NIS netgroups), separated by white-space, that are allowed to access the exported directory.
- A comma-separated list of options, starting with a hyphen.
- Comment text starting with a hash symbol.

Here's a sample **/etc/exports** file:

```
# /etc/exports
# last modified 3/3/95
#
# Export development tools to the developer netgroup
/usr/developer/bin     developers
#
```

```
# Grant read-only access to man pages
/usr/man        developers andromeda pisces orion   -ro
#
# Grant worldwide read-only access (be careful!)
/usr/pub        -ro
```

In this example, three directories are being exported. The first one will only be accessible by machines belonging to an NIS netgroup called **developers**. The second one will be accessible to the **developers** group along with the individual machines named **andromeda**, **pisces** and **orion,** but will be read-only. The last directory is read-only as well, but will be accessible by any system on the network - including any system on the Internet if the machine is connected to it.

You should be very careful about exposing anything to the entire world - this can pose a serious security risk. It's usually a bad idea, unless you have a very good reason to do so. An example of an acceptable application for this is the US Bureau of the Census' datasets on CD-ROM. This Census CD-ROM is exported publicly so that anyone can mount and use it. It's safe because the CD-ROM volume is read-only and contains only data that should be made public.

Mounting a File System

NFS clients make use of exported directories from NFS servers by **mounting** them locally. This is done by using the **mount** command, which operates a little differently under NFS. Before a remote file system can be successfully mounted, it must first be properly exported from another host on the TCP/IP network, as we have just discussed. If the remote file system isn't available to be mounted, then the mount operation can hang, wait, or generate an error, depending on the options available.

mount

The **mount** command can be used to mount a single file system, or it can be used in conjunction with the **/etc/fstab** file to mount several systems as one batch. It can also be used to change the settings for currently-mounted file systems. When mounting a single file system, the syntax is:

```
mount  <remotehost>:<dirpath>  <localpath>
```

where **remotehost** is the network name of the NFS server from which you wish to mount the file system, while **dirpath** is the export you wish to mount and **localpath** is the point on the local file system tree where you wish the new mount to be grafted.

For example:

```
$ mount orion:/usr/local/bin /usr/local/bin
```

This attempts to mount the **/usr/local/bin** directory on the remote NFS server system called **orion** as **/usr/local/bin** on the local machine. This will only work if the directory **/usr/local/bin** already exists on the local machine - the local mount point must exist prior to use of the **mount** command!

The **mount** command takes the following options:

-a	Attempts to mount all file systems listed in **/etc/fstab**. Frequently used in conjunction with the **-t** option.
-o	Sets various options. Some useful ones are:
	nosuid - blocks setuid and setgid from taking effect (for security reasons).
	noexec - prevents binaries from executing from the remote file system - useful when mounting file systems from machines with different architectures.
-p	Prints out information about all currently-mounted file systems. The output is in the same format as the **/etc/fstab** file and can be used to reconstruct it.
-r	Mounts the file system as read-only.
-t type	Restricts the action of the **mount** command to file systems of the given type (**nfs, ufs**, special file system types).
-u	Changes the settings for an already mounted file system instead of mounting a new one.
-v	Turns on verbose mode.
-w	Mounts the file system as read/write (default).

For example:

```
$ mount -a -v -t nfs -o noexec -r
```

attempts to mount all the NFS file systems listed in **/etc/fstab** as read-only, without the ability to execute binaries. The **mount** command will also print out verbose information as it executes.

Mounting Automatically at Boot (/etc/fstab)

Every time a system is booted, all the file systems it uses must be mounted. Rather than issuing individual mount commands for each file system, the usual practice is to list them in a file called **/etc/fstab**, which is then automatically processed at boot. Note that the entries aren't restricted to just NFS file systems, but also cater for other devices and remote file systems as well.

Entry Format

Each NFS file system entry in **/etc/fstab** has six fields in the following format:

```
remotehost:filesystem  localpath  nfs  options  frequency
pass
```

where:

- **remotehost** is the network name of the NFS server from which to mount the file system.

- **filesystem** is the export to mount.

- **localpath** is the point on the local file system tree where the new mount is to be grafted.

- **nfs** is the file system type.

- **options** is a comma-separated list of mounting options.

- **frequency** is the dump frequency for the file system (usually 0 for NFS mounts).

- **pass** is the **fschk** pass number on boot (0 for NFS systems as well).

Options

Some valid options for the **options** field are:

ro	Mounts the file system as read-only.
rw	Mounts the file system as read/write.
soft	If the server doesn't respond, then produces an error.
hard	Keeps trying to connect to the server indefinitely if it doesn't initially respond. However, if your NFS server from which the directory is hard mounted is down, then the client won't boot up at all. This option isn't recommended for medium or large scale NFS networks. There will also be a problem if the system administrator of the file server has unexported the file system without letting anyone else know.
bg	Doesn't wait for the server, but keeps trying in the background.

Example

Here's an example **/etc/fstab** entry for an NFS mount:

```
orion:/usr/developer/bin    /usr/developer/bin    nfs    rw,bg   0   0
```

This will mount the **/usr/developer/bin** directory from the **orion** system at the local mount point **/usr/developer/bin**. The file system type is NFS, and the file system will be mounted with read/write permission. If **orion** doesn't respond right away, the local system will continue, but will keep trying to connect to **orion** in the background. Finally, the file system doesn't need to be dumped or checked.

Always bear in mind that this entry will only work if **orion** is indeed exporting **/usr/developer/bin** and the local machine has been granted access to mount it.

285

umount

File systems can also be unmounted using the **umount** command. Like **mount**, the **umount** command can be used to either unmount a single file system or it can be directed to operate on the file system list stored in **/etc/fstab**. The **umount** command takes as an argument either the local or remote file system to be unmounted. For example, if you had previously mounted locally **orion:/usr/developer/bin** as **/usr/developer/bin**, then either of the following commands would unmount it:

```
$ umount orion:/usr/developer/bin
$ umount /usr/developer/bin
```

The **umount** command also takes a few useful options:

-a	Unmounts all the file systems listed in **/etc/fstab**.
-t <type>	Restricts the action of the **umount** command to file systems of the given type (**ufs**, **nfs**, special file system types, etc.).
-v	Enters verbose mode.

For example:

```
umount -at nfs
```

would dismount all NFS file systems listed in **/etc/fstab**. One small thing to remember is not to attempt to unmount the directory you are currently in. If you do, you'll be informed that the file system is busy. It's a good idea to check with the **pwd** command first.

Monitoring NFS

There are several useful commands you can use to check the status of your NFS servers and connections. Which commands you use will depend on the flavor of UNIX you're using with NFS. The **showmount** command is available on BSD NFS implementations, while the **dfmounts** and **dfshares** commands are native to some System V platforms.

Showing Exported Directories

To show all of the exported directories being shared by a host, use the following command (under BSD):

```
showmount -e <hostname>
```

This command prints out a list that looks something like this:

```
$ showmount -e andromeda
export list for andromeda:
/usr/pub          (everyone)
/usr/local        (everyone)
/usr/developer/bin      cygnus,pyxis,hydra,draco
```

This tells us that the system called **andromeda** is exporting three directories. **/usr/pub** and **/usr/local** are being shared with everyone, while **/usr/developers** can only be mounted from the **cygnus**, **pyxis**, **hydra** and **draco** systems.

On a System V machine, use the following command instead:

```
dfshares <hostname>
```

Listing Remote Mounts

Invoking **showmount** with the **-a** option lists all remote mounts from a server in the format:

client:dirpath

where **client** is the client machine that is remote-mounting the directory **dirpath**.

```
$ showmount -a andromeda
cygnus:/usr/developer/bin
cygnus:/usr/local
pyxis:/usr/developer/bin
hydra:/usr/developer/bin
```

This tells us that the machines **cygnus**, **pyxis** and **hydra** have mounted file systems from **andromeda**'s NFS server.

On System V machines, use the following command instead:

```
dfmounts hostname
```

Invoking **showmount** with the **-d** option lists all the exported directories on the server that have been mounted by remote clients (without indicating which clients).

The Automounter

Automounters maintain a cache of available file system mount points and only mount them when they are needed. When an attempt is made to access a cached file system, the automounter mounts it. After a period of inactivity on the mounted file system, it becomes 'stale' and is automatically unmounted until it is needed again. Automounters are designed to handle network interruptions gracefully, and can even mount alternate file systems in the event that the requested file system is unavailable.

Normally, the file systems to be mounted, including NFS file systems, are listed in the **/etc/fstab** or **/etc/vfstab** file. These are called static mounts, because they are affected at boot and remain mounted until they are dismounted by the user or at shutdown. Automounters don't use the file system static mount table, instead they use **mount maps**, which are text files that describe where to find the file systems that are referenced.

There are two common automounters in use - Sun's **automounter** program and a public-domain automounter called **Amd**. Widely available on the Internet, **Amd** has been ported to most BSD platforms - it can be used on Sun systems as a replacement for the **automounter** program if so desired. Unfortunately though, **Amd** and **automounter** don't share a common map file format. Both are designed to operate in conjunction with NFS, although **Amd** supports some other network file systems as well. Both automounters can work in conjunction with NIS, which centralizes the mount maps and greatly improves the ease of administration for a large network.

Sun Automounter Configuration

The Sun **automounter** makes use of three kinds of maps:

master   The master map tells the automounter on boot up where
           the primary mount points are and where to find the
           direct and indirect mount maps.

indirect Indirect maps list remote resources and simple local
           directories (without slashes) onto which to map them. The
           local directories are mounted under the primary mount
           point listed for the map in the master map file.

direct   Direct maps list mappings from absolute mount points to
           remote resources, much like a conventional NFS static
           mount.

By convention, direct mappings are entered into a file called
/etc/auto_direct.

An Example

Here's a simplified example to show you how everything fits together. The
file **auto_master** might look like this:

```
#
#  /etc/auto_master
#
+auto_master
/net -hosts              -nosuid
/home      auto_home
/-    auto_direct
```

The **+auto_master** entry makes sure that NIS is first used for mapping. The
next entry lets users easily navigate through the exports of other hosts on
the network. Every host will have a virtual subdirectory under **/net**, with
further subdirectories for their exports. This is a convention in the Sun
world. Also note the use of the **-nosuid** option - this is a security setting
to prevent **setuid** security leaks.

auto_home

The **/home** entry references **/etc/auto_home** to indirectly map the home directories of users under the local **/home** directory. This allows users to access their home directories as if they were local, no matter where they log into the network. The last entry is a direct map entry. Direct maps should always list **/-** as their primary mount point.

The **/etc/auto_home** file might look like this:

```
#
# /etc/auto_home
#
+auto_home
tom        orion:/usr/home/tom
dick       orion:/usr/home/dick
harry      hydra:/usr/home/harry
```

These are entries telling automounter where to find each user's home directory. Once again, NIS is used first for mapping.

auto_direct

Finally, the **/etc/auto_direct** map might look like this:

```
#
# /etc/auto_direct
#
/usr/man        orion:/usr/man
/usr/local/bin  orion:/usr/local/bin
```

These mounts are specific grafts onto the file tree - the kind of mounts that have expectations of a specific local file path, and are therefore candidates for direct mounting.

Generally, the automounter is used in conjunction with NIS, and these files are altered using NIS tools (like **nistbladm** and **admintool**) rather than manually with a text editor.

Amd Configuration

To make **Amd** work, it must be run from your **/etc/rc.local** file (or an equivalent file). It reads a mount map (usually called something like **/etc/**

server.map) to determine how to dynamically mount file systems. Let's look at a quick example - say you're currently static-mounting the following NFS file system in **/etc/fstab**:

```
orion:/usr/pub   /net/orion  nfs    rw,bg 0     0
```

To use **Amd** to mount this file system on-demand instead, you would delete or comment out the entry in **/etc/fstab** to prevent it from statically mounting, and then add the following to **/etc/amd.server**:

```
/defaults     opts:=rw;type:=nfs
   orion      rhost:=orion; rfs:=/usr/pub
```

Assuming that **Amd** was told at boot up that the root mount point for dynamic mounts is **/net**, this will accomplish the same results as the static mount above, except that the file system will only be mounted when needed.

Automounters and NIS

Both **Amd** and **automounter** can make use of NIS if it's running. The Sun automounter program is designed to make extensive and almost transparent use of NIS. For example, the indirect map of user's home directories doesn't need to be redefined for the automounter - it can use the **auto_home** map straight from NIS. The automounter file **/etc/auto_home**, which tells the automounter where to get the user home directories under **/home**, can simply look like this:

```
# /etc/auto_home
+auto_home
```

This links directly into NIS's **auto_home** map, allowing NIS to be the central repository (and maintenance point). The combination of NFS, NIS and automounting creates a single virtual system out of many networked machines, with centralized administration and high transparency for the users. If a user logs in at any machine on the net, their password authentication is handled by NIS and their home directory is located by NIS and mounted by NFS and an automounter. Any changes to the user base or system configuration are automatically propagated by NIS without having to reconfigure anything locally, from **/etc/passwd** up to automounting maps.

Summary

In this chapter, we discussed the need for network file systems and surveyed a few of the more popular and important schemes. Then we focused on NFS, the market leader, and discussed how to configure and use it. We discussed how to export a file system, mount it and how to reverse the process. We looked at methods for monitoring the status of an NFS server, such as the `showmount` command, and finally we looked at the two different types of file system automounters. In the next chapter, we'll look at one of the facilities that you can use over the network, the e-mail system.

Chapter

E-mail Systems

Electronic mail (e-mail) is becoming increasingly important for local and inter-organizational communication. Over 30 million people have access to e-mail, many on UNIX systems, so in this chapter we will show you how to set up a UNIX mail system. There are many confusing protocols and standards and here we will discuss all the issues involved in connecting you to the outside world.

The core of this chapter will discuss how e-mail is typically used. There are many issues that need to be resolved when sending a message, and several different programs to send it with. The subjects we will consider are:

- UNIX mail system architecture
- The mail address
- Anatomy of a simple mail message
- The default **mail** program
- The **elm** and **pine** mail programs
- The **MH** and **xmh** mail programs
- Mail standards
- Remote mail access

UNIX Mail System Architecture

In the PC world, electronic mail systems tend to be highly proprietary and closed. Novell, Microsoft and Lotus all provide mail systems that work well by themselves, but are largely inflexible and require cumbersome gateways to work efficiently in a heterogeneous environment.

UNIX mail systems employ an open architecture approach where they are split into two parts - the mail user agent (MUA) and the mail transport agent (MTA). This split accomplishes two major things:

 Mail processing can occur 'behind the scenes' when the user isn't logged in or running the mail program.

 Mail users are free to choose the user-interface to the mail system with which they feel the most comfortable. In fact, different users on the same system can use a variety of different MUAs with the same MTA. Many UNIX MUAs also support multiple MTAs, so even if the MTA changes, users can keep their favorite MUA.

Mail User Agents

The MUA is the user-interface to the mail system. When a user wishes to send a message or view messages in his or her mailbox, he/she performs these actions via the MUA. Essentially, the MUA is responsible for formatting and presenting MTA-received mail to the user and for accepting mail to be sent from the user and forwarding it to the MTA.

Mail Transport Agents

The MTA does all the 'dirty work' in the mail system - it knows how to 'speak' to the mail protocol in order to send and receive mail on the local system. The MTA also sorts incoming mail into each user's system mailbox. The MTA is like a letter carrier for the Postal Service - it picks up mail to be delivered and drops off new mail. It knows how to work within a larger mail-delivery system (like a network) to see that mail is properly routed to its destination.

As a user, you don't need to know what actually takes place in order to get a message or letter across the country - you just have to make sure it's properly addressed and the MTA will sort it out. If your mail isn't delivered, it goes directly into another 'sorting office' system that can deliver it.

Using Mail

Now that we have examined the architecture of the UNIX e-mail system, let's look at UNIX e-mail from a user's perspective.

The user of an e-mail system views it much like conventional postal mail. The main user activities are sending and receiving mail, the system does the rest. Users don't worry about the MTA/MUA architecture or any other technical details.

Usually, an e-mail user has a message to communicate to another user and merely wishes to be given the tools to compose, address and dispatch that message. At the other end, the receiving user needs the tools to view and manipulate incoming mail and possibly reply, forward or save it. All of these functions are features of an MUA and there is a wide range of MUAs that provide these functions in different ways. In this section, we'll survey some of the more popular ones. We'll be looking at how each MUA provides the basic mail functions to the user and we'll review the basic MUA modes and commands.

Before we get down to the details of each individual MUA, let's discuss something that is pertinent to all users of MUAs - how mail addressing works.

The Mail Address

Addressing is perhaps the most basic and important e-mail concept. The most eloquent e-mail message composed in the most sophisticated MUA is useless if it doesn't arrive at its intended destination.

Local Addressing

The simplest kind of e-mail address is a user id of a fellow user on the same system. To send mail to a fellow user on your system, you need only provide that user's id as the address.

UUCP (Route-based) Addressing

Once you leave your own system, addressing can become complicated. It depends on how you are connected to other systems and how your addressee's system is connected.

In the old days, before the Internet explosion, UNIX networking and UUCP (Unix to Unix Copy, an international wide-area network in the US) were synonymous and you had to know something about your UUCP network's topology in order to address your mail correctly. You had to know what all the 'hops' were between your system and the destination system. Once you knew the route that the mail message would have to take to get to your addressee, you could finally address your mail. This kind of addressing is therefore called **route-based addressing**. For instance, let's say that your home system is called **andromeda** and is connected via UUCP to **orion**, which in turn is connected to **cygnus**. If you wish to send a message to the user **aevans** on **cygnus**, then the route-based address would be:

`orion!cygnus!aevans`

As you can see, the address is composed of a list of machines on the UUCP network, starting with the nearest hop, followed by the destination system and ending with the addressee's user id. Each element of the address is separated from the next by an exclamation mark (pronounced 'bang' by UNIX users). Addresses can grow quite long if there are many hops in between.

Internet (Location-independent) Addressing

With the advent of the Internet, mail addressing has become much simpler. The network topology of the Internet presents a far more sensible and organized way to reference remote host machines.

Domains

The Internet is partitioned into sub-networks called **domains**. Each domain can, in turn, be divided into sub-domains, and so on. This domain-based addressing scheme groups related machines together and, in turn, groups related domains in (usually) intuitive ways, making it easier to understand and remember Internet host addresses. Internet host addresses are therefore much more like conventional postal addresses.

One major problem with UUCP addressing is that the address is different when mail is sent to the same person from different places. For example, if you mailed a letter to a friend from home, you'd have to use a totally different address than if you mailed from work, because the route along which the mail travels would be different. Luckily, that's not how Internet addressing works. Instead, you specify *where* to send your letter, rather than *how* - you rely on the Postal Service to figure out the rest. Because the same address works no matter where you send the mail from, Internet host addresses (and Postal addresses) are said to be **location-independent**.

Structure of an Internet Host Address

Let's look at the structure of an Internet host address. As we said before, systems on the Internet are organized into hierarchical groupings called domains. These work like the country, state, city and town in a postal mail address - they systematically narrow down the location of the destination machine. The actual destination machine is the equivalent of the street address.

Internet host addressing works backwards with respect to UUCP route-based addressing. The user id comes first, then the destination system, followed by the smallest sub-domain, up to the outermost domain where the destination system is located. The user id and destination system are separated by an '**@**', while the system and domains are separated by periods. Let's now take a look at some example Internet host addresses:

`root@monster.umz.edu`	The user **root** on the system **monster** in the subdomain **umz** of the domain **edu**.
`jdoe@wrox.com`	The user **jdoe** on the system **wrox** in the domain **com**.
`postmaster@xsol.demon.co.uk`	The user **postmaster** on the system **xsol** in the subdomain **demon** in the subdomain **co** of the domain **uk**.

There are some widely-used domains that are useful for you to know about. Most addresses reside in subdomains of these domains:

Country Domains

All countries that are wired for Internet access have their own domains, for example:

.au	Systems located in Australia.
.ca	Systems located in Canada.
.de	Systems located in Germany.
.fi	Systems located in Finland.
.fr	Systems located in France.
.uk	Systems located in the United Kingdom.
.us	Systems located in the United States (although this is rarely used).

The domain name is mostly taken from the ISO two-character country code (apart from the UK).

Organizational Domains

Some domains represent systems that are related by the activities in which their users participate, rather than their national affiliations:

.com	Commercial systems (operated by profit-making organizations).
.edu	Systems operated by educational institutions.
.gov	Systems operated by the US government.
.mil	Systems operated by the US military.
.net	Subdomains that represent networks operated by specific organizations - usually Internet service providers.
.org	Systems belonging to organizations and associations (mostly trade organizations and non-profit groups).

In the US, the organizational domains take the place of the country domain in the address field. For the rest of the world, the organizational domain and the country domain are both included. For example, **xxx.com** would refer to somewhere in the states while the UK equivalent address would be **xxx.com.uk.**

The Anatomy of a Simple Message

Before we delve into the MUAs, let's review the basic structure of a mail message. The mail message is split into two basic parts - the **header fields** and the **message body**.

Header Fields

The header fields are used to properly route your mail and are, therefore, in a fairly rigid format. The header fields contain the addresses of all recipients, the subject line, the sender's address and a variety of other information depending on the MUA and MTA you are using. The header fields for a typical message look something like this:

```
Date sent:      Mon, 09 Jan 1995 20:05:48
From:           gross@ixxx.org (Gregory Ross)
To:             Andrew Evans <aevans@fake.fake.com>
Subject:        Re: Virus Alert
Cc:             Brian Farmer <bfarmer@fake.fake.com>
```

Message Body

The message body is much more loosely defined. This is the part of the message you are responsible for and can consist of any text you want.

> The contents of the message body get a little trickier with the introduction of MIME (Multipurpose Internet Mail Extensions) and other multipart, multiformat mail types, but you'll generally use a tool that hides the additional complexity from you when you use those types anyway. We will look at MIME later on in this chapter.

E-mail Programs

Now that we've considered the different elements that make up an e-mail message, let's take a look at the different programs that are available to you. Although there are more, we shall consider the main four:

mail	The basic mail program that everyone has.
elm	The next step up from **mail**, fairly user-friendly, but not very configurable.
pine	This is the most user-friendly of all the packages listed here.
MH	Very difficult to use, but quite powerful.

Now we'll compare these mail programs and look at how they deal with checking your mailbox (sometimes called inbox), retrieving messages, composing messages, attachments, uudecoding and encoding, and aliases; we'll end with a command summary.

mail

The **mail** program is essentially the 'default' mail interface on a UNIX system - it's the mail program you have if you haven't installed anything more sophisticated. The **mail** program has a slightly more capable variant on some AT&T systems, called **mailx**, which adds more features to standard **mail** functionality.

Checking Your Mailbox

Perhaps the most basic of electronic mail system functions is that of notifying you when new mail arrives and subsequently allowing you to retrieve and read your messages. To check if you have any mail waiting with the **mail** program, simply run it without any arguments:

```
$ mail
No mail for aevans
$
```

Here, there isn't any new mail waiting for the user, **aevans**. If new mail is waiting for you, **mail** will list out all the messages in your mailbox, showing the address of the sender, the message date and the subject line from each message. Each message in the list is preceded by a number, indicating its position in the mailbox.

Retrieving Messages

To read messages in your mailbox, run **mail** and type the number of the message you wish to view at the **&** prompt. For instance, you might see something like this:

```
$ mail
Mail version 5.5 6/1/90.  Type ? for help.
"/var/mail/root": 2 messages 2 new
>N  1 aevans@wrox.com        Tue Jan 17 12:16   13/283   "Hello there"
>N  2 sponge@clerk.net       Wed Jan 18 23:58   32/391   "Re: ISDN"
&
```

This display indicates that two mail messages are waiting - one from **aevans** at the host, **wrox.com** and another from a user called **sponge** at **clerk.net** - both messages are new and unread. To read the message from **sponge**, you would type **2** at the prompt and press *Return*.

Composing Messages

To begin composing a message, run the **mail** program with the recipient's address as the only argument. For example, to send a message to a machine named **cchuck** on the same host system, you would simply type:

```
$ mail cchuck
```

After you press *Return*, you are in message editing mode (hence the change of prompt) and **mail** expects that you will begin typing your message text. When you have finished entering the text of your message, enter a line with nothing but a period on it. On some systems, **mail** expects a *Ctrl-D* character to end a message.

While this interface to mail message composition leaves quite a lot to be desired, it works and is very simple to use. You can make your life a little easier by using the *~v* escape command (see the Mail Editing Command Summary, a little later) to launch your chosen editor.

You can also compose messages from the **mail** command mode by using these commands:

m   Mail.

r   Reply (including recipients).

R   Reply to just originator (not including recipients).

To compose a new message, type:

```
m <address>
```

where **address** is the address to which you'd like the mail to go.

Replying to a Message

To reply to a message you have received, type:

```
r <message>
```

or

```
R <message>
```

where **message** is the number of the message to which you'd like to reply.

Attachments and Inclusions

Sometimes you will want to send more than just a text message in your mail. For instance, you might want to include a spreadsheet, a picture, or some code with your mail. SMTP with MIME extensions support such mail over the Internet, as we'll see later in this chapter. However, the MUA you use must be designed to take advantage of mail extensions in order to allow you to do this conveniently. Many MUAs now support MIME directly, or have add-ons that enable them to process extensions. The **mail** program doesn't support extensions (some people would argue that you're lucky it supports text). About the only way to include non-text items using the **mail** program is to encode the attachment into 7-bit ASCII text and mail the file as a text message. The recipient, of course, must have the proper decoding software at the other end in order to restore the file to its original form.

uuencode and uudecode

The most common tool for performing this encoding is **uuencode**. A **mail** message, including a file that has been encoded in such a way, can be decoded using the companion program **uudecode**. While this method works for moving binary data, it's not particularly elegant or even convenient.

To Encode a File

Let's say we want to send a spreadsheet file (**payroll.zls**) to a colleague. To encode the binary file, type the following:

```
$ uuencode payroll.xls payroll.xls > payroll.uu
```

The first argument is the file to be encoded and the second argument is what the file will be called when it is decoded (usually they are the same). The encoded text is dumped onto standard output, so you need to redirect it to a file (in this case, **payroll.uu**).

Since **payroll.uu** is now a 7-bit ASCII file, it can now be sent via e-mail.

To Decode a File

First, within your MUA, save the message to a file. Let's say that message **1** in **mail** contains an encoded file. You could enter the following at the **mail** command prompt:

```
& save 1 uu_file
```

Now, message **1** has been saved to a file called **uu_file**.

To decode it, exit the **mail** program and type:

```
$ uudecode uu_file
```

If **uudecode** encounters no errors, the restored binary file will appear in the same directory as **uu_file**. Check the binary file to see if it survived the encode/decode process. If it's okay, then you can safely delete **uu_file**. If it hasn't transferred properly, try to decode it again before asking the sender to repeat the message.

Aliases

The **mail** program, like most MUAs, allows you to set up local **aliases** for addresses that you use quite frequently. Let's say you regularly correspond with **jim_broomfield@betelgeuse.software.xxx.com** and you're getting tired of typing out that long address every time you send Jim a message (this method is also quite error prone). You can **alias** the address to, say, **jimb**, which is far easier to type and remember each time. An **alias** address winds up looking (to you, the sender) like a local user, so be careful - it can get confusing. You set up aliases by placing entries in the file **.mailrc** in your home directory. An **alias** entry looks like this:

```
alias  jimb  jim_broomfield@betelgeuse.software.xxx.com
```

Groups and Nesting

You can also make an alias that represents a group of addresses - your own personal mailing list:

```
alias  conspirators  gknox@garrys-mac.asdg.umd.edu  jimb
aevans@wrox.com
```

Any mail addressed to 'conspirators' would now go to these three addresses. Note that **jimb** is an **alias** within this **alias**, illustrating another feature of **mail** aliases - they can be nested.

Global Aliases

A note about system-wide aliases - the **sendmail** MTA supports the definition of aliases on a system-wide basis. Any mail sent by any user on the system will have the system-wide aliases applied. These aliases are defined in the file **/etc/aliases**, where the entries consist of the alias followed by one or more addresses:

```
jim: jb60679a@huic.fordham.cpsi.com
team:    pwoods, bfarmer, levans, aevans, cchuck
```

Before the aliases can take effect, the program **newaliases** must be run, which actually builds the file **/etc/aliases.db**. This is the file that **sendmail** uses when processing system-wide aliases.

Mail Modes

Like many MUAs, **mail** has two basic modes - **mail** processing mode and **mail** editing mode. When you have new mail waiting for you and you enter the **mail** program, you are effectively in the **mail** processing mode. When you are composing a new message or a reply, you are in the editing mode.

Mail Processing Mode

There are several commands you can use to process your mail; here are some of them:

Full Command	Shortcut	Action
help	?	Prints out a command summary.
!<command>		Shell escape - executes **command** as a shell command.
Print	P	Same as **print**, but includes ignored header fields (see **print**).
Reply	R	Composes a reply to the originator, but not other recipients, of a message.
Type	T	Same as **Print**.
alias	a	Lists all active aliases. If an alias is given as an argument, then it shows the value of that alias.
copy	co	Same as **save**, but doesn't delete the message afterwards.
delete	d	Deletes any messages when you give their message number as an argument.
dp	dt	Deletes the current message and displays the next one.
edit	e	Edits one or more messages given as arguments.

Continued

Full Command	Shortcut	Action
exit	ex, x	Quits without saving changes to the mailbox.
folder	fo	Switches to the folder given as an argument.
folders		Lists the names of all active mail folders.
headers	h, h+, h-	Shows the headers for 18 messages (**h+** moves to the next 18, **h-** moves back 18 messages).
mail	m	Composes a message to the one or more addresses or aliases given as arguments.
print	p	Displays the message or messages given as arguments on the user's terminal.
quit	q	Exits the **mail** session, saving any changes to the mailbox.
reply	r	Composes a reply message to the originator and recipients of a message.
save	s	Saves the message or messages given as arguments to the file which is given as the last argument. If more than one message is given, messages are appended together.
set \<option> =\<value>	se	Sets the mail program options. Useful ones are **VISUAL** for the visual editor to use, and **PAGER** to keep messages from scrolling by too quickly.
type	t	Same as **print**.
undelete	u	Removes deletion marks from the messages given as arguments.
unread	U	Marks the given messages as unread.
write	w	Same as **save**, but only writes out bodies of messages.

Mail Editing Mode

When you run the **mail** program with an address as an argument, or when you use the **m**, **r**, **R**, or **e** commands from the processing mode, you enter the **mail** editing mode. You use this mode to enter and edit the text of your mail messages. While you are entering text, **mail** recognizes some special character sequences in your text, called escapes, which trigger activity in the **mail** program. You can use these escapes to execute certain commands without having to leave the editor. The escape, initialized with a tilde, must be the first thing on the text line and it takes effect when you press *Return*. Here are some useful escape sequences:

Escape	Function Performed
.	Exits the editor, saving the changes made (use *Ctrl-D* instead on some systems).
~!	Executes a shell command.
~b\<addr\> [\<addr\>...]	Blind copies the address or addresses - sends a copy of the message to the given addresses without the knowledge of the other recipients (this means that the addresses won't appear in the message header).
~c\<addr\> [\<addr\>...]	Copies the address or addresses - sends a copy of the message to the given address or addresses (this means that the addresses will appear in the Cc: header field - 'cc' means 'carbon-copy').
~d	Reads in the contents of **~/dead.letter**, if it exists. Useful for continuing an aborted editing session.
~e	Continues editing the current message buffer.
~f\<message\>	Same as **~m**, but not indented by a tab.
~h	Edits the message's header fields.

Continued

Escape	Function Performed
~m<message>	Reads the given message into the message being edited, indented by a tab. Useful when referencing the original message when replying. The **message** parameter refers to the number that is used to identify that message.
~p	Prints out the message being edited as it will appear to the recipient.
~q	Aborts the message editing session and copies the current message text to the file **~/ dead.letter**.
~r<filename>	Reads the contents of the specified **filename** into the body of the message. Useful for including files encoded with **uuencode**, etc.
~v	Invokes a visual editor (typically **vi**) to edit the message.
~w<filename>	Writes the message to a file named **filename**.
~|<command>	Pipes the message body through the given **command** and replaces the message body with the result.
~~<text>	Inserts the given text, preceeded by a tilde, allowing a tilde to appear in the actual message text at the start of a line without triggering an escape sequence.

elm

The original full-screen mail program, **elm**, is still evolving and still very popular. It's simple to use, but not very configurable. In terms of sophistication, it lies somewhere between **mail** and **pine** - **elm** is pretty much a superset of **mail**, but lacks many of **pine**'s built-in features (**pine** was specifically designed to supercede **elm**).

Checking Your Mailbox

When you run **elm**, it immediately shows you summary lines for all the messages currently in your mailbox, much like **mail** does. Here is a typical **elm** display:

```
Mailbox is '/var/mail/aevans' with 62 messages [ELM 2.4 PL23]

  N  1    Jan 12 Paul Woods        (37)    Slinky?
  O  2    Jan 12 Sheila Foster     (48)    Re: Your mail
  O  3    Jan 11 Gregory Ross      (46)    Re: Desert Island Electronics
  O  4    Jan 11 Patricia Thorp    (47)    see ya
  O  5    Jan 10 Howard Rosen      (44)    Re: Fast pizza recommendation




   You can use any of the following commands by pressing the first
character;
 d)elete or u)ndelete mail,  m)ail a message,  r)eply or f)orward mail,
q)uit
    To read a message, press <return>.  j = move down, k = move up, ? =
help

Command:
```

Each message line tells us the following:

Message status	One of the following: **N**=New, **O**=Old (already read), **D**=Deleted.
Message number	An identifier for referring to the message from **elm** commands.
Date received	Normally month followed by day.
Sender	The name of the sender.
Length of the message	Number of text lines.
Message	Subject.

The highlight bar indicates the current message - the message to which all commands currently apply. Some of the available **mail** handling commands are listed at the bottom of the screen.

Retrieving Messages

When **elm** is started, the highlight bar usually sits over the first (most recently received) message in your mailbox. To move the highlight bar to a different message, you can use the *J* (for down) and *K* (for up) keys or the cursor keys. Alternatively, you can type in the message number and hit *Return* to jump directly to that message. To view the message under the highlight bar, simply press the *Return* key. The screen clears and displays your message, one screenful of text at a time.

Many of the **mail** handling commands from the main menu remain active during **mail** viewing. For instance, you can still use the *J* and *K* keys to go to the next or previous message for immediate viewing.

Composing Messages

To compose a new message with **elm**, press the *m* key. You will be prompted with the message header information and you can then start your visual editor. The **elm** system has a native editor based on the original **mail** version, but it usually makes use of external editors for mail composition.

To reply to a message you've received, highlight the message and press the *r* key. You will be asked if you want to copy the original message into the reply (so that you can easily quote or refer to it if necessary). Then **elm** suggests a subject line for the message, based on the original message's subject. You can change it if you like. Next, **elm** asks if you'd like to send a copy to anyone else. Finally, you can edit within your text editor to compose the body of the message.

When you have finished editing your message (whether you're composing a new one or replying), exit your editor. You will then be shown the following prompt by **elm**:

```
Please choose one of the following options by parenthesized letter:
        e)dit message, edit h)eaders, s)end it, or f)orget it.
```

This gives you a last chance to change your mind about message content or header values, or to scrap the whole message before it gets sent. Press the letter corresponding to the action you wish to take.

Attachments and Inclusions

By itself, **elm** doesn't support attachments or inclusions any better than **mail** does (i.e. not very easily). However, a program called **metamail** can be added to your **elm** environment that will allow you to process MIME-compatible mail.

Aliases

Like **mail**, **elm** has its own aliasing mechanism for addresses. It maintains all its aliases in special files - instead of editing them directly, you must use special tools to view and modify them. Several tools are provided with the **elm** installation to accomplish this:

checkalias	Provides a quick check of aliases.
elmalias	The main **elm** alias query tool.
listalias	Generates sorted listings of aliases.
newalias	Adds new aliases to the **elm** alias database.

The easiest way to manage aliases, however, is to use 'alias mode' from within **elm** itself. Just press the *A* key from the main menu and all the alias features become available to you.

```
Alias mode: 3 aliases [ELM 2.4 PL23]


     1    Jim Broomfield, A great guy            Person    jimb
     2    Garry Knox                             Person    gk
     3    Paul Woods                             Person    pw
     4    Charlie Chuck                          Person    ck




     You can use any of the following commands by pressing the first
character;
        a)lias current message, n)ew alias, d)elete or u)ndelete an
alias,
   m)ail to alias, or r)eturn to main menu.  To view an alias, press
<return>.
                j = move down, k = move up, ? = help
Alias:
```

From here you can add or remove aliases, view their values, select one to mail to, or even grab the address of the current message and alias it.

Processing Commands

Here are the principal mail handling commands available from **elm**'s main menu. Note that not all of them are listed at the bottom of the screen, but they are available nonetheless.

Command	Function
Return or *Space*	Views the current message.
Ctrl-L	Redraws screen contents.
`|<command>`	Pipes the message through the specified shell command.
`!<command>`	Executes the specified shell command.
`?`	Displays quick help for commands.

Continued

314

Command	Function
+	Advances to the next screenful of message summaries.
-	Advances to the previous screenful of message summaries.
=	Goes to the first message.
*	Goes to the last message.
/\<pattern\>	Searches for the next occurrence of **pattern** in message headers.
//\<pattern\>	Searches all messages for **pattern**.
a	Enters alias mode.
b	Bounces the current message on to someone else - like **forward**, except that the message retains the original sender's address.
c	Changes the mail folder.
d	Deletes the current message.
f	Forwards message.
g	Group reply - replies to originator and all recipients.
h	Views message with header fields.
H	Turns off help.
j	Goes to the next message.
k	Goes to previous message.
m	Composes a message.
n	Views the current message and then advance to the next message that isn't marked for deletion.
o	Goes to the Options page.
p	Prints out the current message.
q	Quits **elm**.
r	Replies to the originator of the current message.
s	Saves the current message to a folder file.

Editing Commands

The **elm** native editing mode is essentially the same as the **mail** message editor. Note that most of the time, however, **elm** is preconfigured to use an external visual editor for message editing. To see which editor you are using, run **elm** and press the *O* key to see the options. If the primary editor is set to 'built-in', then you are using the **mail** editor. You can also use the Options page to change the editor to your favorite one.

pine

pine is the vanguard IMAP MUA (we'll discuss IMAP later in this chapter). Aside from its IMAP compatibility, **pine** has gained popularity through its sheer ease-of-use. It has a full-screen, menu-driven user-interface, which makes it particularly friendly to first-time e-mail users. It's one of the only MUAs with a built-in spell-checker, and many commercial Internet providers configure **pine** as the default MUA for their customers.

One of the other advantages of **pine** is that it barely needs any documentation - all the commands are displayed in menus at the bottom of the screen and there is extensive online help too.

Checking Your Mailbox

When you first run **pine**, you aren't presented with a summary of the contents of your inbox, as you are with most other MUAs. Instead, you are shown the main **pine** menu, which lists the commands that you can choose from:

```
PINE 3.89    MAIN MENU                        Folder: INBOX   64 Messages


        ?    HELP                  -  Get help using Pine

        C    COMPOSE MESSAGE       -  Compose and send a message

        I    FOLDER INDEX          -  View messages in current folder

        L    FOLDER LIST           -  Select a folder to view

        A    ADDRESS BOOK          -  Update address book

        S    SETUP                 -  Configure or update Pine

        Q    QUIT                  -  Exit the Pine program



    Copyright 1989-93. PINE is a trademark of the University of Washington.
              [Folder "INBOX" opened with 64 messages]
? Help                       P PrevCmd                     R RelNotes
O OTHER CMDS L [ListFldrs] N NextCmd                       K KBLock
```

Your inbox folder is already open by default, so if you want to view its contents then just press the *I* key:

```
PINE 3.89    FOLDER INDEX              Folder: INBOX   Message 3 of 7 NEW

+    1  Dec 21 Aaron Walker       (2,402) Party!
+ A  2  Dec 21 Gregory Ross       (1,721) Re: Desert Island Electronics
  N  3  Dec 21 Jim Reardon        (1,560) Re: Desert Island Electronics
+ N  4  Dec 21 Charlie Chuck      (3,689) One Eyed Dog?
+ N  5  Dec 22 Garry Knox         (3,127) Hey dude
  N  6  Dec 22 Cindy Tobias       (1,992) Help w/Recipe
+ N  7  Dec 22 Barbara Zimmerman  (2,719) Re: Holiday schedule








? Help      M Main Menu  P PrevMsg    - PrevPage  D Delete    R Reply
O OTHER     V [ViewMsg]  N NextMsg   Spc NextPage U Undelete  F Forward
```

This screen tells you that the inbox folder is open and that the current message (the one highlighted) is message 3, a new message from **Mr. Reardon**. Each message summary line contains the following information:

- Message status - either **N** (new message), **A** (answered message), **<nothing>** (read message) or **D** (deleted message).

- Message number (for reference by other commands within **pine**).

- Date received.

- Sender.

- Size of message, in characters.

- Subject line of message.

A '**+**' as the first character of the message summary line indicates that the message was addressed directly to you (i.e. you didn't receive it as the result of a carbon copy).

Retrieving Messages

To view the current message, press either *V* or *Return*. You'll be shown the message in a full-screen viewing mode, with many of the Main Menu and Folder Index options still active. To go to the next message, press the *N* key. To go to the previous message, press *P*. While viewing a message, to go to the next screenful of text, press *Space*. To go back a screenful, press the '-' key.

Composing Messages

pine is one of the only MUAs to come with its own full-screen text editor for composing messages. The **pine** editor is called **pico** and will run independently of **pine**. You can also tell **pine** to use a different editor, but many **pine** users are pretty content to use **pico**.

To Compose a New Message

Choose the Compose Message command (*C*) from the Main Menu. Then **pine** will place you in the **pico** editor, ready for you to fill in the message header fields. **pine** segregates the header fields from the rest of the message text and manages their formats for you, but you are free to edit them at any time during your message editing session.

To Reply to a Message You've Received

Go to the Folder Index screen and select the message you want to reply to. Then choose the Reply (R) menu item from the Folder Index menu. The **pine** system will ask you if you want to include the text of the original message in your reply and, if there was more than one recipient of the original message, **pine** will ask if you want to reply to all the recipients or just to the sender. Then you'll edit your message in the **pico** editor.

When you are done editing your message, you can send it by pressing *Ctrl-X*, or you can abandon it by pressing *Ctrl-C*. These options are listed at the bottom of the message editor screen.

Attachments and Inclusions

Unlike the other MUAs discussed here, **pine** fully supports attachments and multipart mail and is fully MIME-compatible. With MIME though, the recipient also needs a MIME MUA - this restriction doesn't apply with **uuencode**. Adding a simple attachment to a **pine** message is easy - there is a header field for specifying a file to attach. Just fill in the file path of the file to be attached and **pine** does the rest.

When you receive a message with attachments, you can view them when you read the message by pressing the *V* key (view attachments). Then **pine** will ask which attachment you wish to view and whether you wish to view it directly or simply save it to a file in your home directory. For a binary attachment (predominantly used for code), you'll want to just save it to a file.

The Address Book - Better Aliases

pine has a built-in subsystem for managing aliases, called the **address book**. To access your **pine** address book, choose A from the **pine** Main Menu. From there you can add or delete aliases using a full-screen command interface.

The **pine** system lets you use the address book to address your mail - when editing a header field that requires an address, type *Ctrl-T* to immediately open your address book. From there you can browse through your addresses and select the one you want. When you've selected the address, **pine** puts you back in the editor where you left off.

When you are reading mail and you come across a message from someone whose address you want to save, you can press *T* to enter it into your address book.

Processing Commands

In **pine**, the commands available change depending on what screen activity you're conducting. Some commands are always available, others are available in more than one place and some are specific to one function alone. This sounds quite confusing, but remember that the available commands are always listed at the bottom of the screen.

Global Commands

?	Help.
C	Compose a message.
G	Go to (open) a folder.
I	Go to the Folder Index screen.
L	List available mail folders.
M	Go to Main Menu.
O	List other available commands.
Q	Quit **pine**.

Folder Index Commands

-	Go to the previous page of messages.
<Space>	Go to the next page of messages.
J	Jump to a specified message.
N	Go to next message.
P	Go to previous message.

Message Text (Reading) Commands

\<Space\>	Go to the next page of message text.
-	Go to the previous page of message text.
V	View or save attachment.
W	Search for a word in the message.

Folder Index and Message Text Mode Command

|	Pipe the message through a UNIX action command.
D	Delete the message.
E	Export the message to a text file.
F	Forward the message to someone else.
R	Reply to the message.
S	Save the message to a folder.
T	Take the address and store it in the address book.
U	Undelete the message.
Y	Print the current message.

Address Book Commands

-	Go to the previous page of entries.
\<Space\>	Go to next page of entries.
A	Add a simple entry.
D	Delete an entry.
E	Edit an entry.
N	Go to the next entry.

P	Go to the previous entry.
S	Add a list entry (alias for multiple addresses).
W	Find a word in entries.
Z	Append to an existing list.

Editing Commands (pico)

Ctrl-A	Move the cursor to the beginning of the current line.
Ctrl-B	Move the cursor back one character.
Ctrl-C	Cancel the message.
Ctrl-D	Delete the current character.
Ctrl-E	Move the cursor to the end of the current line.
Ctrl-F	Move the cursor forward one character.
Ctrl-G	Help.
Ctrl-H	Delete the character before the cursor.
Ctrl-J	Justify the paragraph.
Ctrl-K	Cut the selected text line(s).
Ctrl-L	Redraw the screen.
Ctrl-N	Move the cursor on to the next line.
Ctrl-P	Move the cursor to previous line.
Ctrl-R	Read a file into the message text at the cursor.
Ctrl-T *(in message text)*	Run the spell-checker.
Ctrl-T *(in header)*	Go to the address book.
Ctrl-U	Paste the last cut text at cursor.
Ctrl-V	Move the cursor down one screenful of text.

Ctrl-W	Search for a word in message.
Ctrl-X	Send the message.
Ctrl-Y	Move the cursor up one screenful of text.
Ctrl-Z	Suspend the editing of the message, saving the draft message.
Ctrl-_	Invoke an alternative text editor.
Ctrl-<space>	Move the cursor on to the next word.
*Ctrl-^*	Mark the text.

MH and xmh

MH (Message Handler) is a flexible mail system distributed by the University of California. At first glance, **MH** appears like the standard **mail** program, divided into several subprograms. However, **MH** is one of the most powerful MUAs available. What **MH** lacks in user-friendliness, it makes up for in flexibility. For example, **MH** is the one of the only MUAs that really lends itself to being embedded in UNIX shell scripts for automatic mail processing.

Checking Your Mailbox

To see if any mail is waiting for you, run the **MH** subprogram **inc** from the shell command line. The **inc** program copies mail from your system mailbox (managed for you by the mail system) to a file in your account called **inbox**. If there is mail waiting for you, then **inc** will print out something like this:

```
Incorporating new mail into inbox...

   1+ 12/20 Garry Knox        Hey!
   2  12/21 Aaron Walker      The meaning of life
   3  12/21 pwoods            Meeting tomorrow?
```

This tells you that three messages are waiting in your inbox. The messages appear in the order in which they were received (the latest is number **3**). This one-line message summary shows:

- The message number.
- The current message (marked with a '+').
- The date the message was received.
- The sender.
- The subject line.

scan

Another useful **MH** subprogram is **scan**, which displays the entire contents of your mailbox, not just the new mail, in the same format as **inc**.

Retrieving Messages

To view your mail with **MH**, you will use three subprograms - **show**, **next** and **prev**. To view the current message, type **show** at the shell prompt. To view the message after the current message (and advance the current-message pointer), type **next**. To show the previous message, type **prev** and the text of the message will be printed to the standard output.

Composing Messages

To compose a new message, run the **comp** subprogram. The **comp** program will prompt you for each header field, then let you edit the text of your message. If **MH** is configured to run an external editor, you'll wind up composing the message with that.

To reply to a message that was sent to you, run the **repl** subprogram. If you run it without any arguments, you'll be replying to the current message. You can pass a message number if you want to reply to a different one. It fills in the To: and Subject: header fields for you and then lets you edit your message, just like **comp**.

When you're done editing the message, exit the editor (if you're using the default **MH** editor, then you can type *Ctrl-D*) and you'll see the **comp** 'What now?' prompt. Some valid options are:

Command	Shortcut	Action
edit	**e**	Returns to editing the message. You can specify an editor to use.
list	**l**	Lists out the whole message on the screen.
quit	**q**	Exits **comp**, but leaves your draft message for later editing. If you specify **q -delete**, then the draft message is discarded.
send	**s**	Sends the message.
whom	**w**	Shows to whom the mail is addressed. If you specify **w -check**, then **comp** actually checks to see if the mail is deliverable.

Attachments and Inclusions

MH is like **mail** in that it provides no direct support for attachments or inclusions - if you want them, then you have to process them yourself. Since **MH** is so open and flexible, it's fairly easy to integrate it with an add-on **MIME** processor like **metamail** to handle complex messages - you just write a shell script or two.

Aliases

You can define aliases for **MH** in a text file in your **MH** directory (usually called **mail**). The file is usually called **aliases**. To make sure that **MH** is using your **aliases** file, check that this line appears in your .mh_profile file:

```
Aliasfile: aliases
```

Aliases in **MH** take this format:

```
<aliasname>: <addr1>[,<addr2>, ... <addrn>]
```

For example, to make a simple alias for our friend Jim, we would add the following line to our **aliases** file:

```
jimb: Jim_Broomfield@software.xxx.com
```

Group Aliasing

To make an alias for a group of addresses, just list them, separated by commas:

```
greatguys: gknox@turtle.asdg.umd.edu, pwoods@wrox.com, jimb
```

Note that **MH** aliases can be freely nested - that's why it's okay to use **jimb** in the **greatguys** alias.

ali

The **MH** subprogram **ali** helps you browse your aliases. Running **ali** with no arguments lists all your aliases. Passing it an alias as an argument displays the addresses that belong to the alias. Running **ali** with the **-user** argument and an address lists all the aliases to which the address belongs - a very useful feature.

Processing Commands

MH is really a set of subprograms and not a command environment. Here are some of the subprograms and what they do:

ali	Browse your mail aliases.
comp	Compose a message.
inc	Incorporate new mail into the inbox.
next	View the next message in the inbox.
prev	View the previous message in the inbox.
repl	Reply to a message.
rmm	Delete messages.
scan	List the contents of the mailbox.
show	View the current message in the inbox.

Mail Editing Commands

The default editor for **MH** is a program called **prompter** that makes the **mail** editor look advanced. There really aren't any commands to document for **prompter**, except *Ctrl-D*, which exits it. You will rarely see **prompter** in use anymore - instead, **MH** is usually configured to use a visual editor like **vi** or **emacs**. If for some reason you're still getting **prompter** as your editor in **MH**, check the file *.mh_profile* in your home directory. It should contain a line like:

```
Editor: vi
```

If not **vi**, then some other reasonable editor should be specified here. If no such line appears, add one for your favorite editor.

xmh

This isn't really an MUA in itself - it is more a front-end for **MH**. In order for you to use **xmh**, you must first have installed and configured **MH**. The **xmh** system is merely an X Windows-based shell that makes it easy for you to access your **MH** mailbox.

We've only just touched on the most basic features of **MH** in this whirlwind tour; if you're interested in doing anything more complex with **MH**, consult the program documentation.

Forwarding with .forward

Finally, a note about UNIX mail forwarding, which is an MTA function and thus not specific to any one MUA.

Simple Forwarding

When you move from one house to another, you can tell the Post Office to forward your mail to you for a period of time after you move. There is a similar facility for your e-mail, if your system is using a **sendmail** MTA. If you move to a new job, or a different department, and your previous system administrator is cooperative, then you can set up the forwarding of your e-mail to smooth over the transition to your new e-mail address.

In the home directory of your old account, create a file called `.forward` and place your new forwarding address in it. You can provide a comma-separated list of addresses if you want to forward to more than one address. If you want to keep copies of the forwarded mail on the old machine (normally you wouldn't), you can add it to the list, preceded by a '\'.

For example, if a `.forward` file contains the following:

```
aevans@wrox.com
```

then all mail going to the account where the `.forward` file resides would be automatically forwarded to **aevans@wrox.com** and wouldn't be held in the forwarding account.

If the `.forward` file contains the following and the forwarding account is '**andy**':

```
\andy,aevans@wrox.com
```

then mail would be forwarded to **aevans@wrox.com** and would be retained in the '**andy**' account on the forwarding machine.

Vacation Forwarding

On some UNIX systems, such as SunOs, there is another use of forwarding. This is vacation forwarding, which is for automatically notifying those who send you e-mail that you are on vacation and unable to respond immediately. That way, they won't think you're ignoring them, and you can give information on who else they can contact in your absence.

Setting Up a Vacation Forward

Create a file in your home directory called `.vacation.msg` and put in it a suitable e-mail message to send to your would-be correspondents. You'll need to include the basic header information (minus the 'To:' line) in addition to the message text. For example, your `.vacation.msg` file might contain:

```
From: aevans@wrox.com
Subject: I'm on vacation!

I'm away from my desk right now, sipping a cool drink on the beach.  I'll
drop you a line in person when I return, at the end of January.  Until
then, you'll have to put up with this lousy automated message.

Cheers,
Andy
```

Run **vacation** with the **-i** option to initialize the vacation database:

```
$ vacation -i
```

Set up the .**forward** file to invoke the **vacation** program when you receive mail. You'll usually want to keep the messages that get handled this way, so you can see them when you return, so be sure to add your local user id. For instance, if you were the user **aevans**, your .**forward** file would contain:

```
\aevans,"vacation"
```

When you return from vacation, be sure to delete your .**forward** file.

An additional note about vacation processing - if you have subscribed to any mailing lists, it isn't recommended that you use a vacation forward! Either unsubscribe during your vacation, or don't use a vacation forward at all.

Mail Standards

SMTP (the Simple Mail Transport Protocol) has been the standard mail protocol for UNIX systems since its introduction in the 1970's, largely due to the fact that virtually every copy of UNIX shipped includes support for it. This doesn't mean that it has a monopoly though; there are many other rival mail systems about. We will now discuss the merits of SMTP and its major competitors.

SMTP

As its name implies, SMTP is indeed simple - it's very concise and fairly straightforward, making it extremely portable to new platforms. Also, SMTP is built on top of (and independent from) the underlying network protocol, further improving its portability. Because of this portability and widespread availability, SMTP quickly became established as the mail standard for the UNIX-dominated Internet.

There are problems with SMTP, however. Mail sent via SMTP must be monolithic - in other words, it can have only one part. An SMTP mail message is just a block of text - in fact, SMTP is only suited for transporting text-based documents. Since it's designed to be simple and portable, it makes use of 7-bit ASCII text (the 'least common denominator' for data communication), making it unsuitable for moving raw binary data, such as images, program code and audio, for example. To get around this limitation, binary data must be encoded into printable 7-bit ASCII and inserted into the text of a mail message, as we discussed earlier with **uuencode**.

MIME

The MIME standard operates on top of conventional 7-bit SMTP, so the current infrastructure of the Internet (and your host system) needn't be changed to accommodate it. MIME provides the following:

Multiple content types	MIME breaks the text-only limitation to allow a variety of message formats, including audio and video.
Multipart messages mail	MIME messages can have any number of parts.
Greater interoperbility X.400	The standards for MIME were drafted with the cooperation of the X.400 community, so great care was taken to make MIME and X.400 gateways as seamless as possible.

MIME Message Content types

The MIME standard explicitly defines seven major types of message content: text, audio, image, video, message, multipart and application. Future content types must be added as sub-types of one of these standards. For instance, one sub-type of 'text' for formatted-text messages is 'richtext' (with fonts, bolding, underlining, etc.).

The reason for this strict adherence to seven basic types with all new type definitions as sub-types is that, if a mail reader defines a way to handle the general basic type, it is more likely to be able to handle mail of an unrecognized subtype.

X.400

X.400 was introduced in 1984 in order to provide a better transport protocol for mail that would support all kinds of documents, including binary files. Many PC mail vendors are scrambling to support X.400, but it isn't yet gaining widespread support in the UNIX world, where SMTP is still dominant. As a UNIX system administrator, you will probably only use X.400 via a gateway (see the next section) rather than as a native protocol.

Why hasn't X.400 taken the e-mail world by storm? Despite the fact that X.400 supports raw binary attachments, many vendors have adopted proprietary extensions to support them, thus defeating the 'standard' nature of that part of X.400. Also, it has proved very complex - complex to implement and complex to use. Users frequently have trouble addressing their mail because the addressing scheme differs from system to system. With the advent of MIME, UNIX systems (and the Internet) will probably remain committed to SMTP.

The X.400 standard (which we will examine shortly) leap-frogged SMTP in this area and, as a consequence, X.400 mail loses its multimedia content when gatewayed to old SMTP systems.

E-mail Gateways

X.400 and SMTP aren't the only mail transports in use. There are many other e-mail protocols and most of them are closed and proprietary. For instance, most of the principal online services - America Online,

CompuServe and GEnie, to name but a few - have their own mail system. Many corporations with PC networks use proprietary mail systems that aren't compatible with SMTP. What do you do if you want to send e-mail to users who aren't connected to the Internet directly?

You have to go through an **e-mail gateway**. A gateway is a machine that 'speaks' more than one mail protocol, is connected to multiple mail systems and knows how to redirect and route mail from one mail system to another. In order for you to send mail to a user on another mail system, there must be a gateway somewhere between the Internet and the other system. When you drive a car on the highway, you can't switch roads unless there is an intersection. An e-mail gateway is an intersection between two mail highways.

Many gateways exist between the Internet and other mail systems. To use those gateways, you need to know how to address your Internet mail in order for it to go through the gateway and reach its destination. Here are a few useful gateways and how to use them:

Destination	Example user id	You would use
America Online	The Sponge	`thesponge@aol.com`
AT&T Mail	user	`user@attmail.com`
BIX	user	`user@bix.com`
CompuServe	70772,744	`70772.744@compuserve.com`
GEnie	user	`user@genie.geis.com`
MCI Mail	John Smith (555-1234)	`John_Smith/` `5551234@mcimail.com`
Prodigy	abcd01a	`abcd01a@prodigy.com`

Sprint Mail	Jane Doe at XYZCorp	`/G=Jane/S=Doe/O=XYZCorp/`
		`ADMD=TELEMAIL/C=US/`
		`@sprint.com` (note that this is an X.400 gateway)

Remote Mail Access

It's becoming increasingly common these days for people to want to read electronic mail from multiple physical locations. For instance, let's say you have an account on a UNIX machine that serves as your principal Internet e-mail account. You check your mail from your desktop PC at work periodically, and you'd like to be able to check it remotely from your home computer, or from a laptop on the road every now and again.

One solution is to **telnet** or direct-dial into the UNIX system from these machines and use a UNIX shell-hosted MUA to read your mail. This is called an 'online' mail approach and has several key disadvantages with respect to an 'offline' approach.

- In the online approach, you must be connected to the remote host during your entire mail session, which could get quite expensive if you frequently check your mail via long-distance telephone connections.

- It doesn't allow you to make use of the growing number of native PC-based MUAs, which offer interoperability with other PC application software and improved user-interfaces.

- This approach may severely limit your ability to take advantage of MIME attachments, since you won't be able to transport the contents of non-text message documents to your remote machine very easily.

Offline Mail Readers

A better solution is an 'offline' mail approach, in which you use an **offline mail reader** program on your remote PC instead of gaining direct UNIX shell access to the mail host for the whole mail session. In general, an offline mail reader connects to your mail server host and block-transfers any mail to be read from the server and any mail to be sent from your remote machine. You compose and review your mail from a native PC program rather than through the UNIX shell. Offline mail readers make use of one of a set of special protocols. The most common protocols are POP (Post Office Protocol) and IMAP (Internet Message Access Protocol).

POP

POP is the oldest and most widely used offline mail reader. Many POP-based remote mail readers are available for a variety of desktop computers, including IBM PC and Macintosh machines. Unfortunately, POP doesn't handle mail access from more than one remote point very well. It is designed to move mail from the host to the remote client, and then let the remote client handle the mail from there. So, if you check your mail from a POP-based offline reader at home but don't read all your mail, and then go into work and try to continue reading mail, you won't see any of the unread messages still sitting on your home machine.

The latest POP version, POP3, provides the ability to leave mail on the server, but POP clients must still move copies of the mail to the remote client. This leaves the user with the task of cleaning up read messages. So, POP only provides a partial solution to remote mail access - IMAP is the only mail protocol that properly supports remote mail access from more than one place, with truly only one copy of all mail on the server. Some successful POP mail readers on the PC and Macintosh platforms are RFD-Mail, Eudora and Pegasus Mail.

IMAP

IMAP is a newer and much more capable offline mail reader. It's specifically designed to address the problem of remote mail access from multiple locations, taking a Client/Server approach to mail access. Rather than moving all mail en masse to the remote machine for processing, IMAP leaves the mail on the server.

The remote machine may update the status of the mail on the server (mark it as read, delete it, etc.) but never actually takes ownership of mail. This gives equal access to the mail from any IMAP mail reader you want to use anywhere, including your old stand-by UNIX shell MUA. The only real disadvantage to IMAP is the limited availability of IMAP-capable mail readers - there are only two, although others are appearing on the horizon. As we noted earlier, the **pine** mail program supports IMAP.

Configuring the Mail System

It's unusual for a system administrator to have to alter the basic configuration of the mail system, but here are a few mail configuration tips anyway.

Setting up the MTA

In a **sendmail**-based SMTP mail environment, if you want to set up **mail**, you need to make sure that the **sendmail** daemon is being run in your **/etc/rc** script and in daemon mode (with the **-bd** option). You'll also want to set the mail update interval using the **-q** option (typically, this is set to something like **-q30m**, meaning that mail will be collected on the system, every 30 minutes). So, you should see a line in **/etc/rc** that looks something like this:

```
sendmail -bd -q30m
```

Unless you have unusual or highly specialized needs, good old **sendmail**, as configured straight out-of-the-box, should be adequate.

Setting up the MUA

How you set up the MUA depends on which MUA you are using. Each one has its own unique installation procedure, which will be documented in the material accompanying the software distribution. Most of them have a well-tested, reasonably idiot-proof installation script that walks you step-by-step through the process (**elm**'s installation is an excellent example).

Summary

In this chapter, we looked at the basic structure of UNIX mail systems. We discussed how mail addressing works and how to use some of the more popular mail user-interfaces. Next, we explored the various mail standards and protocols that are currently in use, and finally we discussed the configuration of UNIX mail systems. Now let's move on from rudimentary Internet access and investigate some of the more exciting ventures on the information superhighway.

Chapter

The Internet

The Internet is easily accessible from a UNIX platform, and there are many UNIX and X Windows applications available on the Internet, most of them at little or no cost.

The UNIX system is very popular with many Internet Service providers due to the robust, multitasking, multi-user environment and all the integrated networking services. Since UNIX is also available on a wide range of platforms, it's a very flexible and popular solution.

The Internet was largely developed using UNIX-based computers and many of its services are actually hosted on UNIX machines. UNIX and the Internet are inextricably linked and are likely to remain so for a long time.

The route we will take for this chapter is:

- The origins of the Internet
- Connecting to the Internet
- Basic Internet services
- The World Wide Web
- Other Internet services
- Finding more information

What is the Internet?

The Internet isn't a single network - it's a truly global network of networks, interconnected using the TCP/IP protocols. Typical sites include government departments, educational establishments, businesses, other organizations and commercial on-line systems like Compuserve and Delphi. The Internet is used for a variety of purposes including e-mail, file transfer, information, participating in discussions and social purposes.

The Internet is being used by all kinds of people, no longer just scientists, academics and computer enthusiasts. Most people initially use the Internet to send and receive electronic mail, but may soon become involved in other aspects. You can participate in discussion forums on thousands of subjects by joining Usenet newsgroups - an excellent way of gathering information on a subject.

Who Runs the Internet?

The Internet has no central control; it's run by co-operation, devolved responsibility and mutual agreement between the operators of the many different networks it is comprised of.

All this is co-ordinated by two 'heavyweight' providers, AT&T and Network Solutions Incorporated. Together they make up the InterNIC.

> **InterNIC is an Information service for Directory, Database and Registration Services, provided by AT&T and Network Solutions, partially supported through a co-operative agreement with the National Science Foundation.**

This is perhaps the closest thing that the Internet has to a central controlling authority. There are also various working parties, such as the Internet Engineering Task Force that help define standards. These standards are necessary to enable all the disparate machines connected to the Internet to run interactively.

The Origins of the Internet

The Internet has its beginnings in the late 1960's when the (US) Defense Advanced Research Project Agency (DARPA) funded an experimental computer network called DARPANET (later renamed ARPANET). This was a great success and the original protocols evolved into the TCP/IP set that has become a standard for inter-network communication.

This fledgling network grew rapidly and, although the ARPANET has now ceased to exist, the Internet, as it's now known, continues to grow rapidly. The original ARPANET design aims, including resilience to network damage (such as that caused by a nuclear strike) have proved very successful in coping with a large and constantly changing network.

The Size of the Internet

This really is an unknown quantity. Since the Internet is managed by co-operation there is no central registry of users, or even of individual machines. Many surveys have tried to assess the total number of people connected to the Internet and the answer depends on your definition of 'connected'. Some approximate estimates for the different levels of connectivity at the end of 1994 are as follows:

- The strictest definition of 'connected' is people having an account on a machine that has a permanent TCP/IP link into the Internet. This numbers 8 million people.

- In addition, there are those with part-time access to interactive Internet services - about 14 million people.

- Finally, there are those who exchange mail with Internet users, and subscribe to non-interactive services by mail. A grand total of 30 million people.

An Internet Connection

Internet connections are either permanent or part-time depending on the organization or network being connected. Each network passes traffic bound for other networks without delay or charge. This 'peering' is what makes the Internet such a valuable and useful resource.

Individuals and smaller organizations may connect to the Internet via a dial-up link to a service provider. This can be achieved with a simple modem connection and some low-cost (or even free) software.

Medium size companies may choose to connect their local network to the Internet via a service provider and a gateway (otherwise known as a firewall - see the chapter on security). Here, all users on the internal network gain access to Internet facilities, but outsiders cannot gain access to internal systems. A small UNIX system is ideal in this situation as it provides an excellent multitasking environment to support the required servers.

Domain Naming

All Internet connected systems have a host name and a domain name. The host name identifies the system within its own network, while the domain name identifies the network itself. For Internet traffic to be routed to the correct location, these domain names have to be widely known. This is where the Domain Name Service (DNS) comes into its own, providing a mapping from these host and domain names to low-level IP addresses.

Internet service providers and larger organizations maintain DNS servers to perform this very function. They will refer to other servers if necessary, moving up the hierarchy which has the InterNIC root name servers at the top. Each domain must be registered with these root servers. Service providers usually register their own domain and can arrange for you to have your own, although most individuals will use the service provider's domain.

For example, a service provider might have a domain, say **provider.com**. A dial-up subscriber will be assigned the host name **subscriber.provider.com**. All traffic bound for this host will be directed, by use of the DNS, to the service provider's machines. Other service providers offer accounts on their machine, often a UNIX host, so the above subscriber would become **subscriber@provider.com**.

Larger organizations may wish to register their own domain name, either through a service provider or directly with InterNIC, so they can use Internet addresses of the form **mycompany.com** or **mycompany.co.uk**.

TCP/IP Services

There are many different services that can be supported by TCP/IP protocols. The following are some of the most important services available across the Internet:

Telnet	Remote terminal access
ftp	File transfer protocol
Usenet	Newsgroups
WWW	The World Wide Web
E-mail	Electronic mail

We discussed e-mail in Chapter 10. The others we'll discuss here.

The two most basic TCP/IP networking applications are **telnet** and **ftp**. They are pretty much guaranteed to be found on any system configured for TCP/IP networking.

telnet

The **telnet** service provides access to remote terminal sessions across the network. It uses its own protocol to manage the connection; the remote machine must be running the **telnet** protocol daemon, **telnetd**, in order to be reachable by **telnet**. This daemon uses the pseudo-terminals to emulate local terminal logins on the remote system.

When a **telnet** connection is established, the session proceeds as if the **telnet** client is connected to a local terminal on the remote machine. Typically, **telnet** is invoked with the hostname or the IP address of the remote system as an argument. The first example will work if the hostname, **andromeda**, is in the host file or if DNS is used:

```
$ telnet andromeda.cpsi.com
```

The alternative is to use the numeric IP address like this:

```
$ telnet 128.8.49.19
```

ftp

The **ftp** service provides a simple means of transferring files from one machine to another over a TCP/IP network. The **ftp** program is actually named after the underlying protocol it uses - the File Transfer Protocol. This protocol is implemented by the **ftp** program on the client, and the **ftpd** daemon on the server. An **ftp** session is established by running **ftp** with the hostname or IP address of the desired server as an argument:

```
$ ftp andromeda.cpsi.com
```

or

```
$ ftp 128.8.49.19
```

Commands

The **ftp** program then requests user authentication on the remote system. If successful, you will be presented with a new command-line that accepts a number of file-handling commands:

ascii	Transfer data as ASCII text.
bin	Transfer data as raw binary data (important when local and remote systems treat binary data differently).
cd	Change to a different directory on the server.
close	Close the connection to the remote server, but don't quit **ftp**.
del	Delete a file on the server.
get	Retrieve a file from the server.
hash	Print **#** marks as data is received.
lcd	Change to a new directory on the local machine.

`ls`	List files on the server machine.
`mget`	Retrieve multiple files from the server.
`open`	Open a new connection to a remote server.
`prompt`	Toggle the confirmation message off/on during `mget` transfer.
`put`	Move a file from the local machine to the server.
`pwd`	Display the current working directory on the server.
`quit`	Terminate the `ftp` session.
`!<command>`	Execute the shell command `<command>` on the local machine.

Anonymous ftp

Some sites offer publicly available files that can be reached via **anonymous ftp**. To access the anonymous `ftp` area at a site, connect to it with the `ftp` program and log in with the userid **anonymous**, using your e-mail address as the password. You will then be connected to the public file area of that site. These `ftp` sites typically offer you public domain software that you can download onto your system. Here's a transcript of a typical anonymous `ftp` session, where we shall retrieve a file called **tripwire-1.2** from the **cert.org** server:

```
% ftp cert.org
Connected to cert.org.
220 cert.org FTP server (Version wu-2.4(1) Mon Apr 3 16:53:11 EDT 1995)
ready.
Name (cert.org:aevans): anonymous
331 Guest login ok, send your complete e-mail address as password.
Password:
230-CERT Coordination Center FTP server.
230-
230-Note:
230-If your FTP client crashes or hangs shortly after login, try
230-using a hyphen (-) as the first character of your password.
230-This will turn off the informational messages, which may be
230-confusing your FTP client.
230-
230 Guest login ok, access restrictions apply.
Remote system type is UNIX.
Using binary mode to transfer files.
ftp> cd /pub/tools/tripwire
250 CWD command successful.
```

```
ftp> ls
200 PORT command successful.
150 Opening ASCII mode data connection for /bin/ls.
total 466
-rw-r--r--  1 cert      cert        462187 Nov 15  1994 tripwire-1.2.tar.Z
drwxrwxr-x  2 cert      cert           512 Sep 10  1993 tripwire1.0.4
drwxr-xr-x  3 cert      cert           512 Dec 21  1993 tripwire1.1
226 Transfer complete.
ftp> get tripwire-1.2.tar.Z
200 PORT command successful.
150 Opening BINARY mode data connection for tripwire-1.2.tar.Z (462187
bytes).
226 Transfer complete.
462187 bytes received in 17 seconds (27 Kbytes/s)
ftp> quit
221 Goodbye.
%
```

The file **tripwire-1.2.tar.Z** has now been copied to the current directory of the local machine. In Chapter 12, we will discuss the role that CERT plays in enhancing the security of your UNIX system.

File Types

The **.TAR** file extension indicates that this is a UNIX **TAR** archive file, and the **.Z** extension further indicates that it has been compressed with the **compress** program. A **.GZ** extension, also quite common, would indicate that **gzip** was used to compress it. To extract the files from the downloaded archive, we'll first have to decompress it, like this:

```
%uncompress tripwire-1.2.tar.Z
```

Then we'll need to extract the archive:

```
%tar xvf tripwire-1.2.tar
```

This expands the archive, recreating the directory tree within it. Notice that we didn't need the **.Z** extension this time - **uncompress** removed it. If the transfer was successful, the software should be ready to use.

If the file has been compressed using the **gzip** compression program (if it has a **.gz** extension), the syntax of the command with which we need to decompress it is:

```
gzip  -d  <filename>
```

Tips for ftp Transfer

When transferring files, it's worth bearing the following points in mind:

- Before you transfer a large number of files, use **prompt** to disable the confirmation messages, otherwise you will have the time-consuming task of having to confirm the transfer of every file.

- Always remember to type **bin** (binary mode) when transferring executables or compressed files.

- Type **hash** before a large transfer if you wish to check throughout the transfer that the transaction is progressing.

- Finally, if you wish to make a rough estimate of how long the transfer will take, open up another window and use the **ls** command to see how much of the file has been transferred into your account, as compared to how long it has taken so far. (Before a transfer begins the total size of the file is given in bytes.)

Setting Up Your Own Site

You may well wish to set up an **ftp** site on your own system so that you can freely distribute information and software, without having to manually send it each time someone outside your system requires it. In UNIX, setting up an anonymous **ftp** server is easy.

First you need to create a non-privileged user, called **ftp**. You need to make an entry in **/etc/passwd** (or shadow password files or NIS maps) such as:

```
ftp:*:404:1::/home/ftp:/bin/sh
```

Notice that the user **ftp** doesn't need to be able to log in directly - the asterisk in the password field prevents this. The **ftp** server will accept 'anonymous' as a login name.

Configuring Your Home Directory

The home directory of the anonymous **ftp** account is also quite simple to create, but remember - it needs to contain everything that the remote user will need. This is because the **ftp** server will restrict the incoming connection so that it only has access to this directory - it won't be possible for remote users to access any other part of your system. A typical home directory contains the following:

pub/	A sub-directory for downloadable files.
bin/ls	A copy of the **ls** program.
lib/*	Any files needed to run **/bin/ls** (shared libraries).
etc/passwd	A dummy password file for user names in **ls** output.
etc/group	A dummy group file for user groups in **ls** output.
incoming/	A directory for user uploads.

Ports

There are two entries for **ftp** in the **/etc/services** file to define the ports used:

ftp-data	**20/tcp**
ftp	**21/tcp**

The **ftp-data** port is used for sending the data during file transfer, whilst the server program, **ftp**, is usually run as a service by the 'Internet superserver', **inetd**. An entry in the **/etc/inetd.conf** file configures **inetd** to start the **ftp** daemon, **ftpd**, when a connection request is made to the **ftp** port.

```
ftp     stream  tcp  nowait  root    /usr/sbin/tcpd  /usr/sbin/
in.ftpd
```

ftp Servers

Suitable **ftp** servers are bundled with many UNIX systems. A popular one, and one which is freely available, is the WU Archive **ftp** daemon as used on the major Internet **ftp** archive **wuarchive.wustl.edu**. It's available from:

```
ftp://wuarchive.wustl.edu:/packages/wuarchive-ftpd/wu-ftpd-
2.4.tar.Z
```

One drawback of **ftp** is that it can be very time-consuming. Logging in to an **ftp** site on the other side of the world carries large time overheads. It can sometimes be several minutes before you get a response to your requests. Your task isn't simplified by the fact that many archives are very large and you need to know where to look for your desired product.

archie

Help is at hand though with another service called **archie**, which is a service for searching **ftp** archives. It's accessible either by **telnet** or by a dedicated client such as **xarchie** (for the X Window System). Each **archie** server maintains a database of files kept at anonymous **ftp** sites - you can query it to find out where you can download a particular file.

The following **telnet** session illustrates an **archie** enquiry. You log in as the special user, 'archie', and query the server. In this case, some of the login messages from the server system have been excised, but the user interaction is shown intact. We ask for archive sites with files that contain the string **gopher2.0** in their names.

```
$ telnet archie.doc.ic.ac.uk
Trying 146.169.17.5...
Connected to phoenix.doc.ic.ac.uk.
Escape character is '^]'.

                    The Archive  —  SunSITE Northern Europe
                    ──────────────────────────────

          SunSITE Northern Europe is located at the Department of Computing,
          Imperial College, London and is running on a SPARCserver 1000 with
          7 CPUs and 42 GB of disk space, kindly donated by Sun Microsystems

          To access Archie,        login as  archie
                                    no password
          To abandon this login, enter a control-D

sunsite.doc.ic.ac.uk (pts/9)  8:35PM on Thursday, 25 May 1995
login: archie
```

```
          Welcome to the SUNSite, Department of Computing, Imperial College, UK
                This is the UKUUG supported archie service.

# Terminal type set to 'dumb 24 80'.
# 'erase' character is '^?'.
# 'search' (type string) has the value 'sub'.
archie.doc.ic.ac.uk> set maxhits 2
archie.doc.ic.ac.uk> prog gopher2.0
# Search type: sub.
# Your queue position: 1
# Estimated time for completion: 8 seconds.
working... O

Host sunic.sunet.se     (192.36.125.2)
Last updated 03:09 26 Mar 1995

    Location: /pub/gopher/Unix
       FILE    -r-r-r-  426337 bytes  01:00 30 Jun 1994  gopher2.016.tar.Z

Host scitsc.wlv.ac.uk     (134.220.4.1)
Last updated 04:12 24 May 1995

    Location: /pub/ourapps
       FILE    -rw-r-r-  426337 bytes  00:00 16 Jun 1994  gopher2.016.tar.Z

archie.doc.ic.ac.uk> quit
$
```

The search type is **sub**, meaning substring, so we get files containing the
string **gopher2.0**, such as **gopher2.016.tar.Z**. The number of results, or hits,
is limited to two by the setting the **maxhits** variable. Some machines will
accept **archie** requests by e-mail, replying to your request with mail
containing the search results.

Efficiency

Although distance appears not to matter when fetching files across the
Internet, you should try and conserve bandwidth and resources. Many
popular sites are 'mirrored' at other locations. These mirror sites normally
maintain an automatically updated duplicate of the master site files. If you
find a mirror site closer to you than the main site, use it. It saves resources
on the main site and reduces the amount of Internet bandwidth you are
using. In addition, it is usually much quicker to fetch a file from a local
mirror site.

Usenet

`ftp` sites are generally fairly static. They are updated, but one of their purposes is to provide exactly the same information or software over a period of time. If you want a more contemporary and changeable bank of information that will give you up-to-date information and discussion of and feedback on various topics, you will need to subscribe to a **newsgroup**. The most common source of newsgroups is **Usenet**, a set of newsgroups, over ten thousand currently, that are available on most Internet-connected machines. Each newsgroup has a name, such as `comp.lang.c++`, giving a clue to those discussions relevant to the group. They are arranged in the hierarchy implied by their names.

Many groups are used as self-help groups for users to lend each other technical assistance. The principal 'top-level' world-wide groups are **alt**, **comp**, **misc**, **news**, **rec**, **soc**, **sci**. In addition, there are other, smaller hierarchies such as **ieee** and **gnu**, as well as regional groups like **de** and **uk**, that serve more localised and specialized areas.

To access a newsgroup you use a newsreader, which will show you the discussions taking place in a newsgroup. The newsreader will also arrange for your postings to be sent to the newsgroup, usually via your service provider. At any one time there can be many different discussions taking place in a single newsgroup. Each separate message in a newsgroup is called a posting, and related postings are normally linked together in threads, so that discussions can be followed in a reasonably structured way.

Etiquette and FAQs

In most newsgroups people are free to post whatever they like - however, it's wise to read a group for several weeks before posting to ensure that your post is relevant to the newsgroup, and not what is known as an FAQ - a frequently asked question. Often there will be a regular posting of FAQs and their answers to help you acclimatize to the newsgroup. If you don't co-operate with the conventions of the newsgroup, you may well receive large amounts of e-mail informing you of the error of your ways. If bad-tempered, this is known as 'flaming'. Usenet only works because readers co-operate.

Some time ago, when a large group of users suddenly gained access to Usenet, many of them joined one of the first groups offered by their newsreader: **alt.best.of.internet**. This newsgroup is for people to re-post some of the most amusing Usenet posts they have seen on other newsgroups. Unfortunately, many of the new Usenet users immediately posted a large number of requests along the lines of 'what is the best XXXXX?'. This upset regular readers and resulted in a lot of flaming - all of which could have been avoided had they taken the trouble to find out what the group was for before posting.

> You can find an FAQ file for almost all newsgroups by anonymous FTP to **rtfm.mit.edu** (or one of its mirror sites) and looking in the directories under usenet-by-hierarchy, where there is a directory structure which mirrors the newsgroup hierarchy. For more information on FAQs, see the section later in this chapter.

A few newsgroups are moderated - only a single person, or small group of people, can post. These are commonly announcement newsgroups. A good way for a new user of Usenet to start is by reading newsgroups with the name 'newuser' in them, such as **news.announce.newuser**, and making your trial postings in a group ending in **.test**. The service provider may have a local testing group for this purpose.

Creating a New Group

One question frequently asked by new Usenet users is 'how do I create a new group?'. Given the large number of newsgroups, the short answer is that there is probably already a group relevant to your topic, it's just that you haven't found it yet. If there isn't a relevant group, and you are sure that you want to try and create one, then you should start by reading **news.groups** and **news.announce.newgroups**, where you will see new groups being discussed and voted upon.

The general procedure for creating a new newsgroup is that a Request For Discussion (RFD) is posted to **news.announce.newgroups** and any related newsgroups. The initial RFD must contain a 'charter', which describes the purpose of the intended newsgroup. Discussions then take place in the newsgroup **news.groups**. If discussion is generally favorable, then a Call For

Votes (CFV) is issued. Voting occurs by mailing a YES or NO response to a special e-mail address provided by a neutral third party. A vote normally lasts for about three weeks, during which time a reminder CFV may be posted. At the end of the voting period the results (including voters' e-mail addresses and how they voted) are posted in the newsgroup **news.announce.newgroups**.

A 'yes' vote is normally considered to be one where at least 100 more people voted yes than voted no, and at least 2/3 of the total votes yes. If no objections are raised to the vote result, then the moderator of **news.announce.newgroups** will send out a control message that causes the new group to be created.

The alt Domain

The **alt** hierarchy is rather different. It stands for 'alternative', though some claim it's actually 'Anarchists, Lunatics and Terrorists'; there are, however, many serious and worthwhile groups. Discussions about a new group take place in the newsgroup **alt.config**, but there are usually no votes taken. Local hierarchies, such as **uk** also have their own rules and conventions.

Many helpful documents about the running of the newsgroup hierarchies can be found on the machine **rtfm.mit.edu** in the sub-directory **usenet/ news.answers**.

If you have a UNIX host connected to the Internet, it is easy to create 'local' groups for internal company use. Of course you should check that these local groups aren't fed back to the Internet. Even if your UNIX machine isn't connected to the Internet, then 'news' is a good forum for enabling discussion of many topics.

Using tin

The **tin** newsreader is a popular UNIX newsreader and posting program. It starts with a group selection screen where you can choose which group you want to read. Here we see a mixture of main hierarchy groups such as **comp.***, regional groups such as **uk.*** and service provider groups such as **demon.***:

```
                    Group Selection (11 R)                    h=help

    1      4   demon.announce             Demon Service Announcements
    2    133   demon.ip.support.unix      Demon Unix Connection Support
    3     52   news.announce.newusers     New Users Start Here
    4   1290   uk.jobs.offered            The UK Workplace
    5     25   demon.archives.announce    Demon FTP Server Announcements
    6    144   alt.humor.best-of-usenet   The Best of Internet News
    7      9   comp.archives              New Uploads to Computer Archives
    8      1   comp.os.linux.announce     Linux Announcements
    9   3099   comp.os.linux.x            Linux X Window System
   10    756   demon.ip.support.win95     Demon Win95 Connection Support


                       *** End of Groups ***
```

If we select a group such as **comp.os.linux.x,** we can see the ongoing discussions in the group. Each discussion, or thread, is listed together with the number of responses to the original posting.

```
               comp.os.linux.x (705T 1302A 0K 0H R)          h=help

    1  + 2   xpaint, no saint                          Eric Hennemann
    2  +     S3 Vision 964 Support ?                   jacques.schmitz.s
    3  +     Need Xconfig for Compaq Deskpro XE560, Dell 4  Marcelo Morenoc M
    4  +     map question                              Casey Claiborne
    5  +     meta-F1 vs. mouse 1                       Larry Blanchard
    6  +     Cvo ???                                   VERLOOVE OLIVIER
    7  +     multiple hardware colormaps like sgi?     Roger Gonzalez
    8  + 3   x from boot up?                           Josh Rivel
    9  +     xdm and XDMCP broadcast feature...HELP!   Jonas Juselius
   10  +     Keypad broken on new X servers            Larry Creech
   11  +     xmcd: endless msgs when no CD present     Dean Edmonds
   12  +     Pentium optimized X server                Mike Big
   13  + 2   Hot Java browser for Linux                Mike Big
   14  +     problems with Xfree3.1.1                  Jochen Kenemann
   15  +     xpilots barfs                             Van den Panhuyzen
   16  +     XWindows fonts - 100 or 75 dpi???         Stephane Du Pasqui
   17  + 16  more memory is worse??????                Stephane Du Pasqui
   18  + 5   netscape 1.1n locks my machine            Andreas Busse
   19  +     @@@@ netscape for LINUX @@@@@@             Michael P. Lindne
   20  + 3   On which LAPTOPS can XFree drive EXTERNAL MON  Misha Rekhson
   21  + 5   Linux Bible, where?                       Matt Welsh
```

If we select a particular thread we can read all of the related postings before moving on to the next discussion. Note that some discussions can lead to lengthy threads!

The World Wide Web

The World Wide Web was devised at the CERN research center in
Switzerland, as a way of disseminating research information. Like many other
services on the Internet, it's used by client programs, and provided by
servers. Each item of information is called a document or page. Web client
programs are normally called browsers.

> Note that there are numerous ways to reference the World Wide
> Web. It is normally abbreviated to WWW or W3, but it can also
> be cut down to 'The Web'.

WWW Documents

A WWW document is a graphical hypertext document featuring embedded
links that allow you to follow ideas in more depth, or to move on to related
subject matter. If you have used IBM's InfoExplorer or MS-Windows Help,
you will be familiar with the idea of a hypertext document. What
distinguishes WWW hypertext links is that the link can lead to almost any
computer site anywhere in the World, all at the click of a button. Some links
may even take you to a totally different service, such as `ftp` or Gopher.

Most WWW pages consist of a magazine-style interface featuring headings,
text, links, static pictures and clickable pictures. Links are normally
highlighted in some way and the text gives you a clue as to where the link
leads. Buttons or images on a page may be linked to some executable code
that is executed on the server when that object is selected, making interactive
pages possible. WWW documents have a very strong multi-media bias. They
may contain not only textual and graphical information, but also sound,
music and video clips.

Uniform Resource Locators and http

WWW documents are normally specified as URLs - Uniform Resource
Locators, pronounced 'earls'. An example of an URL is:

```
http://www.internic.net/
```

353

This refers to the WWW service at the machine **www.internic.net**.

http (Hyper Text Transfer Protocol) is the underlying protocol used to transfer WWW pages. Since in this example no page is specified, a default defined on the remote machine will be shown. A specific page may be requested by appending it to the machine name, separated by a slash. This is much like specifying a file in a subdirectory, for example:

```
http://info.cern.ch/hypertext/DataSources/WWW/Server.html
```

URLs aren't restricted to the World Wide Web either, they also form a useful way of addressing information sources, taking the following general form:

```
<scheme>://<machine  address>/<directory>/<directory>/<resource>
```

For example, the location of a file accessible by **ftp** file transfer might be given as:

```
ftp://sunsite.unc.edu/pub/Linux/kernel/v1.2/patch-1.2.5.gz
```

It is important to realize that the slash character used in URLs to denote a subdirectory should always be a '**/**'. It is the responsibility of the target machine to interpret the URL according to local rules. This is important because it makes properly constructed URLs independent of the target machine. To find out more about URLs you should obtain a copy of RFC1738 (we will discuss RFCs later in this chapter).

SGML and HTML

Documents on the Web are written in a format called HyperText Markup Language (HTML). This is a specific type of structured document defined in Standard Generalized Markup Language (SGML), an ISO standard for portable, structured, documents.

HTML allows the author of a document to specify the layout, style and structure of a document, without knowing in advance what the viewing medium will be. This means that the author will specify that a section of text may be a level two heading, but it depends on the viewer of the document exactly how it is displayed.

Sections in an HTML document are separated with markup tags, which describe how the document is to be formatted. Most tags are paired, with a start tag and an end tag, such as **<TITLE>** and **</TITLE>**. There are other, more complex tags such as anchors that reference a different document, and more complex tag structures for embedded images, lists and fill-out forms. A few of the more common tags are shown here:

Start Tag	End Tag	Function
<TITLE>	</TITLE>	Provide a title
<H1>	</H1>	Provide headings (1 through to 6)
 		Force a line break
<P>	</P>	Paragraph separators
<DL>	</DL>	Definition list
<DT>	<DD>	Definition term and definition detail
<B>	</B>	Bold text
<I>	</I>	Italic font
<TT>	</TT>	Fixed width font
<MENU>	</MENU>	Menu
<LI>		List item in a menu
<FORM>	</FORM>	A form
<A HREF="url">	</A>	A hypertext link
<IMG SRC="url">		Include an inline image

HTML Example

To show you just how easy HTML is to use, here's a short example of some code, followed by a screen shot from an X Window System client showing the displayed page.

355

```
<HTML>
E>Demonstration Record Shop</TITLE>
<H1>Demonstration Record Shop</H1>

<B>Welcome</B> to the demonstration virtual record shop.

<H2><IMG SRC="record.gif" ALIGN=centre> Records Stocked</H2>

<DL>
<DT> <B>Classical</B>
<DD> Many classical records from famous artists.
<DT> <B>JAZZ</B>
<DD> Our speciality - <EM>Big Band</EM> JAZZ <DT> <B>American Imports</B>
<DD> If the record you want isn't in stock please ask.  We may be able to
obtain it for you.
<DT> <B>POP</B>
<DD> A full range of CDs and Videos available for immediate dispatch
</DL>


You may prefer to <A HREF="http://mydomain.com/records/
browse.html">browse</A> through the records available, or fill out the form
below to search for record types that may interest you.

<FORM METHOD=POST ACTION="cgi-bin/scripts/search-form.pl">

<P>Classification:
        <INPUT TYPE="radio" NAME="C" VALUE="A">Classical
        <INPUT TYPE="radio" NAME="J" VALUE="B" CHECKED>JAZZ
        <INPUT TYPE="radio" NAME="A" VALUE="C">American
        <INPUT TYPE="radio" NAME="P" VALUE="D">POP

<P> Send me mail notifying me of future records added to your virtual shop
that match my search criterion:
        <INPUT TYPE="checkbox" NAME="smm" VALUE=1>Yes Please

<P> My mail address: <INPUT TYPE="text" NAME="mailaddress" SIZE=35
VALUE="a.customer@myhost.mydomain.com">

<P> Search: <INPUT TYPE="submit" NAME="search" VALUE="Yes">
        <INPUT TYPE="submit" NAME="cancel" VALUE="Cancel>
</FORM>

Thank you for visiting the
<I>Demonstration</I> Virtual Record Store.
</HTML>
```

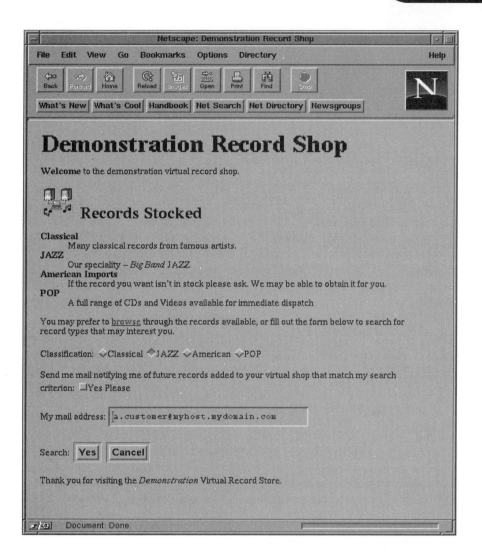

Servers

As the name implies, WWW servers are applications running on machines that serve Web pages. They respond to requests from browsers for pages. Examples include the Netscape Netsite, CERN **httpd** and NCSA **httpd**. Typically, they are hosted on UNIX systems.

Browsers

These are client programs that display the WWW document and allow the user to interact with it. Examples include the Netscape Navigator and NCSA Mosaic. They are available for a wide range of hardware platforms such as UNIX workstations, IBM PCs running MS-Windows and the Apple Macintosh.

Advertising

In general, advertising isn't considered acceptable on the Internet. Indeed some Internet networks have 'acceptable use' policies that specifically exclude advertising. The one area of the Internet on which advertising is considered acceptable, or is at least tolerated, is the WWW. This is because the WWW is passive - no-one has to visit an URL, unlike an unwanted advertisement in a newsgroup that you receive along with the discussion you were following, or unsolicited 'junk' e-mail.

What's on the WWW?

Broadly speaking there are three types of resources to be found on the WWW: public information sources, personal pages and corporate servers:

Public Information Sources

Generally free of advertising, except perhaps for small acknowledgements such as 'server courtesy of Acme Computers', these sources contain a wealth of information on many subjects. Some of them are very comprehensive, and pages may range from details from Library of Congress information, through to education and entertainment pages, sites dedicated to TV shows, and even interactive games.

Personal Home Pages

These are pages created by individuals, for and about themselves. They vary quite a lot, from a simple picture with a few words, to complex demonstrations of skills. Popular features include career resumes and links to the user's favourite web pages.

Corporate Servers

Many companies are now providing WWW pages. Most of these contain some advertising, but since people don't normally visit a Web page just to read the advertising material, they usually contain some helpful information about the company and its services. Some companies are now providing product updates and even demonstration software accessible from their WWW pages.

Setting Up Your Own Web Server

Setting up a World Wide Web server for yourself, or for your organization's internal use is easily done using freely available UNIX software. A corporate Web server can be used by departments to share information with each other, and if connected to the Internet, it can provide information to customers and other Web visitors.

Setting Up the Server

There are various 'free' Web servers available, many of which are widely used and very stable. One popular Web server is the CERN **http** daemon, available from:

```
ftp://ftp.w3.org
```

The server program, **httpd**, responds to requests made on a specific port number; the default is 80. The server is usually started at boot time with the following entries in the **/etc/rc.local** file (or other startup file):

```
echo "Starting Web Server..."
/usr/local/bin/httpd -r /etc/httpd.conf
```

All of the operational details are given in a configuration file, in this case **/etc/httpd.conf**. A minimal configuration might contain:

```
ServerRoot      /usr/WWW
Port            80
UserID          nobody
GroupID         nobody
Pass            /*      /usr/WWW/*
```

This sets the server to use Web pages stored in the directory **/usr/WWW** and its sub-directories, and to listen on port 80 for requests. It will use the non-privileged user identity **nobody** for file access. This user doesn't need to be able to login and will typically have an **/etc/passwd** entry similar to:

```
nobody:*:65534:65534::/:
```

It is possible to set up an **HTTP** server to act as a proxy, that is, it will respond to requests for pages at other sites, download them and pass them on. Coupled with a cache that keeps often-requested pages locally, this can provide a very useful service for corporate networks accessing the Internet via a gateway machine. If more than one user of the local network requests the same page, it is only transferred across the external network once. Both the CERN **httpd** and the NCSA **httpd** can be configured to do this. Conventionally, proxy servers listen for requests on port 8080.

Creating Your Own Web Page

If you have a machine directly connected to the network 24 hours a day, then setting up a set of publicly accessible WWW pages is easy. Just follow these steps:

- You need some server software - if you are running a mainstream UNIX variant, then there is a choice of servers - most of them completely free. Don't confuse 'free' with 'of no value'. Many of the free servers are of excellent quality.

- You now need to create your WWW pages. There are many tools available for automatic generation of HTML, but as we have seen, it is quite easy to write them directly. Most WWW browsers will allow you to see the actual HTML source of other people's documents - so you can always look to see how others have created their pages.

- Having created your pages you need to insert the appropriate links between them. Place your pages in the server directory and test them. Look around the Internet at the many different pages and see what looks good and is easy to use. Remember that many Internet users may be accessing your page through a slow modem link - if you include on your home page a very large graphic image then they might not bother downloading it.

If you aren't directly connected to the Internet, but are using a service provider, you'll need to place your pages on a server elsewhere. Many service providers will rent WWW server space and, for a small fee, will even create your pages for you.

Shorthand

The Internet is a highly interactive, creative and humorous medium, therefore it is only natural that language changes to accommodate the environment. The more prevalent forms of these changes are abbreviations and the use of symbols.

Abbreviations

Abbreviations are often used for common expressions to reduce the time spent typing. Most of them are fairly obvious, once you have seen them a few times. Some of the most common are:

AFAIK	As Far As I Know
AFK	Away From Keyboard
BRB	Be Right Back
BTW	By The Way
FYI	For Your Information
IMHO	In My (sometimes not so!) Humble Opinion
OTOH	On The Other Hand
ROFL	Roll On the Floor Laughing
RTFM	Refer To Manual
SO	Significant Other (i.e. partner)
YMMV	Your Mileage May Vary (i.e. it may not work for you)

Smileys

The other form of shorthand is smileys (or smilies). They are sometimes attractively called 'emoticons' because they are used to convey emotion. Since there are no clues from intonation or facial expression in electronic media, common ASCII symbols are sometimes used to make it clear when the text was intended as a joke or to be taken in a lighthearted manner. Some common smileys are:

`:-)` or `:)`	The 'standard' smiley - used to suggest a sarcastic or joking statement.
`;-)`	Winking - a flirtatious and/or sarcastic remark.
`:-(`	The user is upset/depressed or just didn't like that last statement.
`:-/`	Sceptical.
`:-$`	Put your money where your mouth is.
`:-o`	Shock or surprise.
`%-(`	Cross-eyed (after working all night?).
`|-o`	Bored.
`=):-)`	Uncle Sam.

Please note that smileys are a personal shorthand language, and it is unlikely that everyone will understand them. If you are going to use them, it is sensible to forewarn potential readers.

Other Information Services

Although `ftp` and Web traffic account for a good proportion of interactive Internet use, there are other useful sources of information available by other means.

Gopher

In some ways Gopher is the precursor of the World Wide Web. It presents information archives in a more user-friendly way than `ftp` sites. The interface is menu-based and can be accessed using simple character-based clients.

Gopher can be used to browse a file server. Each menu entry might represent a file and, when selected, that file can be downloaded. The key feature of Gopher is that the menu entries might refer to files or directories on other Gopher servers, in a similar fashion to WWW links.

The University of Minnesota is the leader in Gopher development and they have made available a Gopher server which can run on UNIX systems. The latest unlicensed version is Gopher 1.13 and is available from:

```
ftp://boombox.micro.umn.edu/pub/gopher/Unix/gopher1.13.tar.Z
```

The 'top-level' Gopher server that contains links by region to all the other servers is `gopher.tc.umn.edu`. Some Web clients, notably Netscape Navigator and NCSA Mosaic, can perform gopher server accesses with URLs of the form `gopher://...`

Veronica

Veronica performs much the same function for Gopher servers as `archie` does for `ftp` sites, providing an index to gopher menus and allowing searching. The result of a Veronica search is a list of gopher menu items that contain the given keywords. Many Gopher servers provide a menu item that is a link to a Veronica search service.

WAIS - Wide Area Information Server

WAIS was originally developed by Thinking Machines as a way of indexing large information databases and serving requests for documents from that database. The key attributes of WAIS are the ability to handle large amounts

363

of text and binary data, coupled with a powerful searching technique. The result of a WAIS query is a list of documents that match keywords or logical expressions. Each match is given a score to indicate how close it came to the desired criteria, that is, WAIS is able to offer related material and 'near misses'.

Finding More Information

The Internet is a vast resource of useful information and software. Below we give some pointers for new Internet users on how to find out more.

RFCs

Most of what you need to know about how to connect to the Internet is defined in a set of documents called Request For Comment (RFC) papers. These define not only the protocols in use, but also the services available and the rules and conventions that make the Internet work. These are publicly available documents and may be freely downloaded from many sites. The main one is:

```
ftp://ds.internic.net/rfc
```

If you don't have full Internet **ftp** access, but can exchange e-mail, then you can send mail to:

```
mailserv@ds.internic.net
```

Leave the subject blank and put commands in the body. A good starting request is:

```
help
send rfc-index.txt
```

Beware - the index file is around 250k in size!

FAQs

These are also available by anonymous **ftp** from many sites. The main one is:

ftp://rtfm.mit.edu/pub/usenet-by-hierarchy

Since this is a very busy site, you should use one of the 'mirror' sites if there is one closer to you than MIT.

If you don't have full Internet **ftp** access, but can exchange mail then you can send mail to:

mail-server@rtfm.mit.edu

Leave the subject blank and for more information make the body of the message:

```
help
quit
```

USENET

New users should always start by subscribing to:

news.announce.newuser

Don't forget to digest the information provided.

archie

There are various archie servers available. To obtain some basic help and a list of servers, so you can find one close to you, send mail to:

archie@archie.internic.net

Leave the subject blank and make the body of your message the following:

```
help
servers
```

WWW

To find out more about the World Wide Web, including HTML specifications, free **http** servers and more, start at the home of the World Wide Web:

```
http://www.w3.org/
```

Internet Standards

For more general Internet standards and working party information, try the InterNIC web site, at:

```
http://www.internic.net/
```

Summary

In this chapter, we defined what the Internet is exactly and described its military origins. We mentioned how most companies get connected, and then looked at the different services available and how you can access them with UNIX. We looked briefly at how to make a **telnet** connection, and ran through how you can download files with **ftp** once you have found them with **archie**. We have also learnt how to 'unpack' the compressed files once you've successfully downloaded them. We then looked at other services, mainly the very successful World Wide Web, and how to use a UNIX machine to act as a WWW server.

Chapter

Security

Unix has a reputation of being an insecure operating system. Admittedly, it isn't as secure as some systems, but a properly administered UNIX system can provide a good level of security. In this chapter, we'll be looking at some common threats as well as discussing good security practices and how to implement them. We'll also be taking a look at some of the products that provide a professional level of security.

Here are some of the topics that we'll be covering:

- Physical security
- System security
- Event logging
- Telecommunications, network and mail security
- Security audits
- Data encryption
- What to do if your system is attacked
- Security resources on the Internet

Physical Security

How important is your data? How would you like total strangers to be able to gain access to it without you knowing? In *The Art of War*, Sun Tzu wrote, "Know your enemy and know yourself, and you need not fear the outcome of a thousand battles."

System security is war, especially if your system is exposed to the Internet. If, however, you know the nature of the threat, and you are aware of which processes your system is running, then you can minimize the risk.

You can prevent nearly every possible attack on your system by simply being meticulous in performing a few basic administrative procedures. Most attacks occur when one of these procedures is ignored, exposing a security hole. There are many different precautions that can be implemented, ranging from basic common-sense practices to the installation of physical barriers. Before we look at these though, we'll look at some general security issues that don't just affect UNIX, but are an issue for any computing centre.

System Administrator Selection

The one person who can do the most damage to your system, intentionally or not, is your system administrator. Make sure your that the person you select is trustworthy, pays attention to detail and is very tight-lipped.

Choose the kind of person who will dutifully keep detailed logs and monitor the system regularly. If you are the prospective system administrator and you don't think that you are able to religiously complete these tasks, then you should seriously consider passing the role on to someone more suitable.

Staff Procedures

Once you've found yourself a trustworthy system administrator, make sure you don't become too open about system information with the rest of the staff. The best rule of thumb is to keep all sensitive system information purely on a need-to-know basis. When there's a good atmosphere and everyone is content, it's all too easy to become lax with passwords. If you fall out with someone and they leave under a cloud of ill-will, it's possible that your problems will have only just begun. An enraged ex-employee with root permissions can do a lot more damage with a few keystrokes than most outside attackers could ever dream of.

Even a good employee with a big mouth can unintentionally compromise your system by blurting out restricted information to others. Here are some practical staff security tips to minimize possible dangers:

- Always keep an accurate log of who does what, when and where; this is invaluable in the aftermath of an attack.

- When an employee leaves, remove their account as promptly as possible. It sometimes seems like a nice idea to continue providing an account for an ex-employee for some time after they leave, but a large proportion of system attacks are actually through these accounts (not always from an ex-employee, but sometimes from attackers who seek to exploit dormant accounts).

- If an employee leaves under less-than-amicable circumstances, disable their account immediately. Most system damage or data loss from disgruntled employees occurs while they're still in the building.

- Never give out the root password. It's often tempting, especially when things get really busy, to let experienced co-workers share the administrative burden. Make them wait. Only in a dire emergency, when you absolutely have to do so (you're sick, on vacation, etc.), should you grudgingly give it out to a trustworthy soul. Change the password as soon as the emergency has passed.

371

Site Security

Unless your site is physically secure, even the best electronic security won't protect your systems. If a seasoned hacker can gain physical access to your systems, then it's all over.

Here are some basic physical site security rules:

- Keep your system hardware in a place where access is controlled and make sure you know everyone who has access to the area. Set access rules and always supervise any strangers that are present.

- Never leave an account (especially the root!) open at an unattended workstation; this is very dangerous.

- Keep logs and other important records safe under lock and key. Shred any records that are to be discarded instead of throwing them in the bin - a popular hacker pastime is 'dumpster-diving' (rummaging through institutional and corporate refuse looking for passwords and other account information).

- Keep backup tapes and other electronic media safely locked away. A stolen backup tape is a goldmine for a system hacker - a complete snapshot of your whole system.

System Security

It would be wrong to think that general physical security issues are just common sense and that integral system methods should take precedence. If you don't follow the general security guidelines, your system *will* be compromised. The UNIX system doesn't provide that secure a foundation to work with, but if you are aware of the problems, then your chances of withstanding an attack will be greatly enhanced.

You should be aware of the following fifteen areas of system security and be able to make a careful judgment as to which you wish to address.

Single-User Mode

The most direct way to subvert the security of a UNIX system when you have physical access is to drop down to single-user mode. Most systems allow a machine to give anyone access to single-user mode at some point during the reboot process. The only real protection against abuse of single-user mode is to keep the system and the console physically secure.

Trapdoor Programs

If the 'setuid' permission is set in certain programs owned by the root, they grant superuser privileges to the users that run them. This can cause a 'trapdoor' effect that allows intruders to gain access to your system. There are several valid commands that may be set up like this, such as the mail program, but if you find one in a user directory, then regard it as very suspicious.

File Permissions

Properly configured file permissions on sensitive system files can prevent many attacks. For the most part, these file permissions are what the fight is all about - if you ignore them, you risk losing one of the most effective security techniques available. You should also remember that file permissions only cost the time it takes you to set them up. The following permission tips should be adhered to for optimum success.

Special Permissions

Programs that have the setuid or setgid bits set in their permissions will run with the same authorization as their owner, as well as those of the user currently executing them. This opens up a potentially serious security breach. You should avoid setting these bits for programs other than core system software.

Device Files

Most of the device files should be owned by the root. Disk devices and memory devices (like **/dev/kmem**, the kernel memory device) should only be available for manipulation by the system administrator.

System Directories

Watch out in particular for loose permissions in the root, **/bin** and **/etc** system directories. Bad permissions here can grant attackers free access to highly sensitive files. Only grant a file or directory the minimum level of permission necessary.

Group IDs

When a group of users all need to share the same data, they often distribute the password for the account between them causing a serious security breach. Instead of taking this reckless approach, they should maintain the integrity of their individual accounts and request to become part of a group.

However, this isn't without its own dangers. Users must be very careful about what they make accessible to a group. If just one account in the group is compromised, all group accessible data is compromised as well.

Automated Security Audit Tools

Later in this chapter we'll introduce you to some of the tools that can automate the checking of your file system security, testing the above considerations amongst others. Making efficient use of these utilities will free up a lot of your time - they also mean that you don't have to remember reams of complicated sets of permissions.

Password Security

Passwords are the first line of defence against electronic system intrusion. They are also one of the most obvious and popular targets for intruders. The principal problem with password security, though, is human nature -

users are reluctant to use the very techniques that are effective against intruders. Careful management of user passwords is a must for any system administrator.

Choosing a password isn't as straightforward as you might think. You must choose one that a hacker will *never* think of, or find. Heed the following points when you create a new password:

- Don't tell anyone what it is. Never hint or joke about what the contents of your password are, or might be.

- Never send your password (or someone elses) via e-mail or over a network for any reason.

- Don't give it out over the phone (there was a scam discovered a few years ago, when someone claiming to represent a popular online service contacted subscribers to request their passwords 'for maintenance purposes').

- Don't write your password on a scrap of paper or a Post-it and never leave it next to your computer (a surprisingly common violation).

- If you ever suspect that the integrity of your password has been compromised, change it immediately.

- Never program your password into a logon script or a function key macro.

A good rule of thumb is to pretend that your password is the key to your personal safety deposit box - protect it with the same vigilance.

Selecting Passwords

Taking great care when selecting a password is crucial - any potential hacker can download a password-cracking program from any one of hundreds of dedicated networking sites across the Internet. These programs typically consist of database tables containing hundreds of common passwords, trying each one in turn on various accounts until they find one that works or they exhaust the lists. You must ensure that your password is too obscure to be found in one of these lists.

When selecting a password for your account, avoid the following:

- Single words.
- Your name (or nickname).
- Names of family members or pets.
- Obvious words - 'hello', 'password', 'sesame', 'root', etc.
- Swear words - these are very common.
- Popular numbers, telephone, fax, ISBN, etc.
- Anything that can be easily seen as it is typed - 'qwerty', '123456', etc.
- Any phrases or catchwords that can be seen around the office.

Instead, try to use:

- Multiple, unrelated, small words mixed with non-alphabetic characters, like 'fervor#% spent'.
- Random character strings, like '^cNd9L0(#J$'.
- A mix of upper and lowercase characters.

> **The less obvious and readable the password is, the better. Don't use any of the example passwords given in this book! Such passwords have a nasty habit of finding their way into cracking tables.**

Here's where pesky human nature interferes however - the better a password is, the harder it normally is to remember. If it's too hard to recall, you'll be tempted to compromise by writing it down or hiding it some place. For example, a random character string is a very secure password but is often unreasonably difficult to remember. A two word password with interspersed non-alphabetic characters is pretty secure and much easier to remember.

Password Management

It's a very good idea to periodically change your password, for a number of reasons:

- Some intruders are very quiet - leaving little or no trace of their activity, especially if they are using your system as a 'base camp' for other intrusions. Changing passwords helps to foil this kind of long-term abuse.

- Some hackers break into systems by stealing a copy of the encrypted **/etc/passwd** file. They take it back to their own system (or somewhere they feel reasonably safe) and run password cracking programs against it at their leisure. This is a very time-consuming process and sometimes they won't check back with your system for weeks or even months. If the passwords on your system have changed in the intervening time all their work will have been in vain.

- There are hundreds of ways your password may become compromised without your knowledge - someone looking over your shoulder while you type it in for example. Changing your password regularly helps to reduce the amount of time a compromised password is effective.

Again, human nature interferes. Changing your password regularly is a great idea, but few do it without being prompted. Even with prompting, people tend to cycle through a few favorite passwords rather than come up with a brand new one each time. Thus, a compromised password might make a comeback several months after it was changed - a situation you should strive to avoid.

Habits are hard to break and those who cycle through several passwords often forget which one is the current one. If someone can't figure out their own password then an embarrassing visit to the system administrator is in order.

Several programs have been developed to enable system administrators to force users to manage their passwords in a more secure manner. They attach expiration dates to passwords and keep track of previous passwords to ensure that old ones don't compromise the integrity of the system. Some even analyze passwords using cracking techniques, rejecting ones that aren't good enough. Because of the rigid enforcement of policy and their stern warnings to users, such programs are colloquially referred to as 'fascist password programs'. Two of the most popular are the **NPasswd** and **passwd+**, freely available from various anonymous **ftp** sites on the Internet.

> **Throughout this chapter we will be making references to various tools available on the Internet. At the end of this chapter we give you a table of all the tools and the sites at which you can find them.**

Password Shadowing

We have already mentioned that a system can be compromised if an intruder steals a copy of the file containing all the passwords. Although the **/etc/passwd** file contains encrypted passwords, it still provides the would-be hacker with plenty of raw material to work on.

It seems strange that an intruder can get at your passwords in the first place - albeit in an encrypted form. However, in order to operate, the **/etc/passwd** file must be able to be read by everyone, while at the same time disabling everyone from writing to it (password change utility programs use setuid root).

There is, however, a way to protect your passwords from being viewed or manipulated by anyone without root permissions. A **password shadowing system** allows you to replace the actual encrypted passwords in the **/etc/passwd** file with special tokens that refer to a separate 'shadow' password file that only has root read/write permissions. Existing password systems built into UNIX can be patched or replaced to handle proper shadowing, while newer UNIX flavors (such as SunOS) feature shadowing as a standard part of the system installation. For other UNIX flavors, there are add-on shadowing systems (like **shadow**, available from various sites on the Internet).

However, don't assume that shadowing systems are foolproof - they're not. They are very effective, but like most password systems, they can be breached.

Event Logging

The UNIX operating system includes a number of automated event logging functions that can help you monitor your system for attacks. The following log files accumulate information about certain system events. Note, however, that an experienced hacker with root permissions can alter these files and erase his or her tracks. So don't treat these logs as if they are 100% reliable - they aren't.

last

The **wtmp** and **lastlog** files maintain information about user logins and logouts. These files aren't directly human-readable. The program **last** dumps out a report based on the **wtmp** file. You should periodically look through this information, looking for suspicious logins.

ac

If your system is set up for user time accounting (for personal billing purposes, etc.), you can review the **/usr/adm/acct** file for anomalies. A reporting program, **ac**, is provided to help sort through the information supplied by **/usr/adm/acct**. Another program, **lastcomm**, also provides reporting on this data. Accounting data can help you find suspicious behavior, like users who are consuming unusual amounts of CPU time, possibly running password cracking software. The monitoring of user activity isn't set up by default on most UNIX systems - it usually requires a specially-compiled version of the kernel.

messages

Whenever an important system event or error occurs, a message is logged straight in to a file called **messages**. There are some other useful things that get logged in **messages** as well:

Attempts to **su** as root.

Attempts to login as root.

Repeated login failures - when a user tries three incorrect passwords in a row.

The **messages** file is plain text and can be read and manipulated by anyone with access to it.

Tip

It is a good idea to monitor the number of processes on the system. More mischievous attackers might be aiming just to crash or bring down the system. A favorite method of doing this is by the continual forking of processes (a method of creating one simultaneous process after another), whereby eventually the system runs out of memory. One way around this is to set a limit on the number of processes that one user can run at a time.

Vendor Security Bulletins

New holes in the various implementations of UNIX are discovered from time to time; the vendor of your UNIX 'flavor' will usually notify all registered users of known holes and patches as soon as possible. The moral of this story is to always register your software and make sure you're on the vendor's security bulletins mailing list. When these bulletins cross your desk, act on them immediately. Remember that these bulletins are usually triggered by security breaches that have already occurred on somebody else's system. By the time the word gets out about the system weaknesses, it is already probably part of the cracker 'street knowledge'.

Some vendors maintain online patch archives for their registered users (Sun OS users can find patches on **ftp.uu.net**). Find out if your vendor does this, and check it regularly to make sure you're up-to-date.

Telecommunications Security

Any connection to the outside world exposes a system to attack. Care should be taken to secure any telephone connections to your system. The following advice should be adhered to.

Secure TTYs

The TTY connections listed in the file **/etc/ttys** (or **/etc/ttytab**) on your system can be declared 'secure' - this simply means that root logins will be accepted from the TTY. In general, only the console should be deemed 'secure' in the **/etc/ttys** file. For example:

```
console tty1
console tty2
console tty3
console tty4
console tty5
console tty6
vt100  ttyp0
vt100  ttyp1
vt100  ttyp2
vt100  ttyp3
```

Better still, don't declare any devices to be 'secure' and always use **su** to acquire root permissions (**su** isn't affected by the 'secure' designation). If no TTYs (including network pseudo-TTYs) are designated 'secure', then no one can log in as root from remote network hosts.

Callback Connections

Some vendors are now supplying software and terminal servers that implement callback connections. These systems hang up the line on incoming calls and call the user back to verify that they are indeed phoning from a known and trusted number. Connection is rejected if the given number isn't recognized. This greatly reduces the number of fraudulent practices, but can be very difficult or impossible to manage if users are constantly moving to new sites.

Caller ID Systems

Recent additions to telephone network software have made it possible for subscribers to perform rudimentary traces on all their incoming phone calls. New modems have been developed that can make use of this technology to automatically log the phone numbers of incoming modem connections. Some systems even allow automatic rejection of incoming calls that are from unrecognized numbers.

Internet Security

A UNIX system that isn't connected to the outside world via a network has comparatively little to worry about in terms of system security. The real security headaches come when the system is tied into a large external network like the Internet, where it's suddenly exposed to millions of strangers from all over the world. In this section we'll look at some of the issues that arise when you address securing your system on such a network.

TCP/IP Security Issues

Like the UNIX operating system itself, the TCP/IP network protocol suite and its associated software tools weren't originally designed with serious security in mind. The environment in which TCP/IP was developed was one of collaboration among researchers who had no reason to mistrust one another. Now, however, TCP/IP is being used by the Internet worldwide and is therefore exposed to every security threat that such a public infrastructure involves. Here are some of the major security aspects of TCP/IP.

File Transfer Protocol

The file transfer protocol (or **ftp**) is one of the core communications services used by hosts on the Internet, as we have already discussed in earlier chapters. Configuring **ftp** is as important as configuring user accounts - in fact, **ftp** uses user account information and passwords. An improperly configured **ftp** service presents a major security hole. The principal risks stem from outdated **ftp** software and improperly configured anonymous **ftp** services.

Make sure you're running the most recent version of **ftpd** because there are serious problems associated with versions that pre-date July 1990. Contact your system vendor if you suspect your **ftp** software requires upgrading.

The main danger lies with file permissions. It's possible for people to plant programs into your system which can do a variety of nasty things, ranging from obtaining your password to removing your files. Therefore you should never use your standard password and group files for **ftp**, instead use a stripped-down version. Make sure that your **ftp** home directory isn't writable - otherwise anonymous hackers can plant 'trojan horses' (fake login shells that record your password and then pretend you failed to login correctly). Also, make sure that the **ftp**, **ftp/bin** and **ftp/etc** directories are never owned by the person who logs on to **ftp**, the **ftp** 'user'. They should normally belong to the superuser.

Put all your files that are to be shared across the Internet in a single subdirectory owned by **ftp** (usually **ftp/pub**). Check the **ftpd** manual page on your system for system-specific details on configuring anonymous **ftp** for your system. Note that some security auditing tools (such as COPS) are able to make a pretty thorough check of your **ftp** configuration.

Trivial File Transfer Protocol

The trivial file transfer protocol (or **tftp**) is **ftp**'s brain-dead cousin. This method brings a whole new meaning to the phrase 'world-readable', allowing file transfers to take place virtually without authentication. Most uses of **tftp** are outdated, and most savvy system administrators have simply shut down **tftp** services on their systems. A few uses for it still remain, however - some Sun systems use **tftpd** (the **tftp** daemon) for remote boot services.

Make sure you have the most up-to-date version of **tftp** provided by your system vendor, or even disable the service altogether. You can effectively disable it by commenting it out of your **/etc/inetd.conf** file, i.e. by placing a **#** in front of its entry.

To see if **tftp** poses a threat to your system, try out this simple test, replacing **your.system** with the actual address of your system:

```
% tftp
tftp> connect your.system
tftp> get /etc/passwd
```

If this doesn't produce an error, you have a compromised **tftpd**, and it should either be upgraded or disabled.

finger

The **finger** service allows users of other systems to obtain information about users currently logged onto your system. It can also provide details about one particular user, such as when they last logged in, when they last checked their mail, and even their real name, address, and phone number. By its nature, **finger** is a public service, available to every user on the network. While it may be nice to grant your friends access to such information, you may not want strangers casually browsing through it. The **finger** service is commonly used by hackers to provide raw material for password cracking.

The finger Virus Problem

To make things worse, older versions of **fingerd** (the daemon that controls the **finger** service on your machine) contain more direct security holes that can be exploited by more sophisticated hackers. The most notorious security breach on the Internet, the infamous Internet Worm attack a few years ago, exploited such a hole - a virus brought down about 50,000 computers all over the United States. This virus was a primary cause behind many military organizations removing a large number of their gateways from the Internet. A student at Cornell University figured that as **finger** operates on the privileged level, it has access to any of the computers on the Internet. He wrote code that subverted the **finger** program so that when the system recovered, his own code was operating on the privileged level, replicating itself from one mailbox to another. If your system is running a version of **fingerd** prior to 1989, replace it or disable the **finger** services. On Sun systems, the **fingerd** program is usually found in **/etc/fingerd** or **/usr/etc/in.fingerd**.

The chfn Command

Many system administrators have decided that finger services aren't worth the risk and should be disabled. UNIX adminstrators also face another potential headache with the **chfn** command which allows the user to change their own personal **finger**. This might not seem like a particular problem, but if you trawl through any academic system, you are bound to find obscene or embarrassing remarks that a system administrator could do without.

Disabling finger

If you want to disable **finger** on your system, edit your **/etc/inetd.conf** file and look for the **finger** entry, which will look something like this:

```
finger stream tcp nowait nobody /etc/fingerd fingerd
```

You can either comment this line out, or you can replace the daemon with a 'warning' script. The latter approach is recommended because it doesn't leave legitimate users (such as system administrators) in the dark. For example, **finger** is frequently used by system administrators to locate an emergency contact at another site when they detect a break-in from their own system. A sensible warning script might look something like this:

```
#!/bin/sh
/bin/cat <<"END"

Sorry, but due to security concerns, finger services are not available at
this site. If you need to contact the  system administrator, please call
(301) 555-1234 during normal business hours.  In the event of an after-
hours emergency, please call John Doe at (301) 555-5678.

Thank you!

END
```

Let's say you put this script into an executable file called **/etc/fingermsg**. You would change the **finger** entry in your **inetd.conf** file to read:

```
finger stream tcp nowait nobody /etc/fingermsg fingermsg
```

Now remote users will get this message instead of conventional **finger** responses.

TCP Wrappers

TCP wrappers are programs that act as front-ends to your standard TCP network services. They can help tighten the security on the standard services and aid in tracking both successful and unsuccessful hackers. They can be configured to log the activity of the TCP services on your system and provide rudimentary firewall-like protection by restricting or selectively allowing access from the outside. Wrapper suites are available for free from various sites on the Internet via anonymous FTP.

Protecting Trusted Systems

It's sometimes convenient to grant special permissions to trusted systems with which you regularly share files and services. Such trusted relationships allow users on the remote systems to access certain services without even having to enter a password each time. However, when the security of a system is breached, it may unknowingly compromise every system with which it has a trusted relationship. Try to avoid establishing such trusting relationships with other systems if you possibly can, however, if you can't avoid having to trust a system, then here are some of the ways trusting relationships can be established.

/etc/hosts.equiv

The `/etc/hosts.equiv` file allows a system administrator to declare remote systems as trusted. When a system entry is added to this file the users on the remote system can use **rlogin** and **rsh** to gain access to accounts on the local machine without having to enter a password. This is useful if the two machines have a significant overlap in user accounts, and users frequently switch between the two systems.

One of the first things many hackers will do when they gain access to a system is attempt to read the `/etc/hosts.equiv` file. If they can find a way to read it, they can find out which other systems will let them in without question.

It's a good idea to avoid using `/etc/hosts.equiv` altogether. If you can't live without it, at least confine its use to machines on the same site and preferably under the same administration.

The .rhosts File

The `.rhosts` file works in a similar way to `/etc/hosts.equiv`, but differs in that it allows ordinary users to establish trust with users on remote systems. There is no way to adequately secure a system that allows users to create `.rhosts` files. Therefore it would be wise to not allow them on your system (except for root, which may use a **.rhosts** file to allow for network backups, or other administrative purposes). If you have to trust a system, then at least try to do it through **/etc/hosts.equiv**.

L.sys

This file is used by **uucp** to store account information for connecting to trusted remote systems. Make sure the permissions on **L.sys** make it read/writable only by the user 'uucp', readable by the group 'daemon' and untouchable by anyone else.

NFS

The Network File System (NFS) allows the sharing of file systems over a network. NFS has several security holes, and the best security practice is to avoid using it at all, if possible. Barring that, there are certain steps that you can take to make sure your NFS installation is protected.

/etc/exports

The **/etc/exports** file specifies what directories you are sharing across the net from your system and which remote hosts have access to them. It is possible (actually, it's far too easy) to create world-visible exports. Anyone reading your **/etc/exports** file can find out just what world-visible exports you have and mount them within seconds.

The best practice is to carefully restrict the permissions in your **/etc/exports** file and never add world-visible exports.

NFS and Routers

If your router allows for it, make it block all external NFS traffic. That way no hacker with PC-NFS can come waltzing into your network and begin browsing around your NFS exports.

Root Access

In order to prevent the root user on one system from automatically appearing as root to an NFS-mounted volume from another system, NFS translates root into a dummy user called **nobody**. The **/etc/exports** file on the remote system must explicitly grant root access to mounts from your host if you want true root access to the volume.

> **Be very careful about granting root access to any remote host via NFS. It's best to avoid doing this if possible.**

Preventing Root Access Across the Network

We have already covered this in the previous section on telecommunications security, but it's also relevant here.

> **You can prevent remote users from logging in as root over the network by removing the 'secure' designation from all entries in /etc/ttys (or /etc/ttytab on some systems). To acquire root permissions, log in under a different account and use su.**

Mail Security

Electronic mail services have been extensively exploited by system hackers. The Morris Internet Worm took advantage of a serious flaw in some UNIX e-mail services. Pranksters have exploited such flaws to send 'mail bombs' - messages containing destructive scripts that could be made to execute on the unwitting recipient's machine. Most of the holes are plugged as they are discovered, but you need to make sure your software has the necessary fixes. Even with these fixes though, a determined hacker may still find ways to *read* your mail. Never send sensitive information (like passwords) through electronic mail. If you are concerned about the interception of your mail, you can use encryption, which we will discuss later in this chapter.

sendmail

Old versions of the **sendmail** program are notorious for having serious security holes, so make sure you have an up-to-date version (versions 8.6.4 or later are highly recommended). To determine the version of **sendmail** you are running, try the following:

```
% telnet localhost 25
quit
```

The **sendmail** version should be printed. If it isn't, you will have to refer to the documentation that details installation of the system.

PEM

For further mail security there is Privacy-Enhanced Mail (PEM), a commercial public-key encryption system built on top of an MH mail transport. PEM is available from Trusted Information Systems, Inc.

Network Firewalls

One of the most secure ways to connect your network to the Internet is through a network firewall. A firewall acts as a single point of contact between your network and the Internet - all traffic must pass through it. The firewall is just another host system, except it runs special network software, and it generally works full-time as a network router and watchdog.

With a firewall, none of the services on machines are directly visible to the Internet - everything passes through the firewall first. All e-mail is sent to the firewall, which then forwards it to the appropriate hosts and users. The routing on your local network is totally invisible to all those on the outside. Most firewalls make use of a system called proxy services to allow applications to access services in a highly controlled manner through the firewall.

Creating a Firewall

There are three ways to create a firewall at your site - you can buy a preconfigured firewall machine, hire a consulting firm or systems integrator to help you, or you can download firewall software from the Internet and set up a firewall yourself on one of your own machines. Preconfigured

389

firewalls, like Gauntlet from Trusted Information Systems and solutions built around BorderWare (formerly JANUS), generally consist of a desktop PC running an Intel port of UNIX with all of the firewall software pre-installed. The main disadvantage is that preconfigured firewalls usually cost US$15,000 or more.

Many UNIX network consulting and systems integration firms are value-added resellers of firewall systems; they will sell you the firewall, set it up and show you how to use it. If you have a UNIX machine lying around doing nothing, you can put it to good use and save yourself some money by installing firewall software yourself. A fully-fledged firewall system, The Firewall Toolkit from Trusted Information Systems, is available via anonymous **ftp** from **ftp.tis.com** in **/pub/firewalls**.

If you are serious about securing your hosts and routers on the Internet, acquire a firewall. It can be configured to accommodate most of your needs whilst effectively thwarting most external attacks.

Security Audits

"An ounce of prevention is worth a pound of cure," or so the old adage goes. The best security measure you can apply to your system is vigilance. Constantly checking up on your system's status and taking corrective action as needed will deter most security threats.

A Simple Checklist

To be deemed vigilant, a system administrator must regularly perform a comprehensive routine. The best way to do this is to check off items from a list such as this one:

 Check your system for **.rhosts** files. The following line should do this:

```
find / -name .rhosts -ls
```

Check your system for **setuid** programs noting any new or suspicious ones. This should do it:

```
find / -type f -perm -4000 -ls
```

- Look in **/etc/passwd** for new or suspicious entries.

- Run a password cracker on your **/etc/passwd** file. If it is capable of cracking your password file, your password file is unsafe.

- Look in the system messages file for suspicious login or **su** attempts.

- Check the size, permissions and dates of all executable daemons and other key system binaries (like **/bin/sh**, **ps**, **cat**, **sum**, **ls** and **ifconfig**) against a list derived from the original install media.

- Check the **exports**, **hosts.equiv**, **ttys**, **inetd.conf**, **crontab** and **rc** files for new or altered entries.

- Run **ps** to look for suspicious tasks.

- Periodically check to see who's logged on. If you've been away from the console, use **last** to look at the recent account history.

- Check for other users with a user id of zero - they're logged on as root.

- Make regular system backups and store them in a secure place.

Automated Security Auditing

The audit outlined above is a good start, but it is hardly all-inclusive. Even so, going through it by hand on a regular basis would be time-consuming and potentially prone to error and misjudgment. Because of this, several automated auditing tools have been developed to take a lot of the drudgery out of security auditing. They can even be set up to be run by **cron** and then e-mail the results to you. Running (and paying attention to) such tools goes a long way towards keeping your system secure. Here are some of the most popular automated security auditing tools that are available.

Computer Oracle and Password System (COPS)

COPS is a freeware security auditing toolset. When you run it on your system, it checks a wide variety of things about your system configuration to determine if there are any security risks present. It doesn't actually fix the problems it finds - it merely reports them, although later versions of COPS build rudimentary repair scripts that the administrator can run to fix those problems found. The package also includes a program called **chkacct** that all users can run to check the integrity of their accounts.

Here are some of the things that COPS looks for:

- Bad passwords.
- Suspicious entries in **/etc/passwd.**
- Problems with **cron** and **/etc/rc.**
- File permissions on critical files and devices.
- Problems with **setuid.**
- Some CERT-reported security holes (we will be discussing CERT later on in this chapter).

Crack

Crack is the foremost freeware password security auditing tool for UNIX. It's a powerful password cracker program, designed specifically for system administrators, rather than would-be intruders. Crack is much more powerful than the password cracking tools in COPS and makes a nice complement to COPS in a complete security auditing suite.

Crack uses an extensive (and extensible) dictionary to attack your **/etc/ passwd** file - if Crack breaks a password, it's certain that an intruder can too. It's designed so that it can be run unattended, and will automatically send a 'nastygram' (a warning via e-mail) to users whose passwords it manages to break.

There is also an add-on to Crack called UFC that inserts a faster crypt algorithm into Crack.

ISS

The Internet Security Scanner (ISS) checks your network service configuration for a variety of recognized holes and common misconfigurations. It shouldn't be confused with COPS, which concentrates mainly on file system and user account issues. In fact, ISS and COPS complement each other well and could be used together to provide a formidable security audit for Internet-connected systems. ISS is also available from various anonymous **ftp** sites on the Internet (we'll discuss where later).

TripWire

TripWire is yet another freeware security tool. It isn't an auditing tool, it's an intrusion-detection system. TripWire is designed to be installed on to a 'clean' system configuration, where it generates checksums for sensitive system files. If any of these files are altered without permission, TripWire generates an alarm helping to prevent viruses, trojan horses and other malicious tampering on your system. TripWire is free and widely available on the Internet via anonymous `ftp` (again sites are given at the end of this chapter).

Data Encryption

You can also take further steps to protect your data by passing it through encryption software. This can keep it safe even if an intruder manages to gain access to it. There are two principal families of encryption techniques in use, private-key and public-key. Keep in mind that no matter how good the encryption scheme, your data is only as safe as the key, and keeping keys safe presents its own set of problems.

Private-Key Systems

In a private-key encryption system, data can only be encrypted or retrieved by someone who knows the password. Therefore, if one party wants to encrypt a message to send to another party, both parties must know the same password. This has some serious security problems - for instance, the password will probably need to be communicated from one party to another via an insecure medium, like e-mail or the telephone system. Private-key systems work best when data is encrypted for archival purposes rather than for communication. The `crypt` system in UNIX and the DES (Data Encryption Standard) system are common examples of private-key systems.

Public-Key Systems

A much more sophisticated way to encrypt shared data is to use a public-key system. Here the key is split into two parts - a public-key and a private-key. The public-key alone can be used to encrypt, while both are required to decrypt. Therefore, you can distribute your public-key freely to those who wish to send you encrypted messages, as long as you protect the private portion of the key.

The RSA (Rivest-Shamir-Adleman, named after its inventors) scheme is currently the most popular public-key encryption scheme. Commercial products from RSA Data Security Inc. make use of this scheme, as does the controversial freeware program Pretty Good Privacy (PGP). RSA is exceptionally strong - so much so that products employing it are classified by the U.S. Government as *munitions* and are subject to severe export restrictions.

Key Management

An encryption key is like a root password - you don't want to forget it, but you also don't want it to fall into the wrong hands. In most serious public-key encryption systems, the key is more than just a password - it's a block of binary data that must be stored electronically. Sometimes it is further encrypted with a private-key password just in case it falls into the wrong hands. Remember that your unbreakable, military-grade public-key system is rendered useless if someone gets your key.

A common technique is to store keys on removable media, like floppy diskettes, physically under lock and key. This keeps them very safe when not in use and helps ensure you'll be able to find them when you need them. For keys you use in lower-security applications or high-volume automated encryption (like e-mail), you may want to take your chances and leave your key in a reasonably secure part of your file system. Just make sure to keep your password safe!

There is a problem with public-key systems where one person can publicize a key and claim it belongs to someone else, allowing them to intercept and decode encrypted traffic to the victim. You can get around this by allowing third-parties to "witness" the creation of all new keys. If you don't trust the source of a key, check with the supposed owner and compare it with a witnessed key. Eventually, there may be centralized key-notary services on the Internet that can verify the authenticity of keys for you.

In the Event of an Attack

There are several ways in which you might become aware of a possible attack on your system:

- The system begins to exhibit strange behavior not attributable to other system conditions.

- You notice a user logged in whose account is long dormant.

- You notice suspicious processes running that you can't trace to a legitimate source.

- Your system crashes unexpectedly.

- A routine security audit (either by hand or with a tool like COPS) turns up suspicious system conditions, like altered file permissions or bad system file checksums.

- A system administrator from another site contacts you, complaining of attacks originating from your system.

Close the Hole

Your first task is to plug the hole to prevent further attacks.

Change All Administrative Passwords!

Immediately change all passwords on privileged and vulnerable accounts. Remove or disable any accounts that have been granted root access by the attacker. If you have a small number of users, it's worthwhile recommending that everyone change their passwords. Otherwise, run Crack on your **/etc/passwd** to suggest any weak passwords. Your attacker may have used Crack itself to attack your system.

Block Suspicious or Compromised Accounts

If you know the account from which the attack is occurring, disable it immediately and notify (or even disable) any accounts with bad passwords. Ideally, you'd like the user of a potentially compromised account to have to contact you in order to get the account re-enabled so that you can be sure that the attacker doesn't continue to exploit it.

Many administrators keep small programs on their systems that can act as shell replacements in emergency situations like this. The administrator changes the login shell for the compromised account to the replacement program, which usually prints out a message like:

> Your account has been temporarily disabled. Please contact the system
> administrator (phone: 555-1234) for more information or to arrange for
> reactivation of your account.

This accomplishes a couple of things. It directs a legitimate user to you for
specific details, providing more information about what's going on than the
login incorrect message, which would be displayed if the account was
actually removed or disabled with an asterisk in the **/etc/passwd** password
entry. At the same time, however, it also effectively blocks further attacks
through the compromised account.

Take the System Off-Net

If the attack came through a network connection or over a
telecommunications line, you may wish to consider disconnecting the system
from the outside world, at least until you're reasonably confident that
you've blocked further attacks.

Locate the Hole

Your next task is to try to track down the weakness in your system that
was exploited by the attacker. If you are unsure, here are a few pointers.

Check the Logs

In some cases, like the suspicious 'resurrected' user, the problem is self-
evident - a password was compromised. If you didn't actually see a
suspicious user, look in the **/etc/passwd** and **/usr/adm/wtmp** files for
suspicious entries and recent activity in dormant accounts (the program
last will produce a human-readable log). If your system is using
accounting, look in the accounting records as well (usually **/usr/adm/acct**)
with the **ac** program.

Perform an On-the-Spot Security Audit

This is starting to sound like a routine security audit, isn't it? Well, if your
system hasn't been crippled by the attack, you should do a thorough

security audit immediately to try and locate system elements that were compromised during the attack. In particular, watch out for users with root privileges - if the attacker manages to sneak in a new account with root privileges or someone grants them access to an existing account with a compromised password, you're exposed to a serious repeat attack.

Survey the Damage and Clean Up

Now it is the time to fix anything that you found to be amiss during your on-the-spot security audit. Take a close look at the home directories of any compromised accounts - look for hidden files and directories, and check the `.history` files to see if you can piece together the activities engaged in by the hacker. Try to ascertain whether your system was used as a waystation for attacks on other systems (via the `telnet`, `rlogin` commands in the `.history`).

Contact Other Possible Victims

If your system was used to attack other systems, and the adminstrators of the remote systems haven't already tracked *your* system down as the source of the attack, then be a good net.samaritan and make an effort to reach them. There are several tools that you can use to help locate the administrator for a certain machine on the Internet.

finger

The first thing you should try is `finger root@attacked.system`. If `finger` services are running at the remote site, then there is a decent chance that the system administrator has placed contact information in their plan.

whois

The `whois` utility is used in conjunction with the name of a network, domain or user. It returns information about the network address number, and sometimes, extra technical and administrative support information, and maybe a postal or e-mail address and phone number. On some systems this has been replaced by the `fwhois` command, which has the same format:

```
$ fwhois sunsite.unc.edu
[rs0.internic.net]
University of North Carolina at Chapel Hill (SUNSITE-HST)

   Hostname: SUNSITE.UNC.EDU
   Address: 152.2.22.81
   System: SUN running UNIX

   Record last updated on 01-Feb-94.


To see this host record with registered users, repeat the command with
a star ('*') before the name; or, use '%' to show JUST the registered
users.

The InterNIC Registration Services Host contains ONLY Internet Information
(Networks, ASN's, Domains, and POC's).
Please use the whois server at nic.ddn.mil for MILNET Information.
```

The Network Information Center (NIC)

The most comprehensive directory of network contacts is maintained by the
Internet's Network Information Center (NIC). Anyone can anonymously
access the NIC's database lookup service via telnet at **nic.internic.net**.

traceroute

If you can't find a contact at the attacked site, you may want to try looking
up the domain's contact information instead. You can use **whois** and the
NIC lookup to do this, but sometimes you can get a good lead on who to
contact by running the command **traceroute** on the address, which will
show you all the intervening network hops between you and the attacked
system. You may be able to locate an intermediary service provider who has
contact information for the attacked system.

The Last Resort

If you can't find a quicker way to reach the attacked systems'
administrators, then there's always e-mail. It's better than nothing. One
thing to remember, however, is that the mail system on the remote machine
may be compromised and the hacker may be watching for and deleting
your mail. If you're going to send an e-mail message, your best bet is to
send it to the root account or postmaster account.

Internet Resources

The Internet itself is perhaps the best security information resource for the UNIX system administrator. Here are a few places on the Internet where you can find valuable security tools, tips and advice. Many will point you to a variety of other resources as well.

CERT

The Software Engineering Institute at Carnegie-Mellon University operates the Computer Emergency Response Team (CERT), which serves as the Internet's main security body. CERT gathers security information and coordinates with system vendors to ensure that potential security holes are fixed. CERT operates the **cert-advisory** mailing list, which is an important source of up-to-the-minute information about Internet security issues. To join **cert-advisory**, send a request via e-mail to **cert@cert.sei.cmu.edu.**

If your system has been attacked, it's a good idea to contact CERT immediately. CERT operates a 24-hour hotline at +1 (412) 268-7090. If your e-mail system hasn't been compromised, you can send e-mail to CERT at **cert@cert.org**.

Security Tools via Anonymous ftp

Here's where to find some of the tools mentioned in this chapter:

Tool	FTP Site	Directory
COPS	**cert.org**	**/pub/cops**
Crack	**ftp.uu.net**	**/usenet/comp.sources.misc/ volume28/crack**
ISS	**iss.net**	**/pub/iss**
Passwd+	**dartmouth.edu**	**/security**
Shadow	**ftp.uu.net**	**/usenet/ comp.sources.misc/volume38/ shadow/usenet/comp.sources.misc/ volume39/shadow** (you need the sources from both directories)

Continued

Tool	FTP Site	Directory
TCP Wrappers	`cert.org`	`/pub/tools/tcp_wrappers`
TIS Firewall Toolkit	`ftp.tis.com`	`/pub/firewalls/toolkit`
TripWire	`cert.org`	`/pub/tools/tripwire`

Usenet Newsgroups

The Usenet News system carries a number of security-related groups:

Newsgroup	Topic
`alt.security`	Covers general security issues, not just those concerning UNIX.
`comp.security.misc`	Similar to `alt.security`, but it's a bit more serious in tone.
`comp.risks`	Discusses risks to the public posed by computers. Covers several system security issues.
`comp.protocols.tcp-ip`	General discussion of the TCP-IP protocol suite, including security issues. Carries the same traffic as the TCP-IP mailing list.
`comp.security.unix`	Deals specifically with the security of UNIX systems.
`comp.security.announce`	Announcements.
`alt.2600`	This group is mostly dedicated to *breaking* security, normally the domain of hackers. A good systems administrator might want to keep an eye on some of the issues raised here.

Mailing Lists

If you don't have access to the Usenet news system, information is available directly via e-mail:

List	Topic	How to Join
CERT-Advisory	Up-to-the-minute security bulletins from CERT	Send a request via e-mail to: **cert@cert.sei.cmu.edu**
TCP-IP	General discussion of the TCP-IP protocol suite	Send a request via e-mail to: **tcp-ip-request@nic.ddn.mil**
Virus-L	Discussion of virus incidents, protection, etc	Send a request via e-mail to: **listserv%lehiibm1. bitnet@mitvma.mit.edu**

World Wide Web Pages

There are several sites on the World Wide Web that carry excellent security resources. These sites are basically launch pads to various other Internet security resources:

Page	URL	Contents
SAIC Security Page	**http://mls.saic. com/docs.html**	An archive of security documents made available on the Internet by SAIC Corporation.
Computer Security Resource Clearinghouse	**http://csrc. ncsl.nist.gov/**	A compilation of security resources put together by the National Institute of Standards and Technology.
Computer and Network Security Reference Index	**http://www. tansu.com.au/ Info/security. html**	A large archive of documents and references to other security resources on the Internet. An excellent resource.

Summary

In this chapter we looked at some of the security threats facing a UNIX system and how you can defend against them. We saw how good administrative practices alone can make a big difference in system security. We explored the special security problems that are posed by external connections via the telephone and network systems. We suggested both new working practices and some freely available tools and utilities which could help. We looked at methods for auditing the security of a system and we surveyed some techniques for encrypting sensitive data. We discussed the steps you should take if you feel your system has been compromised by an intruder. Finally, for reference purposes, we listed most of the useful tools mentioned within the chapter and the addresses of the sites from which they are available.

Chapter

PC Connection to UNIX

You should by now have a fairly good 'feel' for the whole UNIX system. We've looked generically at the commands that UNIX uses and have considered most of the main functions that you could use UNIX for, from accessing the Internet to administering a network of workstations. This would be of more practical use if you could simply hook up to a UNIX system via your PC. A common configuration in an office environment is one or more UNIX 'servers' and a larger number of PCs, perhaps one per desk. In this chapter we'll look at how these can be connected together, and how the facilities available on the UNIX machines can be made available on the desktop.

First, we will deal with the question of making the actual physical connection. Once this has been made, then there is the problem of getting your applications to communicate with the hardware. We will also look at the task of transferring files between a PC and UNIX and sharing resources. Finally we will consider a range of commercial products which will facilitate different aspects of the UNIX/PC integration. The order of play is:

- Direct Serial connection
- IP connection
- Network connection
- Methods of file and text transfer
- Improving the integration
- Commercial products

Types of Connection

There are two main ways of physically connecting an MS-DOS/MS-Windows PC to a UNIX box: you can use a direct serial cable or connect them via a local area network (LAN). The serial connection is, in general, easier to set up initially, but the LAN connection offers higher performance and more flexibility in the long term.

If your PC is connected by a serial cable, it can either act as a single 'dumb' terminal, or run multiple terminal emulations and file transfers, simultaneously.

Direct Serial

For a direct serial connection you simply need to connect a serial port on your UNIX machine to a serial port on your PC. Most PCs have an unused serial port, and almost all UNIX machines will support additional serial ports: larger UNIX machines are easily capable of supporting more than 60 concurrent serial ports. This is probably the simplest method of connection, but it is also the least flexible.

The cable used will depend on many things, such as the line speed you intend to use over the link, the length of cable required and the amount of electrical noise in the area around the cable run. The absolute minimum number of wires required in the cable is three, though this is only suitable for the simplest connections. Five wires should be used for a direct serial connection and seven if a modem is being used.

The layout of connections will be a star, at least logically:

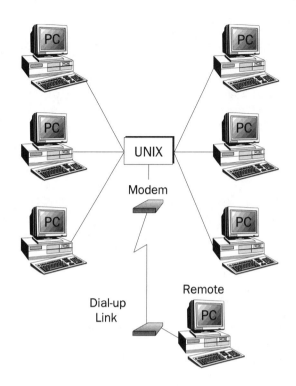

Terminal Emulation

Having physically connected the UNIX machine and the PC, the simplest option is to configure the UNIX machine as though a simple terminal was connected on the serial port. Then run a terminal emulation program on the PC, so that it behaves as a simple terminal. There are many different terminals that can be configured and emulated - the most common are probably the Digital Equipment Corporation (DEC) VT100 series and the ANSI standard series.

There is a wide range of PC terminal applications available, both for MS-DOS and for MS-Windows. If you only need to access UNIX from the PC for simple commands and responses, then a budget priced terminal emulator or even a shareware package may be suitable. If you need to run a UNIX application that uses more sophisticated output, such as color and line drawing, then you may need a more fully featured terminal such as Tektronix or VT320 color terminals.

File Transfer

If you are running a simple terminal emulator, then transferring files between the UNIX machine and your PC can be quite difficult. For a limited amount of text information, it may be possible to 'cut and paste' between the terminal emulation and a PC-based editor, but this would be unworkable for larger or more complex files.

To transfer larger files you need to use a file transfer program. There are several available, including Zmodem and Kermit, and they sometimes come as a built-in feature in terminal emulators. We will look briefly here at Kermit, since this is the most commonly used.

Kermit

First of all you will need a Kermit program available on both your local PC and the UNIX machine. To establish a Kermit connection:

1 Start Kermit on the PC.

2 Establish a terminal session (via Kermit) to the UNIX machine.

3 Start the remote Kermit program.

4 Escape back to the local Kermit program, which will then allow you to transfer files in both directions.

A sample Kermit session is shown below. Notice the use of *Alt-X* which is the key sequence used to tell the local Kermit program that you wish to access its command mode, rather than send characters to the remote machine. The

connect command is used to start or resume a session, and here it resumes passing characters to the remote machine. The session below assumes the serial connection to the UNIX machine is connected to port COM2 of the PC, and the UNIX machine is expecting the serial port to run at 9600 baud.

```
C:\>
C:\>kermit
MS-Kermit
Copyright (C) Trustees of Columbia University 1982,1990
Type ? for HELP for help
MS-Kermit>set speed 9600
MS-Kermit>set port com2
MS-Kermit>connect
UNIX (sales)

login: jim
Password:
Last login: Mon Jan 16 11:27:58 from jj
Welcome to sales.

You have mail.
There is news to read

/home/jim 1 $ kermit
C-Kermit, 5A(100)
Type ? for help
C-Kermit>receive
Alt-X
MS-Kermit>send list.txt
MS-Kermit>connect
C-Kermit>send hello.c
Alt-X
MS-Kermit>receive
MS-Kermit>connect
C-Kermit>exit
/home/jim 1 $ exit
Alt-X
MS-Kermit>exit
C:\>
```

IP Connection

Rather than use your serial cable for a simple terminal emulation, you can choose to run a protocol over the serial cable, allowing a much higher level of integration. This allows applications to pass data across the serial link as though it was a local area network, enabling multiple applications and simultaneous bi-directional data transfer.

Traditionally, the majority of UNIX machines use TCP/IP for accessing networks. It's possible to use the same protocol over a serial link, by using an additional lower level protocol, normally SLIP, CSLIP or PPP. These protocols are also probably the most common form of dial-up access to the Internet. To use one of these protocols you need support on both the host and the PC. Some UNIX machines may provide TCP/IP support over serial lines, otherwise you will need to obtain a shareware or commercial product. We'll take a look at PC-based software later in this chapter.

Once a TCP/IP connection is established over a serial link to a TCP/IP host on a local network, it allows multiple higher level protocols to simultaneously use the serial link. If you have the appropriate software, it becomes possible to run multiple terminal sessions, file transfers, mail transfers and other applications simultaneously. This access is limited by the speed of your serial link, but for many practical purposes it provides similar functionality, if not performance, to a local area network (LAN) connection.

Serial Line IP (SLIP)

This protocol came into being in the early 1980's. It's a packet framing protocol that allows IP packets to be transferred over a serial line. SLIP is a very simple protocol, easy to implement and widely distributed. Since it's so simple, it is a good option to choose when initially setting up an IP connection over a serial link.

Compressed Serial Line IP (CSLIP)

This is a variation on SLIP, improving the speed of connections across a serial link by compressing the IP packet headers.

Point to Point Protocol (PPP)

This protocol was designed more recently than SLIP. It is a much more general protocol for allowing the transfer of encapsulated datagrams over a serial link with error correction. PPP has the ability to negotiate IP addresses without user intervention, which may be necessary in circumstances where clients are allocated a dynamic IP address on connection to a network. This is sometimes required on dial-up networks.

Although PPP is a more complex protocol than SLIP, it's generally more popular than SLIP because of its greater efficiency and end-to-end error correction. However, on a link with error correcting and compressing modems (such as the V42 and V42bis modems) the practical performance differences between SLIP and PPP can be quite small.

A simple representation of a hierarchy of protocols, usually referred to as a protocol stack, with bi-directional data flow to multiple applications is shown below:

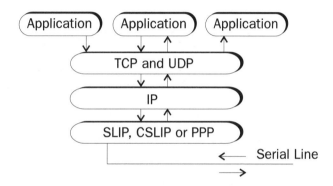

Network Connection

A direct serial connection has very limited bandwidth. Using a local area network for connections provides a substantial increase in performance.

There are many different types of LAN in use and each has its own physical characteristics and hardware interface, or Media Access Control (MAC) layer. Perhaps the most common forms of LAN for connecting to UNIX machines are 10base2 and 10baseT. 10base2 is commonly referred to as 'cheapernet', as it is derived from the original 'Ethernet', but uses a cheaper form of cabling. 10baseT uses twisted pair cables and may have a lower installation cost, at the possible expense of less flexibility in the positioning of network connections because of its 'star' topology. All of these LANs require the use of a network card in your PC. Many different cards are available, in both 8-bit and 16-bit versions.

Whatever physical topology your network has, it must support the TCP/IP protocols, since networking on the vast majority of UNIX machines is designed around the use of TCP/IP. Many of the products available for accessing UNIX machines with TCP/IP are compatible with other networking products at the physical level, so it's usually possible to run many protocols on the same physical network. This enables machines using Novell and MS-Windows for Workgroups, for example, to use the same physical network as machines using TCP/IP. Indeed a single PC may be able to work concurrently with many different protocols - this is usually referred to as using dual protocol stacks.

Here is an example 'Ethernet' or 'cheapernet' LAN with a backbone and multiple spurs:

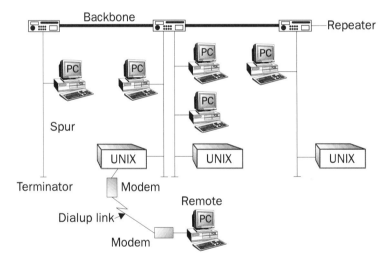

TCP/IP for MS-DOS and MS-Windows

Once you have physically connected the PC to the network with a network card, you have to run software on the PC to interface with the network card and provide access to the TCP/IP protocols on the LAN.

When you use TCP/IP over a LAN, the protocol stack is logically very similar to the one in place when you use a serial cable.

Interface Software

There is a wide variety of interface software available, some of it is shareware. The main decision you need to make is whether you need access to the network from MS-DOS, MS-Windows, or both, and whether you need part of the UNIX file system to be mapped to a local drive-letter on the PC.

Network Cards

Network cards are normally supplied with some software to access the card, often some drivers for specific operating systems such as MS-Windows, MS-DOS, OS/2 and Novell. Manufacturers often include a diagnostic test suite for ensuring that the card is functioning correctly and can access the lowest layer of the network protocols. Sometimes additional software is required to enable applications to access the higher levels of the network protocols.

MS-DOS Applications

A common way of adding support for a network card is a 'terminate and stay resident' (TSR) program called a packet driver. This may either be a packet driver that accesses the hardware directly, or a hardware independent interface, such as an NDIS or ODI driver, which is normally provided by card manufacturers. Since many applications support a packet driver interface, there are also packet drivers available that access the card via an NDIS driver. This double layer is sometimes referred to as a 'shim'. The packet driver interface presented via a software interrupt to the application (or TCP/IP software), between the hexadecimal range of 60 to 7f. To ensure that the TSR is as small as possible, each packet driver normally only supports a single type of card, but there are many packet drivers available.

Depending on your application, if your application doesn't feature built-in support, you may have to run an additional TSR program to provide support for the TCP/IP protocol. The packet driver itself doesn't provide any protocol support.

Here are some of the different ways for an MS-DOS application to access the network:

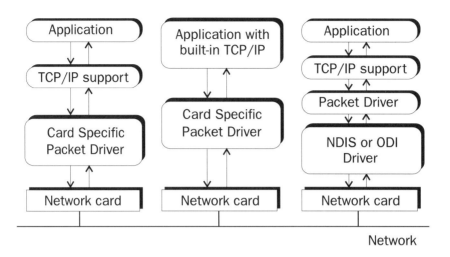

MS-Windows Applications

Until recently, accessing the network from an MS-Windows application wasn't standardized very well (the Windows NT client now comes with built in support for TCP/IP). A common way of providing access was to run an additional TSR after the packet driver, that provided an additional higher level interface to the packet driver for MS-Windows applications.

Winsock

There is now a standard Applications Programming Interface (API) called 'Windows Sockets', often abbreviated to 'Winsock', developed by a large number of individuals and supported by many companies. It is based on the successful 'socket' paradigm in an early (but still very widely used) network programming interface used in Berkeley System UNIX and some early specifications work done by JSB Corporation and Net Manage, Inc.

This specification has almost gained universal acceptance now for accessing TCP/IP networks from MS-Windows applications, with a multitude of both shareware and commercial products available. Even commercial vendors who originally had a proprietary interface now often offer Winsock as an option.

Winsock DLL

All Winsock implementations provide a DLL file called **winsock.dll.** This DLL (dynamic link library) provides a standard set of functions that MS-Windows applications can call to access the TCP/IP network. It's very important to realize that each vendor's version of **winsock.dll** is different - only the higher level interface to applications is standard; the lower layer is vendor-specific. The current version of the Winsock standard is 1.1a, but there are ongoing discussions about a version 2.0, which will probably appear be released towards the end of 1995.

There are many advantages to the Winsock standard. Firstly, it doesn't matter to the application which physical hardware is providing the physical transport, or whose TCP/IP implementation is in use. A Winsock application should run on a dial-up serial line just the same as on an Ethernet network, if a little slower.

Secondly, once you have installed a protocol stack that provides a Winsock interface to your physical network, you can mix and match applications from different vendors. So even if your terminal program comes from one supplier, and your **ftp** application from another, they should both run simultaneously without problem on a third vendor's Winsock-compliant protocol stack.

The only significant drawback occurs in the (slightly unusual) situation where you wish to run two different versions of **winsock.dll** at different times, perhaps one for using a dial-up serial connection and one for using an Ethernet connection. In this situation you must arrange for the two different versions of **winsock.dll** to reside in different directories, accessed at appropriate times, depending on which network connection is currently in use.

On the next page is a representation of a Windows protocol stack, showing the level where the Winsock API is standardized:

415

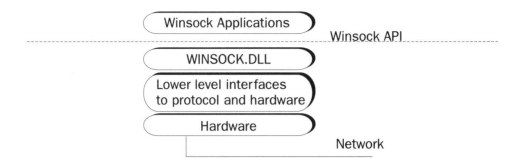

Providing your physical network supports multiple protocols, there is no reason why you shouldn't run multiple protocols, with different applications accessing the different protocols simultaneously. For example, you could be running an application that uses the NetBEUI protocol, a TCP/IP **telnet** session and a TCP/IP **ftp** session simultaneously.

The underlying stack would then look something like this:

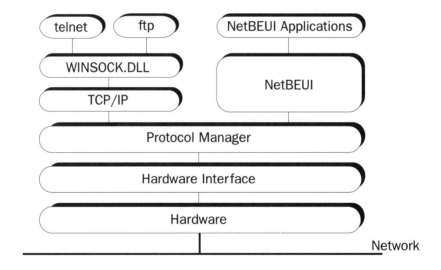

telnet and rlogin

These are probably the most widely used applications over TCP/IP. They provide a terminal emulation and allow a remote machine to access another as though it was a local terminal. MS-DOS versions are normally very similar to the original UNIX versions. To access a remote machine you use a command such as:

```
C:\>telnet sales.widget.com
```

You are presented with a login prompt as if you were connected locally. After logging on you are presented with a command prompt (from the remote machine) which you can use as though it was a direct connection. When you log out from the remote machine, the connection is automatically closed and you return to your local command prompt.

Here is some example dialog:

```
C:\>telnet sales.widget.com

Trying ...

UNIX (sales)

login: jim
Password:
Last login: Mon Jan 16 12:17:18 from jj
Welcome to sales.

You have new mail.
There is news to read

/home/jim 1 $ exit
Connection closed

C:\>
```

The **rlogin** command is one of a set of remote commands found on most UNIX machines.

NFS

The Network File System was developed by Sun, originally to allow UNIX machines to transparently share remote disk drives across a network. It's possible to allow PCs running MS-DOS and MS-Windows to access remote UNIX files in a similar fashion. Since MS-DOS and MS-Windows permissions and filename restrictions are different from the UNIX equivalents, names and permissions are mapped to valid MS-DOS names and permissions.

Additional MS-DOS drives are normally added by assigning or mounting the remote file system to a MS-DOS drive letter. NFS is a 'stateless' protocol and considers each request for reading or writing a block of data independently from the last. This has both advantages and disadvantages. It has the considerable advantage that if the PC crashes, or is turned off without the remote file system being un-mounted, then normally no harm will have been done. The disadvantage is that each write request to the UNIX machine must finish before the client (the PC) can be allowed to continue, and this can make writing to a drive that NFS accesses rather slow. Later versions of the NFS protocol incorporate speed improvements that alleviate this difficulty.

SMTP and POP3

These two protocols are used for transferring mail across networks and were originally discussed in Chapter 10. The first is Simple Mail Transfer Protocol (SMTP) and is used mainly for exchanging mail between two machines, independently of user names. One machine simply connects to the remote machine, sends all the mail for the remote machine and those systems that can only be accessed via that machine, deletes the local copy of the mail and then closes the connection. SMTP is commonly used for mail backbones, where there is a number of different e-mail packages connected through the backbone.

The POP3 protocol (Post Office Protocol version 3) is a much more complex protocol. It allows individual accounts to access `mail` from a remote machine. The remote machine connects to the server and must then specify a mail account and password. It may then query the state of the mail box, list the mail headers, retrieve individual mail messages and finally delete the remote copy of the mail.

Mail is normally transferred across a large network using SMTP. However, where there is a single UNIX server with mail and many permanently connected PCs, POP3 would normally be used. You should check out which protocols are used with different clients. It's quite common for PC mail applications to use POP3 for retrieving mail from the UNIX server, but to use SMTP for sending outgoing mail back to the server. Most PC mail programs just require the mail protocol to be configured once and then hide the implementation details from the user.

MIME

An important feature to look for in mail applications is MIME (Multi-purpose Internet Mail Extensions) support. Originally Internet mail only allowed 7 bit characters to be transferred and some nodes limited message sizes to 64k. This wasn't a problem when only small text messages were being sent, but is a problem for mailing large messages or messages containing binary data.

NNTP

This is Network News Transfer Protocol. It is used for transferring news articles across the network. News transfer can operate in two modes, on-line and off-line.

Off-line Mode

With off-line news transfer, the client requests a list of articles that have arrived for a newsgroup since the last news was transferred. The server responds with a list of article identifiers, which the client then requests. When all the articles have been transferred, the connection is closed and the news articles may be read by users.

On-line Mode

With on-line news, articles are requested one at a time by the user and the connection remains open while the news is being read.

Off-line reading is normally used where there's a charge for connection time, (such as over a dial-up link) or between two news servers distributing news. On-line news reading is more often used where the network connection is permanent. Its advantage is that the client can arrange to transfer individual news articles as they are requested for reading and then delete them. This minimizes the storage space required on the client machine.

HTTP

This is Hyper Text Transfer Protocol, the protocol used by the World Wide Web. Various browsers are available, mainly for window systems (Microsoft, the MIT X-Window System and the Macintosh). Some of these browsers are also capable of accessing other services such as **mail**, **news**, **ftp** and other information providing services such as Gopher and WAIS. By configuring external 'helper' applications, it's also possible to include moving images and sound.

PC as an X Terminal

Sometimes you may wish to use a UNIX program that uses the MIT X Window System (usually called X), but access the program from your PC. There are some products available that are able to interpret the X information and display it using MS-Windows. These are PC-based X servers that provide display facilities for UNIX X client programs. Servers exist for MS-DOS and, more commonly, MS-Windows. They may turn the PC into an X terminal, as if you were running X on a UNIX workstation, or they may allow X clients to display in MS-Windows windows. These normally work best on more powerful PCs with large screen sizes.

X as MS-Windows

If you primarily wish to use X, but occasionally need to use an MS-Windows program, then there are some products that allow programs written for Microsoft Windows to execute on a UNIX machine giving X output. This is more difficult than the former case and, at the time of writing, only a small number of products are available - examples being WABI from SunSoft and SoftWindows from Insignia Systems.

Smoothing the Connection

If you use both MS-DOS and UNIX, you may wish to try and make the transition a little easier - there are several things you can do:

- Make UNIX more like MS-DOS.
- Make MS-DOS more like UNIX.
- Make the dual work environment more integrated.

Usually it's easier to use the flexibility of UNIX to mimic MS-DOS than vice versa, although several products are available that provide a UNIX emulation under MS-DOS.

If you are going to be using both systems a lot, it's much better to learn the new system, rather than hide it away. This is also more convenient if you ever need to use a machine that doesn't have your familiar emulation facilities installed.

Aliasing UNIX Commands

> **Most UNIX shells support either aliasing or functions, permitting new commands to be created efficiently. By creating shell aliases you can use new commands to both mimic MS-DOS commands and to replace existing UNIX commands with MS-DOS equivalents.**

It's usually easiest to add extra commands that convert MS-DOS commands that don't exist in UNIX into working UNIX equivalents, such as aliasing the MS-DOS command **TYPE** to represent the UNIX **cat** command. See Chapter 5 for further details on aliasing.

Turning MS-DOS into UNIX

Making MS-DOS more like UNIX is generally more difficult, since MS-DOS doesn't provide the functionality for many of the UNIX commands or file attributes.

However, there are two main ways of superficially turning MS-DOS into UNIX. The easiest way is to buy a commercial product that performs this very function. The other method is to write new commands, programs, or even simple batch files to emulate UNIX commands. This isn't as difficult as it might at first seem, since many UNIX commands have an open version available as source code. The major problems are programs that access devices, since MS-DOS devices are very different from UNIX devices, especially where UNIX programs assume a large 32-bit flat memory model, but require an extender in MS-DOS.

Improving the Integration

If you are using NFS on your MS-DOS PC, then there is one very simple, but very worthwhile, arrangement that can make the integration appear almost seamless. If at all possible you should arrange that your home directory on UNIX is also mounted as a drive-letter under MS-DOS.

This deceptively simple step means that you have files accessible to both operating systems at the same time. You could, if you wanted to, use a UNIX program to create the files, extract data from them with an MS-DOS program and then use UNIX's sophisticated backup tools to back them up. You could read your UNIX mail on a MS-Windows machine using an MS-Windows program and save the message to a file on a network drive, which means the saved file appears both in your home directory on the UNIX machine and as a file on your PC. Since MS-DOS only supports short file names (eight characters plus a three character extension) and isn't case sensitive, you will probably find it easier and a more cohesive transition, if you restrict your UNIX file names to valid MS-DOS names.

Commercial Products for PC Connection

There is a wide range of products available for UNIX and PC integration, ranging from some free and shareware products, to comprehensive commercial products that cost considerable amounts of money. Here we will give an overview of a small selection of some of the more popular products available. Since new products are appearing all the time and existing products are continually being updated, you should always consult your supplier, checking your individual needs against the facilities available before purchasing.

The facilities available fall into several categories:

- NFS for MS-DOS
- NFS for MS-Windows
- TCP/IP protocol stacks for MS-DOS
- TCP/IP protocol stacks for MS-Windows
- TCP/IP applications for MS-DOS
- TCP/IP applications for MS-Windows
- X display programs using MS-Windows
- MS-Windows hosting environments for UNIX and X.

Many products provide more than one of these facilities.

Microsoft

If you are running Windows for Workgroups 3.11, Microsoft has a TCP/IP add-on available for download (Winsock) from its publicly accessible **ftp** site, **ftp.microsoft.com**. Alternatively, contact your local dealer for a floppy disk version at nominal cost.

Primarily Winsock is an MS-Windows Virtual Device Driver, or VxD, that provides a Winsock API for MS-Windows applications. It comes complete with **telnet** and **ftp** programs - reasonably simple but functional applications.

Since this is an MS-Windows only VxD, it provides no support for MS-DOS programs, but it doesn't use significant amounts of MS-DOS memory either.

PC/TCP

There are several **ftp** software products available. The one we will look at here is PC/TCP with NFS. This package provides TCP/IP support, NFS for MS-DOS and MS-Windows, protocol support and a set of applications.

423

It has NFS support for both MS-DOS and MS-Windows, with the additional NFS drives appearing on the file manager toolbar. At the moment, MS-Windows for Workgroups 3.11 doesn't have built-in support for PC/TCP.

Like most packages that provide NFS drives for MS-DOS programs, there is a significant base memory overhead, although careful use of the MS-DOS **loadhigh** command can minimize the loss of base memory. A **winsock.dll** that will use the underlying **ftp** TCP/IP support to give a Winsock-compliant interface is also available. This enables you to use Winsock applications from other vendors over **ftp**'s TCP/IP implementation, if you wish.

A suite of applications, such as **telnet**, **rlogin** and **ftp** is provided with both MS-DOS and MS-Windows versions of most applications.

Trumpet Winsock

This is a shareware package from Trumpet Software International Pty Ltd, and is available for download from many Internet sites for free. It is a Winsock-compliant stack that provides a Winsock API for other applications. At the time of writing, the 'home' site for trumpet Winsock is **ftp://ftp.trumpet.com.au** and you are permitted to evaluate it for 30 days before you need to register and pay for it.

You can use Trumpet Winsock with either a serial interface (using SLIP, CSLIP or PPP) or by accessing a LAN via a network card with a packet driver. Both types of interface are fully configurable and are complemented by a large number of options.

If you are using a serial line, then Trumpet Winsock has a built-in dialer and a powerful scripting language. It's possible to write complex scripts for controlling modems and logging into remote machines. Also provided are several 'tracing' options; these are useful diagnostic tools to help you when things don't seem to be working!

Chameleon NFS from NetManage

This is an MS-Windows only package that removes the support for MS-DOS applications, allowing the package to use a very small amount of base memory - only 6KB on the current version. Installation is straightforward, with support for many different types of LAN, as well as support for serial lines for both SLIP and PPP. It also works concurrently with many other network types.

Once installed the MS-Windows file manager toolbar is modified to integrate the additional NFS options. Although NFS drives are accessible to other MS-Windows programs, they don't seem to be accessible to MS-DOS programs running in an MS-DOS box under MS-Windows. A suite of MS-Windows applications is provided, including `ftp`, `telnet`, `news`, `lpr` and `mail`.

The mail client is a fully featured application with support for both SMTP and POP3 protocols. The mail agent can handle MIME mail, allowing it to send and receive binary attachments with mail messages. The mail application also features handy folders for categorizing and storing received messages.

Chameleon also provides a `winsock.dll` interface. This wasn't mentioned in the manual available at the time of writing, but provides comprehensive Winsock 1.1 support, allowing other Winsock applications to run simultaneously with Chameleon's own applications.

Netscape

This is a World Wide Web browser and doesn't come with a protocol stack. Versions are available for several platforms, including both MS-Windows (using a Winsock interface) and X. At the time of writing, the product may be evaluated free of charge, although most classes of user should register after the designated trial period if they wish to continue using the product.

Netscape was designed to be usable over modem links, and downloads the text of WWW pages and displays it before fetching and decoding any embedded graphical information. This saves a lot of download time if you are only 'passing through' a page and are limited by a slow modem.

WinQVT/Net

This is a shareware package for MS-Windows providing a set of linked applications. The main interface is to a 'launcher' window, allowing configuration, as well as the invocation of separate `telnet`, `mail`, `ftp`, `news` and printing programs. Versions are available for both a packet driver and a Winsock interface to the network.

The **mail** program supports both SMTP and POP3, and has a background check facility for those permanently connected to a network. Since WinQVT/ Net provides several applications in a tightly integrated form and is low cost shareware, it's a package worth investigating.

JSB Multiview DeskTop

JSB Computer Systems' Multiview Desktop is a product that runs on MS-Windows for accessing UNIX machines. It can connect over serial lines, its own Winsock-compliant TCP/IP stack or via various other networking products, such as IPX/SPX.

Multiview provides various terminal emulations, complete with scripting and 'learn login' features, a file transfer utility and remote printing facilities. Unusually, it also provides desktop icons that can be used to directly invoke remote commands on UNIX machines (without the need to start a terminal session), and the ability for remote programs running in a desktop terminal window to invoke local PC applications. An additional Host Support Server is available which enables multiple simultaneous sessions, even over serial lines, without needing SLIP or PPP support on the UNIX machine.

JSB can also supply a Remote Execution Kit - a set of 'C' libraries for developers to use to access the communications provided by JSB Desktop. In addition there is a Remote Execution Kit Custom Control which allows Visual Basic developers to link to UNIX machines using JSB communication channels.

XVision from Visionware

This is a package that brings the MIT X Window System to the MS-Windows PC - in UNIX parlance, it's an X Server. This package also provides remote printing, terminal emulation and file transfer facilities. XVision will run over a wide range of networks, mostly TCP/IP versions. To run over a serial line, additional programs are required.

When XVision is installed, it runs a series of tests to optimize its performance on your graphics card. It then creates a new program group with a set of icons. You can use XVision in two distinct ways. If you use it for providing access to a small number of UNIX programs that use X, you can remain within the MS-Windows window management style and execute iconified X programs by clicking on them. If, on the other hand, you prefer to run a UNIX Window Manager, then you can set XVision to run a single MS-Windows window and use your X window manager to manage your X applications inside the virtual desktop.

Wabi 2.0 from SUN Microsystems

This is one of a range of products from different vendors that allow UNIX users to run MS-Windows applications on a UNIX machine with an X display. It is intended to run on a UNIX workstation sitting on a user's desk. Most of the products in this area are quite new and only support a finite set of MS-Windows applications. Wabi 2.0 supports about 24 applications, including Lotus SmartSuite and Microsoft Office. If you have a UNIX workstation on your desk and mostly run UNIX and X, only needing to run a small number of MS-Windows applications, then this might be an effective solution. You may also need to purchase a copy of MS-Windows to use some of these emulators.

MKS Toolkit from Mortice Kern Systems

This is a set of utilities primarily for MS-DOS, providing a range of utility programs to make the UNIX user feel 'at home' with MS-DOS. As well as 'small' utilities such as **diff**, **rm**, **grep**, **find**, **uniq** and **sort**, there is a set of development utilities including **make**, **rcs**, **awk**, **lex** and **yacc** - and even **vi**! There is also a Korn shell and archiving programs such as **tar** and **cpio**. Some of the MS-DOS utilities are 32-bit memory-extended, to ease memory constraints on larger datasets.

A version of the MKS toolkit is also available for Windows NT.

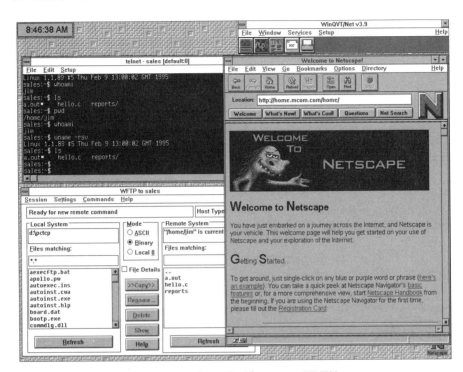

Bringing the PC Closer to UNIX

This screen shot is from a PC running MS-Windows for Workgroups 3.11, connected over a TCP/IP network to a UNIX (Linux) machine. TCP/IP networking (and a Winsock interface) is being provided by PC/TCP from FTP Software. The `ftp` session is an application provided with PC/TCP; the `telnet` session is from WinQVT/Net and the World Wide Web browser is an MS-Windows version from Netscape, accessing the Internet via a UNIX gateway machine.

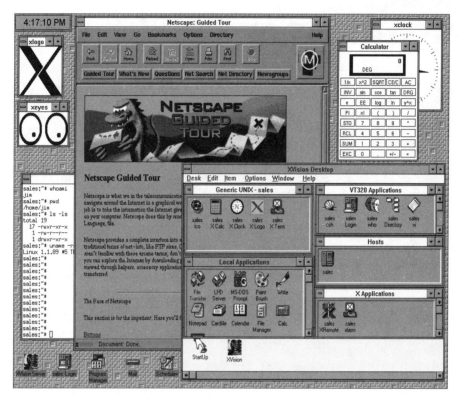

Bringing UNIX to the Desktop

This screen shot is from the same PC, still running MS-Windows for Workgroups 3.11, but now running XVision from Visionware. It shows various UNIX X application programs running, displaying their X output in MS-Windows form, as well as a remote login and XVision Desktop window. This version of Netscape is a UNIX (Linux) binary, executing on a remote UNIX machine, still accessing the Internet, but now providing its X display output remotely to the PC.

UNIX Variants for the PC

Many of the available UNIX variants will run on a PC. Most require the minimum of an Intel 386 (or compatible) processor and at least 4 megabytes of memory, although as with many operating systems nowadays, more would be preferable! If you wish to run X, then you should budget for a reasonable specification of an Intel 486 (or compatible) and a minimum of 8 megabytes of memory.

Most products are commercial, but there are some 'free distribution' UNIX systems available, most notably Linux, which we'll be looking at in detail in the next chapter. Remember to check your requirements and hardware compatibility before purchasing any of these products.

Novell Unixware 2.0

Unixware is available in two flavors: Personal Edition and Application Server. Initially only available for Intel-based computers and based on the latest System V Release 4.2 MP, it comes with X, the MOTIF graphical user interface, and networking (TCP/IP and NFS). The Personal Edition supports two simultaneous users, whilst the Application Server version is an unlimited user system. Both require a CD-ROM drive for installation.

Both versions of Unixware support multithreaded UNIX applications and can also run some real mode MS-DOS programs and even standard mode MS-Windows 3.1 applications. (MS-Windows itself isn't included.) The iBCS2 standard is supported, allowing any UNIX application that complies with iBCS2 to be executed without recompilation. For the developer, the system conforms to POSIX 1003.1, X/OPEN XPG4 base profile as well as earlier standards.

Novell are also working on providing the API for X/OPEN Ltd.'s SPEC1170 standard. Novell will provide code to OEM customers to allow them to convert it to other platforms; they are also working with various other companies to try and establish Unixware on other hardware platforms.

Solaris x86 2.x from SUN Microsystems

This is a version of Sun's Solaris version of UNIX, more usually seen on SPARC workstations. It is identical in features to the Solaris SPARC product and includes networking, X capability and Wabi 2.0. This product will be of particular interest to companies or individuals already running, or familiar with, Sun's popular UNIX based SPARC workstations.

SCO UNIX

One of the first vendors to sell a 'UNIX' for the PC was the Santa Cruz Operation (SCO), who sold a product called XENIX, which was available for PCs even before the Intel 386 was available.

The current SCO products are SCO UNIX and SCO Open Desktop, available with various numbers of user licenses. Both versions require a minimum of a 386 class CPU. The core of both products is the same, with the SCO Open Desktop version including X and MOTIF support, coupled with extra functionality.

SCO UNIX is sold as a set of smaller packages, so you can choose which facilities you wish to pay for. For example, a development machine might use the basic operating system plus the development system, the text processing system, TCP/IP networking, NFS, X-sight (X11/MOTIF) and SCO Merge for running MS-DOS applications. A single user's machine might only require the base operating system to be purchased.

FreeBSD

FreeBSD is a full source code 4.4BSD Lite variant for PCs based on Intel 386/486/Pentium (or compatible) systems. It's mostly based on software from the University of California at Berkeley, but contains software from other sources as well.

It is available on the Internet and on CD-ROM.

Summary

In this chapter we have seen how it's possible to connect PCs to UNIX machines. Indeed, the problem now is more one of choosing between different solutions, although the advent of the Winsock standard for MS-Windows applications has made it much easier to mix solutions from different vendors, whereas previously, applications usually had to be from the same vendor as the protocol supplier.

There is much you can do to integrate PCs and UNIX machines, especially if you have a TCP/IP LAN. If you don't wish to go as far as running UNIX on PCs (probably the ultimate integration!), then you could do any of the following instead:

- Install a local area network that can use TCP/IP protocols. Many other integration tools need this as a pre-requisite.

- Run NFS on both UNIX machines and PCs, giving tightly integrated disk areas.

- Run terminal emulators on the PCs to allow them to act as UNIX terminals.

- Emulate MS-DOS commands on your UNIX machines.

- Emulate UNIX commands on your MS-DOS machines.

- Run an X server on MS-Windows, for X capability on a PC.

- Run an MS-Windows translation for MS-Windows applications under X, on the UNIX machines.

- Run news, mail and WWW applications across the PC and UNIX machines.

It seems quite unlikely that any organization would need all of these simultaneously, but it does show you just how much can be achieved!

Chapter

Getting Started with Linux

Linux represents a chance for anyone interested in UNIX to operate a UNIX-like environment on almost any modern PC. Although UNIX implementations for PCs are available from a number of vendors, including Santa Cruz Operation (SCO UNIX), Novell (UnixWare) and Sun (Solaris 2.4 for Intel), they can be quite an expensive option, especially for home, hobbyist or evaluation use.

Linux started life as 'just' a UNIX kernel. However, through the efforts of many people on the Internet, it's now a complete UNIX environment and will run on most modern PCs. It uses the GNU project development tools and can run an X display. And of course, just as significantly, Linux is free.

This chapter will cover the following points:

- How and where to obtain Linux
- Linux installation
- Booting Linux
- Slackware distributions
- Linux applications

A Quick Note

Although we have tried to make the instructions for the programs in this chapter as generic as possible, you may find that the code shown in the examples doesn't work with your system. If this is the case, then you probably require different installation files to the ones we are using - these files are available in the Slackware distribution. To get Linux running correctly probably requires some experimentation with different files to find those that best suit your system.

You should also be very careful that you don't inadvertently alter your partitions when experimenting with installation files.

What is Linux?

Linux is a completely free clone of the UNIX operating system for 386/486/ Pentium class of personal computers. Linux itself is just a kernel, written in the first instance by a Finnish student named Linus Torvalds. Over several years the kernel has been extensively enhanced by volunteers exchanging ideas, source code and progress reports over the Internet. Many applications such as C compilers, editors and networking utilities have been written for, or ported to, the Linux environment. Most of the programs produced by the Free Software Foundation's GNU project are available as is MIT's X Window System.

Linux provides support for a wide variety of hardware components, network cards, processors, motherboard technologies, hard disk controllers, CD-ROM drives and video cards. Drivers for new hardware are developed and distributed almost as soon as a member of the Linux development community gets a hold of the appropriate information. With gigabytes of software available for Linux, and comprehensive software support available on the Internet or from independent support organizations, Linux represents a truly astonishing achievement in co-operative development.

Where Can I Find Linux?

Linux is available from many Internet `ftp` sites, notably **sunsite.unc.edu** and its mirror sites. However, downloading the Linux kernel and installing it yourself isn't the easiest thing to do, since you have to start with raw kernel sources. Thankfully, a number of individuals and organizations have arranged Linux and some application software into installable sets called Linux distributions. Some of the best known are Slackware, SLS, MCC, Debian and TAMU and they are available from `ftp` sites.

A Linux distribution is typically very large. In this chapter, the Slackware distribution that we will use as an example is well over 200Mb in size. Transferring that much software by modem from an `ftp` site would take a very long time and be very expensive. Luckily, some organizations offer Linux distributions on floppy disks, tapes and CD-ROMs. CD-ROMs are probably the best media since they're relatively inexpensive and feature extra applications, utilities and documentation.

Popular CD-ROM Linux distributions include Morse Slackware Pro, TransAmeritech CD-ROM and Yggdrasil Plug and Play Linux. These are easy to use and easy to install and come with technical support from the suppliers. Some even allow Linux to be run directly from the CD-ROM with little or no installation, although this feature is probably best used only as a pre-installation trial.

The InfoMagic Linux Developer's Resource CD-ROM set contains a number of Linux distributions, including Slackware, and several images of Linux `ftp` sites. It's a cost effective way of obtaining a good Linux distribution and a wealth of additional Linux software.

Installing Linux

Usually Linux is installed into two or more empty partitions on a PC hard disk. One is used for swap space to provide virtual memory; another stores the root directory and is known as the root partition. The others are used to store system files and user data.

UMSDOS

By using a facility known as UMSDOS (Unix on MS-DOS), it's possible to install a Linux file system into part of an existing DOS file system. The DOS disk must not be accessed via compression software such as MS-DOS DoubleSpace/DriveSpace or Stac Stacker and should have between 10Mb and 150Mb free space. UMSDOS provides a convenient way to try Linux before committing your system to the re-organization of your hard disk, a process that might require a complete backup and restoration of all files on the disk.

For the purposes of this chapter, we will look at a Linux installation using this technique. We will use the Slackware 2.1.0 distribution as found on an InfoMagic CD-ROM set. For information on installing on Linux native partitions, refer to documentation files supplied with any Linux distribution.

Note that the UMSDOS system does impact Linux performance. This is because the DOS file system isn't as efficient as the native Linux file system, and UMSDOS must cope with the added complication of mapping UNIX file names into the restricted DOS format. It does this transparently, but there is a performance penalty associated with it.

An Example

Let's consider a fairly normal PC. It's a 386DX-40 with 8Mb RAM. It has two IDE hard disks, with capacities of 201Mb and 41Mb. The larger disk has been partitioned into two drives and the second of these is largely empty. The second disk has been compressed with DOS DoubleSpace.

The available DOS drives are:

C: 101Mb First Disk, First Partition (Primary)

D: 41Mb Second Disk, First Partition (Primary), DoubleSpaced

E: 100Mb First Disk, Logical Drive in Second Partition (Extended)

The DOS **FDISK** program reports:

```
Display Partition Information

Current fixed disk drive: 1

Partition  Status   Type     Volume Label   Mbytes   System   Usage
   C: 1       A     PRI DOS                    101    FAT16     50%
      2             EXT DOS                    100              50%

Total disk space is  201 Mbytes (1 Mbyte = 1048576 bytes)

The Extended DOS Partition contains Logical DOS Drives.

Drv Volume Label  Mbytes  System  Usage
E:  DRIVE_E         100   FAT16    100%

Current fixed disk drive: 2

Partition  Status   Type     Volume Label   Mbytes   System   Usage
   D: 1       A     PRI DOS    ALEX            40     FAT16     98%

Total disk space is   41 Mbytes (1 Mbyte = 1048576 bytes)
```

In this example, we shall install Linux into the free space on the uncompressed **E:** drive.

Boot Disks

To start a Linux installation you need to boot your computer from a special disk that contains a Linux kernel. This disk, similar in concept to a DOS bootable diskette, formatted with **FORMAT /S**, is known as a **boot disk**. A Linux kernel may contain drivers for many different hardware combinations. There are a number of different boot disks in the Slackware distribution, each containing a slightly different Linux kernel supporting a variety of different options.

Three boot disks of note are **NET**, **SBPCD** and **SCSI**.

NET

The **NET** boot disk contains a kernel with a multitude of network drivers and can be used with a suitably equipped PC to install Linux from a network NFS server (either UNIX or Linux).

SBPCD

The **SBPCD** boot disk contains support for CD-ROM drives connected to the popular SoundBlaster Pro sound card. It can be used to install from a CD-ROM distribution. Note that this boot disk is only useful for CD-ROM drives connected directly to the Panasonic CD-ROM interface of the SoundBlaster Pro card (or to a separate LaserMate or SPEA interface card).

Some multi-media kits use Sony or Mitsumi CD-ROM drives. For these you'll need to use a different boot disk (**CDU31A**, **MITSUMI** or **MODERN**) - see the relevant documentation in your boot disk's sub-directories.

SCSI

The **SCSI** boot disk contains support for SCSI devices, including disks, tapes and CD-ROM drives. These and other boot disks are available in the **BOOT144** and **BOOT12** directories of the Slackware distribution, for 1.44Mb 3.5 inch and 1.2Mb 5.25 inch floppy disk versions, respectively. Those with the **GZ** filename extension will have to be uncompressed using the **GZIP.EXE** utility.

Making a Boot Disk in DOS

Make a boot disk now using the DOS **RAWRITE.EXE** utility. This can often be found in a subdirectory of a Linux distribution CD-ROM. In this example we are using the InfoMagic CD-ROM on the **F:** drive:

```
C:\> F:\DOS_UTIL\RAWRITE
RaWrite 1.2 - Write disk file to raw floppy diskette
Enter source file name: F:\DISTRIBU\SLAKINST\BOOT144\SBPCD
Enter destination drive: A:
Please insert a formatted diskette into drive A: and press - ENTER - :
Number of sectors per track for this disk is 18
Writing image to drive A:. Press ^C to abort
Track: xx Head: xx Sector: xx
Done.
```

The **RAWRITE** program prompts you for the name and path of a boot disk image, for example **SBPCD**, and a disk drive to copy it to, say the **A:** floppy drive. It's important to choose a boot disk image that is the appropriate size for your boot floppy drive, in this case 1.44Mb.

Making a Boot Disk in UNIX

From a UNIX or Linux computer you can make a boot disk using **dd**:

```
# mount -r /cdrom
# cd /cdrom/distributions/slakinst/boot144
# dd if=net of=/dev/fd0 bs=18k
80+0 records in
80+0 records out
```

Root Disks

A **root disk** is very similar to a boot disk and is created in just the same way as a boot disk. The root disk contains a Linux root file system that the kernel on the boot disk can use. Once running, this floppy disk-based Linux system can be used to configure your hard disk and install software packages. Usually it's only used once because, by the time the initial installation is done, Linux can be booted from the hard disk, or from a single, customized floppy boot disk created especially for this installation.

There are a number of different root disks available in the directories **ROOT144** and **ROOT12**. The most common are **COLOR144**, **TTY144** and **UMSDS144**. **COLOR144** contains a full-screen, color version of the setup program. **TTY144** has **tty**-based scripts for installation. The **UMSDS144** root disk is a version of **COLOR144** to be used when installing Linux into a DOS partition using the UMSDOS facility.

Now make a root disk using the **GZIP** and **RAWRITE** command, but specify an appropriate root disk image such as:

F:\DISTRIBU\SLAKINST\ROOT144\UMSDS144.

Starting the Installation

Now place a boot disk in the **A:** drive and reboot. Make sure that the PC is configured to boot from a floppy drive if a disk is present. You will see the following:

```
LILO
Welcome to the Slackware Linux 2.1.0 bootkernel disk!
If you have any extra parameters to pass to the kernel, enter them at the
prompt below after one of the valid configuration names (ramdisk, mount,
drive2)
...
If you would rather load the root/install disk from your second floppy
drive:
   drive2

DON'T SWITCH DISKS YET! This prompt is just for entering extra parameters.
If you don't need to enter any parameters, hit ENTER to continue.

boot:
```

Now press *Return*.

```
Loading ramdisk......
Uncompressing Linux......
Console: colour EGA+ 80x25, 1 virtual console (max 63)
Serial driver version 4.00 with no serial options enabled
tty00 at 0x03f8 (irq = 4) is a 16450
tty01 at 0x02f8 (irq = 3) is a 16450
lp_init: lp1 exists, using polling driver
ftape: allocated 3 buffers aligned at: 001b8000
Calibrating delay loop.. ok - 6.65 BogoMips
Memory: 5448k/8192k available (724k kernel code, 384k reserved, 1636k data)
Floppy drive(s): fd0 is 1.44M
FDC 0 is a 8272A
Swansea University Computer Society NET3.017
Swansea University Computer Society TCP/IP for NET3.017
IP Protocols: ICMP, UDP, TCP
eth0: EtherExpress at 0x300, 00 aa 00 29 9e 1f, IRQ 5, Interface BNC.
eexpress.c:v0.07 1/19/94 Donald Becker (becker@super.org)
Checking 'hlt' instruction... Ok.
Linux version 1.1.59 (root@fuzzy) (gcc version 2.5.8) #7 Sat Oct 29
03:50:25 CDT 1994
Partition check:
   hda: 94354-230, 201MB w/32KB Cache, CHS=954/12/36, MaxMult=64
   hda: hda1 hda2 <hda5>
   hdb: Seagate Technology ST157A, 42MB w/2KB Cache, CHS=977/5/17, MaxMult=0
   hdb: hdb1
RAMDISK: 1474560 bytes, starting at 0x1e3268
```

```
Please remove the boot kernel disk from your floppy drive, insert a
root/install disk (such as one of the Slackware color144, colrlite,
tty144, or tty12 disks) or some other disk you wish to load into a
ramdisk and boot, and then press ENTER to continue.
```

When we insert a suitable root disk, in this case the UMSDOS one (i.e.
UMSDS144), the installation continues and Linux starts up.

```
VFS: Disk change detected on device 2/28
RAMDISK: Minix filesystem found at block 0
RAMDISK: Loading 1440 blocks into RAM disk...............
done
VFS: Mounted root (minix file system).
Jan 20 16:09:03 init[1]: version 2.4 booting
none on /proc type proc (rw)
Mounting remote file systems...
inetd

Slackware Linux UMSDOS install disk v. 2.1.0.

Hello, and welcome to Linux. Unless have more than 4 megabytes of RAM,
you'll need a swap file to install. This should be created on the DOS
partition that you plan to install on.

    Device Boot   Begin   Start    End   Blocks   Id  System
   /dev/hda1    *      1       1    477   103014    6  DOS 16-bit >=32M
   /dev/hda5         478     478    953   102798    6  DOS 16-bit >=32M
   /dev/hdb1    *      1       1    976    41471+   6  DOS 16-bit >=32M
```

Note that the extended DOS partition we're going to use is referred to by
Linux as **/dev/hda5**. This is because Linux uses the device names **/dev/hda1**
through to **/dev/hda4** to refer to (at most) the four possible primary
partitions. Extended partitions that represent logical drives are referred to as
/dev/hda5, /dev/hda6, etc.

```
Use which device (such as /dev/hda1, or ENTER to skip)? /dev/hda5
Mounting device /dev/hda5 under /mnt:
UMSDOS Alpha 0.4 (compatibility level 0.3)
Making directory /mnt/linux/dev:

What size swap file would you like to create?

To give you an idea, you will specify a number such as 4096 if you want
to use 4 megabytes of your DOS partition for a swap file. Assuming you
have 4 megabytes of RAM, you will need a swap file of size 2048 to install
the system and try a few things out. If you're planning to run X, you'll
probably want to use a larger swapfile (around 8192 or so).
```

```
Enter swap file size: 8192

Creating a 8192K swapfile in your /dev directory:
8192+0 records in
16384+0 records out
Running mkswap on the new swapfile:
Setting up swapspace, size = 8384512 bytes
Activating swap partition:
Adding Swap: 8188k swap-space

Memory status:
            total      used      free    shared    buffers
Mem:         5444      4672       772       468      3838
Swap:        8188         0      8188

You should see your swapspace indicated on the table above.

Now just go ahead and log in, run the 'setup' program and give it
the same partition that you used here for your swap space.

Press ENTER to continue.
```

Press *Return.*

```
Jan 20 16:17:45 entering runlevel 4

Welcome to the Slackware Linux installation disk, (v. 2.1.0-UMSDOS)

###### IMPORTANT! READ THE INFORMATION BELOW CAREFULLY. ######

This is a special distribution of Linux designed to be installed on an
existing DOS partition without reformatting it or damaging your existing
data. You will need anywhere from 10 to 150 megabytes of free space,
depending on how much of the software is installed. You will also require 8
megabytes of RAM, or 4 megabytes plus a swapfile or swap partition. A swap
partition is more efficient, but requires repartitioning of your hard
drive. See the Installation-HOWTO if you need information on creating a
swap partition.

Once you have prepared a swap partition (if you need one), type 'setup' to
start the installation process.

You may now login as "root".

slackware login: root

Linux 1.1.59. (Posix).

If you're upgrading an existing Slackware system, you might want to
remove old packages before you run 'setup' to install the new ones. If
```

```
you don't, your system will still work but there might be some old files
left laying around on your drive.

Just mount your Linux partitions under /mnt and type 'pkgtool'. If you
don't know how to mount your partitions, type 'pkgtool' and it will tell
you how it's done.

To start the main installation, type 'setup'.

# setup
```

The main installation program, **setup**, presents you with a menu, help and instructions on selecting the displayed items.

Mapping the Keyboard

Linux, like DOS, needs to know about the layout of your keyboard. It will install a map of the keys in a similar way to the DOS **KEYB** command in your **AUTOEXEC.BAT**. The default layout is for a US keyboard.

For a non-US installation select **KEYMAP** and scroll through the list of options until the appropriate keyboard is selected. The list shows keymap files to be installed in **/usr/lib/kdb/keytables**. For example, for the UK, choose **uk.map.gz**.

You now have a chance to try out the keyboard. If it isn't working correctly, then try another selection. Pay special attention to the keys that tend to be in different places on different keyboards, such as **#~'@"'\|**.

Swap Space

If a swap partition hasn't been set up, as is the case when using an UMSDOS install disk, the **setup** program will ask if you wish to continue without a swapfile. Choose the **YES** option.

Target

You need to tell **setup** where to install Linux. For this example, specify **/dev/hda5** (drive **E:**) as before.

The **setup** program can also arrange for the other DOS and OS/2 partitions to be made available to Linux. Since Linux can read and write MS-DOS disks and partitions, this will enable us to share files with DOS applications. Note that Linux can currently only read OS/2 files, not write them. There is a utility in development that will allow Linux to read DoubleSpace compressed drives, but this isn't yet distributed with Slackware.

We can arrange for **/dev/hda1** (drive **C:**) to be made available - mounted as a file system under the directory **/dosc**. Similarly **/dev/hdb1** (drive **D:**) can be mounted under the directory **/dosd**. The choice of mount points here is arbitrary, but the ones we have chosen are often used.

The **setup** program reports these additions to the system file **/etc/fstab**, used to make disks available to Linux:

```
/dev/hda1  /dosc msdos defaults
/dev/hdb1  /dosd msdos defaults
```

Source Media

Linux can be installed from a variety of distribution media. It's probably the simplest though to install directly from a CD-ROM distribution - easily achieved if there is an available boot disk supporting your type of CD-ROM drive.

CD-ROM

The **setup** program is configured to know about the following CD-ROM drives and distributions:

Drives: SCSI CD-ROM

Sony CDU31A

Sony 535

Mitsumi

Sound Blaster Pro (Panasonic)

NEC 260 IDE CD-ROM

Distributions: Slackware Pro

TransAmeritech CD

Linux Quarterly CD-ROM

InfoMagic CD-ROM

You can install Linux from almost any source, even from another CD-ROM distribution, or a DOS hard disk partition - you simply need to specify the directory where they can be found. The representation of the install files are based on a set of floppy disks, the contents of which are kept in a separate directory for each floppy disk. For example, the four disks in the Linux base set (the A set) are kept in directories called **a1**, **a2**, **a3** and **a4** (we'll discuss the Slackware directories later).

Floppy Disk

Alternatively, Linux can be installed from a real set of floppy disks or even across a local area network from a server that can make the floppy disk contents available via NFS.

From UNIX/Linux:

```
# mount -r /dev/cdrom /cdrom
# cd /cdrom/distributions/slackware
# mcopy a1/* a:
```

Note that the syntax of the **mount** command will vary from system to system depending on the operating system and CD-ROM hardware.

From DOS:

```
C:\> COPY F:\DISTRIBU\SLACKWAR\A1\*.* A:
```

Repeat this procedure for each floppy disk in each set that you intend to install.

447

Series Selection

Slackware is composed of a number of series of disks. Each series contains a group of related software packages, some required, others optional.

The Slackware disk series consists of the following directories:

A	Base Linux system (must be installed).
AP	Various Applications (don't require X).
D	Program Development (C, C++, Lisp, Perl, etc).
E	GNU Emacs.
F	FAQ lists, HOWTO documentation.
I	Information files - documents readable with info or emacs.
IV	InterViews Development, Doc and Idraw Applications for X.
N	Networking (TCP/IP, UUCP, Mail, News).
OOP	Object Oriented Programming (GNU Smalltalk 1.1.1).
Q	Extra Linux kernels with UMSDOS/non-SCSI CD drivers.
T	TeX.
TCL	Tcl/Tk/TclX, Tcl language and Tk toolkit for X.
X	Base Xfree-86 3.1 X Window System.
XAP	X Applications.
XD	XFree-86 3.1 X11 Server Development System.
XV	XView 3.2 release 5 (OpenLook Window Manager, applications).
Y	Games (don't require X).

Options

For a first-time install, it's usual to allow the **setup** program to offer you a prompt for each optional package. You can enable this by selecting **Normal** in answer to the **setup** program question about prompts. If you try to install all of a series at once, it's possible to end up with a system where two mutually incompatible options have been chosen. This is especially true of some of the packages in the A, N and X series.

The minimum functional Linux installation can be achieved by installing just the A series. Once up and running with Linux, you can always add further packages by running the **setup** program again.

For a floppy disk installation, the **setup** program will prompt you to insert each disk of the series as it is required. Other types of installation automatically locate the files they need.

When installing the A series be sure to select the appropriate kernel option: **idekern** (for systems without SCSI) or **scsikern** (for SCSI systems). Users of non-SCSI CD-ROMs and other special hardware will need to install a kernel from the Q series, or rebuild one using the tools and kernel sources from the D series.

It's also important to install the A series package **keytbls** if you have a non-US keyboard and choose to install a new keyboard map file during initial installation.

Installation Tips

To use the printer spooler, **lpd**, you'll either need to install the TCP/IP package from the N series, or rebuild a Linux kernel without network support. This is because the print system can operate over a network and will try to do so if it finds network support in the kernel. You don't need to be physically connected to a network to install TCP/IP support as it can operate over a loopback interface.

It's recommended that you install the **loadlin** package (part of the A series) when the system needs to run both DOS and Linux. This utility allows you to start Linux from DOS.

The **tcsh** package ought to be installed from the A series at this stage, since these programs and utilities aren't re-installable, while the other series may be installed by running the **setup** program at a later time. The **tcsh** package provides a version of the C-Shell that some other Linux packages require, such as the Andrew User Interface system from Carnegie Mellon University.

Setting the time zone under Linux will allow the system to automatically adjust to daylight saving time. The setup program offers a list of many time zones. For example, for the UK choose **GB-Eire**. To keep the DOS time (which doesn't use time zones) the same as that seen by Linux, you need to execute **/sbin/clock -s** in your **/etc/rc.d/rc.S** file and **/sbin/clock -w** in your **/etc/rc.d/rc.0** file. These commands set the Linux clock from the CMOS on startup, and re-write the CMOS on shutdown. For more information on the **clock** command see **man 8 clock**.

Booting Linux

There are many ways to boot Linux after it has been correctly installed:

- You can use a floppy boot disk with a kernel on it.
- You can use the Linux Loader, **LILO**, to boot a kernel on the hard disk.
- You can use a utility such as **LOADLIN** to boot Linux from the DOS prompt.

The **setup** program will offer to configure the Linux system, including setting up the manner in which the Linux system will be started. One very reliable method of starting Linux is to use a boot diskette, similar to the one that starts the installation process, and that uses the hard disk for its root partition. It's strongly recommended that you make a boot disk when **setup** offers you the chance.

When you have installed all the disk series you need, you can exit **setup** and reboot Linux using the boot floppy you made.

So that we can see the disk space being used by the installation of Linux, we'll include an indication of the remaining disk space by using the **df** utility after the installation of the A series:

```
# df
Filesystem        1024-blocks   Used   Available Capacity Mounted on
/dev/hda5             102580    27272     75308     27%    /
/dev/hda1             102796    89732     13064     87%    /dosc
/dev/hdb1              41374    40342      1032     98%    /dosd
```

The figure for **/dev/hda5** includes 8Mb swap file plus 8Mb DOS data already present, so a minimal installation is 10Mb. Note that **/dev/hdb1** is a DoubleSpace drive and appears to be full, since it contains one very large file, the compressed drive. We'll omit the lines for **hda1** and **hdb1** in the output from **df** in future.

Booting from DOS

The **LOADLIN** package (installed as **lodlin15.zip** in the **root** home directory) can be used to boot Linux from a DOS prompt. The simplest way to install this is to create a subdirectory **C:\LOADLIN** and copy the required files into it.

```
# cd
# unzip -d lodlin15.zip
```

This creates a subdirectory called **LOADLIN** containing the **LOADLIN** executables, documents and source code. The files we need at the very least are **LOADLIN.EXE** and **LINUX.BAT**:

```
# mkdir /dosc/loadlin
# cp LOADLIN/LOADLIN.EXE LOADLIN/LINUX.BAT /dosc/loadlin
```

Now copy an active kernel to the **LOADLIN** directory on the DOS hard disk - this is needed to boot from.

```
# cp /vmlinuz /dosc/loadlin
```

Now you can boot Linux from a DOS command prompt with the commands below. If you are running DOS SmartDrive, make sure that its cache is emptied before booting Linux.

```
C:\> SMARTDRV /C
C:\> C:\LOADLIN\LOADLIN C:\LOADLIN\VMLINUZ root=/dev/hda5 rw
```

Note that the root device must match the actual partition Linux was installed on. The **rw** parameter indicates that the Linux root should be mounted as read-write, because this is needed for UMSDOS installations.

For native Linux file system installations, the parameter must be **ro** to indicate that the root partition should be initially mounted read-only. This allows the file system checking software to run automatically when Linux starts up.

The Linux boot commands can be placed in a batch file, and an example is provided in the **LOADLIN** package, **LINUX.BAT**. If you edit this to suit your installation and place it in a directory in your DOS path, you can boot Linux from DOS with the command:

```
C:\> LINUX
```

The Slackware Disk Series

The Slackware Disk Series consists of 17 directories crammed full of programs, utilities, files and information. We'll discuss some of them here:

Networking Linux

Networking support in Linux is very similar to that included with most commercial versions of UNIX. It's based on the TCP/IP protocols and includes all UNIX tools and commands; it's also possible to use Linux as a network file server using NFS.

The N Series

The Slackware N series contains all of the packages used in networking Linux. This also includes dial-up or direct point-to-point networking via serial lines with SLIP, CSLIP and PPP. There's also a version of IP that runs over parallel ports, called PLIP.

Even if you're not connected to a network, but you intend to use a printer with Berkeley style **lpd** printing, you'll need to install networking support.

There are many packages in the networking software series, some of which are mutually exclusive. For example, don't install both C-News and INN as they both define different versions of the news handler, **inews**, which results in severe problems with Usenet news.

A reasonable selection from those packages on offer, assuming that you are connected to either a local area network, or to a dial-up Internet service provider, would be:

elm	A popular mail program, **pine** would be an alternative.
netcfg	The **netconfig** script, used to configure the network interface.
tcpip	The base networking functions (essential).
mailx	The Berkeley mail program.
dip/ppp	Dial-up support for SLIP and PPP.
sendmail	The mail delivery system (needs **m4** from series D).
cnews	Usenet news handling.
tin	A threaded newsreader and poster.
bind	The Domain Name Server, optional.

After the installation of these packages from the N series, **df** reports:

```
# df
Filesystem        1024-blocks  Used Available Capacity Mounted on
/dev/hda5            102580    34662   67918     34%    /
```

Configuration

If you choose to install the **netcfg** package on initial installation, the script **netconfig** will be run automatically. If you add networking at a later date you need to run **netconfig** to set up network addresses properly.

The **netconfig** script configures TCP/IP and **mail**. You'll need to have the following information available:

hostname:	**alex**
domain name:	**mydomain.co.uk**

If you aren't connected to a network, then you'll use the loopback interface and **netconfig** will ask you to confirm if this is the case. If you are using the loopback there'll be no need for you to answer the questions that follow. (This would be true only if the networking package was installed to allow the printer to run correctly.) Note that the IP addresses here are just examples, you must use your own.

IP address: **192.168.17.23**

Gateway: **192.168.17.4** (or your own IP address if you don't have a gateway)

Netmask: **255.255.255.0** (for Class C)

If you're going to use a name server, **netconfig** will ask you for its IP address and make an entry in your **/etc/resolv.conf** file.

Now when you reboot, your computer will be ready to communicate on a local area network. The difference will be shown by some additional information lines appearing on the console:

```
Going multiuser...
Mounting remote file systems...
Starting daemons: syslogd klogd inetd lpd

Welcome to Linux 1.1.59.

alex login:
```

Help

Dial-up access to network service providers can also be configured. Setting up modem control and the automatic delivery of mail and news is a task that needs to be undertaken with some care. A help package, created by John Phillips, called **slack2.1.help.tar.gz** is available on the Internet at

ftp://ftp.demon.co.uk/pub/linux/Demon/

This excellent system covers all the configuration needed to set up a SLIP or PPP connection to a service provider (in this case Demon Internet, but others are very similar). It also details the configuration of mail (**sendmail**) and news (**C-News**).

Full Networking Capability

With the establishment of low-cost dial-up Internet access, it's possible to turn your personal computer into a fully-fledged networked workstation. All that's needed is a modem (from as little as $60 for a V32bis 14k4 model), a telephone and a dial-up account (usually a fixed monthly charge, with just the cost of telephone calls to add). Some providers may even be able to provide local call access to keep the telephone charges down. Many of the common networking tools, including graphical network browsers such as NCSA Mosaic and Netscape Navigator are available for Linux.

Newsgroups

There are a number of Usenet and local newsgroups devoted to Linux and of particular interest to Linux users. These include:

`comp.os.linux.announce`	Linux Announcements.
`comp.os.linux.answers`	Linux FAQs and other useful information.

These two groups are moderated and provide a lot of information about new package releases, changes to the kernel and new commercial products.

Other newsgroups of interest to Linux users:

`comp.os.linux.advocacy`	Discusses which version is the best.
`comp.os.linux.setup`	Discusses Linux setup problems.
`comp.os.linux.hardware`	Discusses hardware problems.
`comp.os.linux.misc`	General Linux discussion.
`comp.os.linux.networking`	Discusses Linux networking problems.

Applications

Another major Slackware disk set is the AP series of applications. These contain many useful programs that make up a typical UNIX user environment, such as editors, manual pages and tools.

An example selection from the AP series packages might be:

jove	A text editor that shares some of **emacs** features.
man	The manual page program.
manpgs	The basic manual page set.
diff	The difference utility.
jed	A programmer's editor.
jpeg	A program for displaying JPEG images.
shlbsvga	The SVGA shared libraries, needed for **jpeg**.
mc	Midnight Commander, a Norton Commander-like file manager.

After the installation of these packages from the AP series, **df** reports:

```
# df
Filesystem        1024-blocks  Used Available Capacity Mounted on
/dev/hda5           102580    37458    65122      37%    /
```

The X Window System

Slackware provides a complete X environment based on the MIT X11R6, together with a wide range of additional contributed X programs. These are contained within the X and XAP (for applications) series. There are many different X server programs for many different video chip sets. You only need to install one of these - the appropriate one for your own video hardware. There are also many optional fonts that can be added.

The X Series

A recommended subset of the packages in the X series is:

oldlibs, xf_lib, xpm, fvwmicns	X libraries
xf_bin, xf_ctrb, xman, xlock	X client programs

`config86`, `xf_cfg`, `xf_doc`	Configuration and documentation
`xfnt`, `xfnt75`	Basic fonts

plus one of the X servers `XF86_xxx`.

The XAP Series

From the XAP series, a good compromise would be to choose:

`libgr`	Graphics library
`seyon`	Communications program
`vgaset`	Utility for fine tuning your X display
`gnuplot`	The GNU graph plotting program
`xv`	The XV graphics file viewer
`gchess`	GNU chess and a graphical chess board
`xfm`	A file manager for X
`xpaint`	A painting program
`xfract`	The fractal program `FRACTINT`, for X
`xgames`	A collection of games for X
`xspread`	A spreadsheet for X

Note that the graphics file viewer and editor, `xv`, is unregistered shareware and a fee must be paid to the author should you decide to use it. Note also that the `libgr` package is required to run both `xv` and `InterViews`.

After these packages from the X and XAP series have been installed, `df` reports:

```
# df
Filesystem          1024-blocks   Used Available Capacity Mounted on
/dev/hda5             102580      61914    40666     60%    /
```

Installing X can be difficult, but in the end it's also very rewarding since it provides a PC workstation environment.

The XV Series

The XV series contains the OpenLook Graphical User Interface developed by Sun Microsystems. Included is the OpenLook Window Manager, **olwm**, that provides a look and feel very much like Sun workstations. However, among workstation vendors an alternative look and feel, OSF/MOTIF from the Open Software Foundation, is more common. This is also available for Linux from several suppliers at extra cost.

To obtain a good OpenLook user installation, without the development libraries or examples, install the following packages:

xvo132	Basic binaries
xv32_so, xv32_sa	Basic libraries
xvmenus	Menus for the OpenLook window manager

After these packages from the XV series have been installed, **df** reports:

```
# df
Filesystem          1024-blocks  Used Available Capacity Mounted on
/dev/hda5              102580    70010   32570     68%    /
```

X Configuration

X provides an extremely useful graphical user interface for Linux, which is very flexible and can support a wide range of PC-compatible video cards and monitors. The version supplied with Slackware 2.1 is XFree86 3.1, a port of X11R6 to Intel or compatible personal computers. However, it can be difficult to get the most out of it, since video cards and monitors must be carefully configured.

> Please remember that it's possible to damage your computer monitor if XFree86 is misconfigured. Therefore, it's important to read the supporting documentation provided with XFree86 and gain an understanding of your computer's capabilities. You will need to know the specifications of your video card and monitor, often found in the user guides that accompany them.

There is a utility, **ConfigXF86** (in subdirectory **/usr/X11R6/lib/ConfigXF86**), that can help with the initial configuration of X. As a guide, if your computer is capable of running MS-Windows at a resolution of 1024x768 in 256 colors non-interlaced, then X should run fine without risk of damage.

If you are in doubt, try to install X using conservative choices, such as 640x480 on a standard VGA card. Later you can experiment with the higher resolutions and the accelerated functions of any SuperVGA card you may have.

SuperProbe

You can determine exactly what your video hardware is by running the **SuperProbe** utility. This program probes the hardware and reports the chip sets used for generating the display.

For example, on the machine **alex** which has a generic S3-based video card, **SuperProbe** reports:

```
# SuperProbe

First video: Super-VGA
        Chipset: S3 86C911
        Memory:  1024 Kbytes
        RAMDAC:  Sierra SC1148{2,3,4} 15-bit or
                         SC1148{5,7,9} 15/16-bit HiColor
                 (with 6-bit wide lookup tables (or in 6-bit mode))
```

The ConfigXF86 Setup Program

We can configure X by running **ConfigXF86**. It will prompt you for some information about your hardware, typically the following:

Mouse type	Several different types of mouse are supported, including some bus versions (support for these needs to be built into the kernel). The most common is probably Microsoft serial, although a 3-button Logitech or Mouse Systems mouse have advantages under X, as all three buttons can be used.
3-button emulation	X-based workstations have historically used 3-button mice. To gain access to functions normally provided by the missing middle button on 2-button

	mice, the X server can be configured so that if you press both buttons at the same time, the server acts as if a middle button has been pressed. To do this it needs to know that you have finished pressing buttons, so a slight movement may be needed in the mouse before the mouse click is registered.
Mouse port	If you set up the mouse in the original installation, you can specify **/dev/mouse**. If you have a bus mouse and are running the **gpm** (general purpose mouse) utility, you may have problems starting X, because it will regard the mouse as being in use - you'll have to disable **gpm** to use X.
Mouse baud rate	You can choose 1200 for any serial mouse, although some Logitech mice will work at 9600. Bus mice don't require this.
Video card	The configuration utility will present a menu of video cards with over 80 choices. You must select the one closest to your card.
Monitor	A menu of different monitors will be displayed. You may like to try the generic VESA modes if your monitor isn't listed.
Virtual desktop	X can use a display larger than the size of your screen and arrange to see a portion of it at a time, automatically scrolling as you move the mouse off the edge of the screen. The default size of the 'virtual desktop' is 1024x768.
Viewport	This is the location of the initial view into the 'virtual desktop'. There is little reason to change it from the default, where the top left hand corner is (0, 0).
Option flags	These are options to the X server itself. Refer to the manual page for the server you are using, e.g. **man XF86_S3**. These options may be used to enable some features of the video card that aren't automatically detected, such as setting the RAMDAC to 8-bit mode allowing the card to run in 64,000 color mode. For now just accept the defaults.

Fontserver   If you're running a stand-alone workstation then there is little need to run a fontserver - enter **No**.

ConfigXF86 Video Options

ConfigXF86 will then calculate the video modes that you have available, i.e. the resolutions that your hardware can achieve. The VESA modes include 640x480, 800x600, 1024x768 and others up to the bandwidth limit of your monitor.

Choose the safe standard VGA, 640x480 with a clock of 25MHz as the first mode, then pick any others. You can change modes by using *Ctrl-Alt-+* and *Ctrl-Alt--* to scroll through the list, then if one doesn't work you can quickly backtrack to one that does.

Saving Your Setup Choices

Save the **config** files as the default ones. You will need to edit the resulting **XF86Config** file in **/usr/X11R6/lib/X11** to initialize the actual characteristics of your monitor. For example:

```
Bandwidth 75
HorizSync 30-60
VertRefresh 50-90
```

Be careful here - be sure to get them right. It is possible to over-drive your monitor with XFree86. Refer to the manual pages for X, XFree86 and your server for more information on configuring and fine tuning X. There are also useful documents installed in the directory **/usr/X11R6/lib/X11/doc** if you have any problems.

Executing X Windows

Run X with the **startx** command. To start OpenLook use the command **openwin** instead.

Adding Users

Slackware has a utility called **adduser** that can be used to simplify the creation of user accounts. It prompts you for all the information it needs:

```
# adduser

Enter login name for new account (^C to quit): jim

Editing information for new user [jim]

Full Name: James Jameson
GID [100]:

Checking for an available UID after 500

First unused uid is 501

UID [501]:

Home Directory [/home/jim]:

Shell [bin/bash]:

Password [jim]: Watchout-this-is-echoed

Information for new user [jim]:
Home directory: [/home/jim] Shell: [/bin/bash]
Password: [xxxx] uid: [501] gid: [100]

Is this correct? [y/N]: y

Adding login [jim] and making directory [/home/jim]

Adding the files from the /etc/skel directory:
./.kermrc -> /home/jim/./.kermrc
./.less -> /home/jim/./.less
./.lessrc -> /home/jim/./.lessrc
./.term -> /home/jim/./.term
./.term/termrc -> /home/jim/./.term/termrc
```

We can let the Group identifier default to group 100 - the 'users' group. User identifiers start at 500 by convention on Linux, so we can allow **adduser** to default to 501. We can choose a home directory for the new user and select a suitable shell. The default shell is the GNU shell, **bash**. The system adminstrator can customize the environment for all new users by adding or modifying the default startup files held in the **/etc/skel** directory.

Note that in the **adduser** utility, the password allocated to the user is echoed to the screen - don't follow this procedure unless you're sure you aren't being observed. Alternatively, use the **passwd** command to immediately change the new user's password.

The Printing System

Linux uses the Berkeley BSD printing system. To configure it you need to make an entry for your printer in the **/etc/termcap** file. Many filters for producing various printing effects are available via newsgroups or **ftp** archive sites.

ghostscript

ghostscript is a fully-featured PostScript interpreter. It can be used to convert PostScript into a number of different forms, including many graphics formats such as Group 3 FAX, and into printer formats such as Epson and Hewlett-Packard.

By combining **ghostscript** with the printer filter system, it's effectively possible to turn a humble HP DeskJet printer into a PostScript device. Many X applications expect to have access to a PostScript printer, and **ghostscript** can provide it at no cost, except the CPU processing time in the conversion.

ghostview

ghostview is an X application that interfaces to **ghostscript** in order to provide an on-screen previewing facility for PostScript files.

Fax

There are a number of packages available for Linux that can use a FAX modem to transmit facsimile documents to a Group 3 FAX machine, or another FAX modem. One successful fax program that works well with Class 2 or Class 2.0 modems is **mgetty+sendfax**, which allows the modem to be shared for both FAX and dial-up access.

IBCS2

Another exciting development in the Linux community is the creation of a kernel interface for IBCS2, the Intel Binary Compatibility Standard. Using this package, it's possible to run many SCO UNIX and System V programs directly under Linux. In particular, there's a IBCS2 version of WordPerfect that runs under Linux. Many more new applications are also being supported in this way.

463

Development Tools

A large range of development tools are available for Linux. Slackware contains compatible versions of most of the tools found on UNIX systems including a C compiler (**gcc**), a parser generator (**bison** or **byacc**), a lexical analyzer generator (**flex**) and a make file (GNU **make, pmake**).

Other programming languages available for Linux include Lisp, Prolog, Forth, Ada, Fortran, Modula-2, Pascal, Eiffel, Tcl, Perl, Smalltalk, C++ and Objective-C. Interface toolkits used to develop X programs with graphical user interfaces include InterViews and Tk.

TeX and MetaFont

Donald Knuth's typesetting and fonts packages, TeX and MetaFont, are available for Linux, as are Leslie Lamport's LaTeX system and a wide variety of extra macros, utilities and fonts.

Andrew

The graphical user interface system from Carnegie Mellon University, Andrew, is also available, providing a multi-media mail package, sophisticated editor/ word processors and a complete user interface development environment.

Summary

We have seen in this chapter that Linux is a widely available, UNIX-like operating system that is being co-operatively developed by many individuals communicating over the Internet.

Many distributions of Linux are available at low cost from suppliers of CD-ROM software. These contain both the Linux kernel and many software packages, including development tools and the X Window System.

A fully configured Linux-based PC can now rival the functionality of mid-range workstations. Linux certainly gives many commercial versions of PC UNIX a run for their money.

Try it, you might like it!

Where Do We Go From Here?

Whatever your preconceived ideas about UNIX were before you read this book, we are sure that you've found it an enlightening, informative and eye-opening tour. Not only have we tried to remove the excess baggage that traditionally drags UNIX material down, but we've also attempted to pack everything you need to know into a compact, cost-effective reference guide.

There is no doubting the sheer immensity of the UNIX world - developers have been developing, users have been using and suppliers have been supplying UNIX systems for well over 20 years. During that period, UNIX applications have matured into fine examples of their genre and, of course, software written as long ago as 1975 can still be found in use today. It's difficult to represent such a vast back catalog of existing software in a single publication, but wherever possible we have included the best sources, references and directions.

Now you've had a taste of our refreshing style, would you like to know more about Wrox Press and our other publications? If you do, then why don't you ask for a catalog, or check out our Web page. And remember, when you're down at your local bookstore, look out for our distinctive red binding - your guarantee of Wrox value.

Are you interested in writing or reviewing any of our future books? We warmly welcome any willing contributors that can help Wrox to publish *even* better books. If you're interested, contact us right away - see the details at the back of this book.

You can contact Wrox via the reply card at the back of this book, or you can correspond with us by any of the following means:

Snail mail	Wrox Press Ltd., Unit 16, 20 James Road, Birmingham, B11 2BA, United Kingdom.
Electronic mail (e-mail)	johnf@wrox.demon.co.uk
World Wide Web	http://www.wrox.com
CompuServe	100063,2152
Telephone	(44121) 706 6826
Facsimile	(44121) 706 2967

INSTANT

UNIX

Index

Symbols

475

477

P

Wrox Press present
their new *bestselling* author:

Could this be you?

Have you ever thought to yourself "I could do better than that"?

Well here's your chance to prove it! Wrox Press are continually looking for

new authors and contributors. It doesn't matter if you've never been published before.

If you are a professional programmer, or simply a great developer,

we'd be very interested to hear from you.

Contact John Franklin at:

Wrox Press, Unit 16, 20 James Road, Birmingham, B11 2BA, UK

from US call: **800 814 3461**

or

e-mail: **johnf@wrox.com**

compuserve: **100063,2152**

Notes

Notes

Notes

Notes

WIN FREE BOOKS

TELL US WHAT YOU THINK!

Complete and return the bounce back card and you will:

- Help us create the books you want.
- Receive an update on all Wrox titles.
- Enter the draw for 5 Wrox titles of your choice.

FILL THIS OUT to enter the draw for free Wrox titles

Name _____

Address _____

_____

_____

_____ Postcode/Zip _____

Occupation _____

How did you hear about this book?

☐ Book review (name) _____

☐ Advertisement (name) _____

☐ Recommendation

☐ Catalogue

☐ Other _____

Where did you buy this book?

☐ Bookstore (name) _____

☐ Computer Store (name) _____

☐ Mail Order

☐ Other _____

I would be interested in receiving information about Wrox Press titles by email in future. My email/Internet address is:

_____

What influenced you in the purchase of this book?

☐ Cover Design

☐ Contents

☐ Other (please specify) _____

How did you rate the overall contents of this book?

☐ Excellent ☐ Good

☐ Average ☐ Poor

What did you find most useful about this book? _____

_____

What did you find least useful about this book? _____

_____

Please add any additional comments. _____

_____

What other subjects will you buy a computer book on soon? _____

_____

What is the best computer book you have used this year?

_____

Note: This information will only be used to keep you updated about new Wrox Press titles and will not be used for any other purpose or passed to any other third party.

WROX PRESS INC.

Wrox writes books for you. Any suggestions, or ideas about how you want information given in your ideal book will be studied by our team. Your comments are always valued at WROX.

Free phone in USA 800 814 4527
Fax (312) 465 4063

Compuserve 100063,2152
UK Tel. (44121) 706 6826 Fax (44121) 706 2967

Computer Book Publishers

NB. If you post the bounce back card below in the UK, please send it to:
Wrox Press Ltd. Freepost BM6303, Unit 16, 20 James Road, Birmingham, B11 2BR

NO POSTAGE
NECESSARY
IF MAILED
IN THE
UNITED STATES

BUSINESS REPLY MAIL

FIRST CLASS MAIL   PERMIT#64   CHICAGO,IL

POSTAGE WILL BE PAID BY ADDRESSEE

WROX PRESS
2710 WEST TOUHY AVE
CHICAGO IL 60645-3008
USA